THE POLITICAL ROLE
OF THE
UNITED NATIONS

THE POLITICAL ROLE
OF THE
UNITED NATIONS

Advancing the World Community

John W. Halderman

PRAEGER SPECIAL STUDIES • PRAEGER SCIENTIFIC

Library of Congress Cataloging in Publication Data

Halderman, John W.
    The political role of the United Nations.

    Includes index.
    1. United Nations.   2. Arbitration, International.
3. Pacific settlement of international disputes.
I.   Title
JX1977. H229   341. 23   81-13948
ISBN 0-03-060322-6   AACR2

JX
1977
H229
1981

Published in 1981 by Praeger Publishers
CBS Educational and Professional Publishing
A Division of CBS, Inc.
521 Fifth Avenue, New York, New York 10175 U.S.A.

© 1981 by Praeger Publishers

123456789   145   987654321

Printed in the United States of America

To Elenor Halderman

This great country of ours is not like the cork that is tossed on the waves over which we have no control. Our enormous capacity to act imposes upon us a responsibility to make history and to take a large part in shaping events.

> Dean Rusk, responding to the announcement of his designation as Secretary of State, December 12, 1960

A new administration . . . must recognize that, in the field of foreign policy, we will never be able to contribute to building a stable and creative world order unless we first form some conception of it.

> Henry Kissinger, "Central Issues of American Foreign Policy," in K. Gordon, ed., Agenda for the Nation, at 614 (1968)

[T]he pledges of each new Administration are like leaves on a turbulent sea. No President-elect or his advisers can possibly know upon what shore they may finally be washed by that storm of deadlines, ambiguous information, complex choices, and manifold pressures which descends upon all leaders of a great nation.

> Henry Kissinger, White House Years, at 16 (1979)

ACKNOWLEDGMENTS

I wish to acknowledge, with thanks, my indebtedness to Duke University and its School of Law and libraries for support and assistance in the preparation of this book. Much of the research was done while I was a member of the Rule of Law Research Center, of which Professor Arthur Larson was Director. He and Dean Elvin R. Latty were instrumental in my coming to Duke, and I am grateful for their assistance and that of all deans of the School of Law in the ensuing period.

I am also indebted to many librarians for their always generous assistance. These include the late Mr. Benjamin Powell, former University Librarian, Miss Marianne Long, former librarian of the Duke University School of Law, Mr. Elvin Strowd, presently Acting University Librarian, Miss Wilhelmina Lemen, formerly librarian of the government documents section of Perkins Library, and Mrs. Elizabeth Graham, formerly of that section.

The manuscript was read and valuable suggestions made by Professor Daniel G. Partan of Boston University, Professor John Dugard of the University of the Witwatersrand, and Professor A. Kenneth Pye of Duke University. I am further indebted to Professor Partan for other assistance in connection with this book.

CONTENTS

PREFACE

In the context of seeking world peace and security, a valid distinction can be drawn between two battlefields of international conflict. The first is the verbal arena, embracing arguments over particular disputes and, more broadly, over ideas and ideologies. The second involves the disposition and use of force and other tangible pressures for purposes of defense and deterrence, as well as more aggressive pursuits of policy goals.

The psychology of an insecure world is such that apparently little can be done, internationally, in the second area to lessen that insecurity. Such seems to be the lesson of international efforts to control armaments, constant since World War I with the significant exception of the period of World War II.

This book is concerned not with this second arena but rather with the first, the verbal battlefield of issues, arguments, and ideas, which is believed to have potential for progress toward world peace and security.

To try to draw some coordinates to locate our position in a world of confusion, it may be observed that this potential was not mentioned in the recent U.S. presidential campaign of 1980, whereas it was frequently said that SALT (strategic arms limitation talks with the Soviet Union, and resulting treaties and proposed treaties) constituted the most important issue before the country.

The basis of orderly societies apparently lies in the minds of the people in them. Democratic societies rest upon a consensus of their respective concerned populations, at least in a general sense, as to the meaning of justice. Dictatorships have a similar requirement, requiring the support of dominant elements of their populations. However, it is the case of democracies that is of interest here, since, short of World War III, international peace and security must evidently be attained on the basis of some consensus.

Minds can be shaped by words, including international debates on international issues.

One of the requirements of democratic systems capable of maintaining order is the existence of a pattern of agreed and limited powers for the handling of disputes. Such patterns must, of course, exist in the minds of the people concerned, and not just in written constitutions.

We have what may be a starting point for endeavors in this direction in the existence, in the U.N. Charter, of limited and agreed-on powers conferred on the organization for the handling of disputes. These have existed only as paper commitments. It is the purpose of this book to offer some suggestions as to how, through proper use, they may be transformed into the necessary foundation, in the minds of informed elements of the world's public, for international peace and security.

It may seem at first glance a foolhardy venture to bring out, in this day and age, a new book on the search for peace through the United Nations. Part of the justification is found in the obvious elementary need, if peace and security are ever to be achieved, for some sort of mediatory international agency capable of softening the sharp edges of direct state-to-state conflict. The U.N., under its Charter as written, would be well adapted to fulfilling this need if the Charter were observed. It contains, moreover, the rudimentary elements of a system, consisting mainly of its limited powers in the political, or dispute-handling, area. It is impossible, in the present state of world relations, to contemplate the establishment of a new world security organization. Such an organization could not be better, basically, than the U.N. in its formal structure. The problem is always to transform written provisions into reality.

To achieve the goal under discussion through the U.N., this organization must be used as it has never been used before—as the basis for the limitation of international powers of dispute-handling, rather than, as in the past, as an instrument for attempting to extend those powers.

It may be emphasized, in concluding this introduction, that this book does not suggest any impingement upon what the United States or other states feel they must do physically to safeguard their security, to ensure deterrence, and to achieve related aims. The purpose is rather to suggest how, gradually, over a period of time, world community may be built and international tensions correspondingly lessened, with the effect of reducing, and ultimately eliminating, the need for armaments and military alliances.

The main thesis of this study is set forth in the first two chapters.

For those who think sufficiently well of the thesis to desire to explore it further, the remainder of the book attempts to show (1) how basic limitations in the Charter came to be ignored and buried, and (2) how they might have been applied in a number of past cases. The latter type of exposition is intended to indicate, broadly and generally, some of the kinds of problems that might be encountered in future attempts to apply these principles properly. Some complexities are here encountered not because the basic Charter is complicated, but because of complex and devious courses that the organization has been compelled to follow, by governments and supporting majorities, in pursuit of policy goals.

THE POLITICAL ROLE
OF THE
UNITED NATIONS

1

INTRODUCTION

THE UNITED NATIONS, WORLD COMMUNITY, AND WORLD PEACE

A study of the efforts of the League of Nations and the United Nations to deal with international disputes has led to the following conclusions, which seem fairly basic:

1. The effort to find international methods and procedures capable of solving all significant disputes and situations that arise under the present format of international relations seems doomed to failure. The "system" seems to give rise to the occasional intractable dispute (by definition beyond available means of settlement) and to the occasional war.

2. It therefore seems necessary, if the search for peace and security is to succeed, to find means of lessening international tensions to the point at which no intractable disputes would arise. Stated affirmatively, this means the building of world community sentiment to the requisite degree. Even the beginning of such a development would entail a change in the traditional format of relations. To add to the apparent difficulty of meeting this challenge, the necessary degree of community sentiment must be built not just among governments but among the peoples of the world.

3. The United Nations Charter contains essential elements— perhaps the essential elements—of an adequate constitutional instrument. Most important, it outlines dispute-handling procedures incorporating a pattern of uniform and limited powers. If applied, these provisions would tend to free and strengthen the international debating process, enabling it to perform the traditional consensus-building role performed by legislative debates in democratic societies within individual countries.

A first question of practicality might be: What chance would we have of transforming a mere paper instrument into an effective constitution, capable of converting our turbulent and anarchic world into one of peace and security? A partial answer is that unless we make the effort, we have no chance whatever and a nuclear holocaust, sooner or later, is inevitable. Beyond this, we do not know. Skeptics might ask: If, for example, the Weimar Constitution could not be given effect in Germany, a relatively disciplined community, how could we hope that the U.N. Charter could transform the whole world scene from one of disorder to one of peace and security? Certain differences in the two cases can be perceived. During the Weimar period there was obviously a growing wish on the part of the German people to institute a totalitarian regime that could carry out certain desired policies. The written Constitution was thus doomed. On the world scene today, the predominant wish must be to avoid world rule by a single power. The vast majority must hope for a high degree of pluralism in a system capable of maintaining peace. The present discussion aims at such a goal and will find certain useful analogies in individual democratic societies. Another part of our answer is that democracies have sacrificed their best assets in the world political struggle by acquiescing in the traditional battleground of crude pressure and counter-pressure. Antidemocratic powers do best on this kind of terrain. Democratic regimes, it is here believed, would do better if the issues could be taken up in the marketplace of ideas, through full and free debate.

We do not know how distant the goal of security would be if sound policies directed to this goal were followed. As will be further discussed in this chapter, the framers of the U.N. Charter thought that the goal was closer than it was in fact; however, they did not follow a sound approach. They thought that the necessary consensus had already come about, and did not contemplate any change in the basic traditional approach.

The consensus has proved not to exist and world insecurity, fueled in part by efforts to achieve balance or superiority in arms, seems to have deteriorated. The downward spiral does not seem to have been materially slowed by intermittent gestures toward coexistence or detente, nor by the efforts, especially during the 25th anniversary observances of the U.N., to reiterate the principles of the Charter.

The present proposal is to go to a deeper level by initiating a public and visible struggle to install a basically sound constitutional system, however elementary, grounded in world public sentiment. Whatever the nature of the plan that might be followed with any hope of success, the effort required would be even greater than any hitherto made because it would entail the necessity of discarding some established ideas and adopting and implementing some new ones.

A more optimistic consideration is the possibility that success might prove not too distant once correct approaches were adopted. Certainly the world is at one in desiring an end to war. A moderate and, perhaps, largely imperceptible advance in world community might bring us to the point at which unrestricted violence would no longer be resorted to. Success would then only require that the effort be sustained. This would be so, even though some disputes might drag on for a long time.

It is, of course, conceivable that the unaided forces of history will bring about an effective system capable of maintaining world order. However, the absence of such a development in the several centuries since the present pattern of relations originated with the beginning of the modern state system (and, indeed, back to the dawn of history) seems to indicate the desirability of a strong effort to find and carry out a program designed to end the world's chronic state of insecurity and recurrent wars.

Little seems needed in elaboration of the first conclusion set forth at the outset of this chapter, namely that there is little or no prospect of being able to devise means of peacefully solving all the disputes that arise under the traditional system of conducting relations.

The League of Nations and the United Nations, representing the major efforts in this century to achieve permanent world peace, as well as other organizations, treaties, and related instruments, have concentrated mainly on developing methods and procedures of dispute-handling. While not every possible method or combination of methods can have been tried, a sufficient number have to justify the conclusion that no better results can be anticipated as long as the basic format of relations remains unchanged.

The second conclusion thus becomes inescapable. Specifically, in the context of disputes, if no means can be found of peacefully managing all those that arise under traditionally prevailing conditions, it becomes necessary to seek out means of reducing their intensity so that all are within manageable proportions. The problem is to bring about the requisite degree of world community sentiment. The realization of this objective would mean that, in fact, a basic change in the format of international relations had been carried out.

An answer would thus be provided for the problem that can be stated more informally, but no less accurately, as follows: If people are going to talk about world peace, they must be prepared to talk about changing the world. This seems to be a commonsense statement of the problem as derived from a glance at modern history, the present condition of world armament, and the impending problems of world population, environment, and related matters that threaten the future of planetary life.

Community sentiment, for the purposes of this study, is defined as the requisite consistency of thought patterns among influential elements of the world population to ensure that no disputes capable of leading to war will arise.

If there are ways of bringing about the requisite degree of consistency on the part of governments, as distinct from peoples, they are unknown to this writer. Part of the efforts since World War I to establish peace and security have been directed to this goal, but without success. The U.N. Charter's requirement that all members of the organization be peace-loving states[1] was a gesture in this direction. Equally futile are exhortations to governments to incorporate morality and the search for justice as factors in policy-making. The problem is that states differ in their views on such matters.

If, on the other hand, bonds of community grow among peoples across national borders, the resulting fabric, if sufficiently strong, can hold the governments concerned within the required patterns of consistent policy-making. The governments and peoples of the Scandinavian countries and Finland have, in this century, developed a shared sense of justice sufficient to permit the peaceful settlement of several disputes of kinds that in other times and places could well have led to wars.[2] Leaders in this situation were not, it is believed, acting with "all options open" but within limitations imposed by a web of common relationships extending across boundaries. The interplay of relations between publics and leaders, together with other factors contributing to the shared thought patterns, must have operated on regional as well as national levels. The possibility of such a degree of community on a world basis may appear remote; however, it is necessary to consider the possibility that some significant development of this kind is the only alternative to ultimate world war.

Our third conclusion is that the U.N. Charter outlines the essential requirements of an effective international constitutional instrument, embracing functions and procedures capable, if applied, of gradually building the required degree of world community sentiment. The problem, of course, is their application, and we have already considered what must be a foremost question of practicality in this respect.[3]

An effective constitutional system, written or unwritten, must incorporate uniform and limited powers for the solution of disputes. The traditional approach to the conduct of international relations has, by contrast, been characterized by the freedom of states and groups of states to apply any available pressures deemed appropriate in pursuit of their policy objectives. States have acted accordingly, with resulting anarchy. The uniform and limited powers found in the dispute-handling provisions of the Charter have been largely ignored or overridden from the outset, notwithstanding that those herein considered most important were agreed to by states in the full and deliberate understanding that they could be applied against themselves.

These are the provisions defining the organization's "peaceful settlement" function, which is concerned with the solution of substantive issues in dispute. Member states desired that the new organization be able to assist in finding such solutions. However, they had no intention of relinquishing the traditional attribute of "sovereignty" by which each remained its own final judge of matters of concern to it.

Consequently, provisions were incorporated in Chapters IV and VI of the Charter enabling the General Assembly and the Security Council, respectively, to discuss disputes and make recommendations as to their solutions; neither was authorized to decide them on their merits.

There was general agreement on this limitation, and the provisions were incorporated virtually without debate on this point.

The second major function of the U.N. in the dispute-handling, or political, area of its activity is that of collective measures, frequently referred to as the "enforcement" function. It authorizes the use of tangible pressures, force, or measures less than force (such as diplomatic and economic sanctions) in order to deal with aggressions, other threats to peace, and breaches of peace. This function received predominant attention at the time the Charter was formulated, since it was designed to enable the organization to deal with situations such as had, only recently, given rise to World War II. It was thought that the provision for the use of force was the greatest advance of the new organization over the League of Nations and that it would enable the U.N. to succeed where its predecessor had failed.

The peaceful settlement function was in the shadow of the collective measures function in the meetings at San Francisco to establish the U.N., and there it has remained. This is not at all because it is considered to be of lesser importance, but rather because in the perspective from which people ordinarily view the world organization, which relates to its major role of maintaining peace and security, it is the collective measures function that captures attention. It was apparently a widespread initial anticipation on the part of the ultimately victorious allies that the major powers would preserve the peace, as world policemen, in the post-war world. [4] This view was substantially retained in the structure of the U.N. Security Council, with its requirement for unanimity among the permanent members when the collective measures function is to be applied.

The function may be said to correlate, to a considerable extent, with the traditional view, which leaves states, and groups of states, free to use such pressures as they see fit in pursuit of their objectives. Here, of course, the freedom was to be exercised by the major powers, as a group, with the objective of maintaining peace. However, the usual perception of the "enforcement" function is not that of a uniform pattern of powers and restraints.

The difference in the general perception of the two functions may be better appreciated by noting the anticipation, at least at the outset, that the collective measures function was brought into being primarily to deal with wrongdoers such as those who had recently precipitated World War II. Governments and national populations generally do not regard their own countries as being in this category. The Charter basically carries out the conventional concept of collective security by which peace-loving states, comprising the great majority, will be able to recognize and identify aggressors and combine to keep them in check or defeat them.

On the other hand, the peaceful settlement function was intended to deal with the kinds of disputes that are bound to arise from time to time among the peace-loving states themselves.

It was also recognized at the time the Charter was formulated that situations might arise in which the collective measures function would impinge on the safeguards of state sovereignty incorporated in the peaceful settlement function and that it might be abused with this effect. Some interpretive declarations, designed to prevent the violation of sovereign rights by use of the collective measures function, were placed in the record, and there were other indications of the importance attached to safeguarding those rights.

Perhaps the most important threat thus foreseen was related to the proposal to authorize the Security Council to recommend terms of settlement on the merits of disputes. The Dumbarton Oaks Proposals, which served as the basis of discussion at San Francisco, would only have authorized the Council to recommend procedures or methods of settlement. It was well understood that the major function of the Council was to be in the sphere of collective measures, or "enforcement," which was carefully restricted to dealing with breaches of and threats to peace. The power to enforce substantive decisions was excluded because the organization was to be given no power to make such decisions. When the proposal was made at San Francisco to empower the Council to recommend terms of settlement, there was hesitation on the grounds that the two functions might be confused. The then-recent Munich settlement was invoked to illustrate the danger.[5] The competent committee of the San Francisco Conference, in approving the proposal, placed a note in the record making it clear that this power was to be truly recommendatory and without binding effect.[6]

Clarifications were also made giving a negative answer to the question whether, if failure to resolve a dispute should be perceived as giving rise to a threat to peace, the Council should have the power to make and enforce a decision on the merits of the case. [7]

It may be worth mentioning in this connection that whereas an intense debate took place at the Conference over a proposal to confer general automatic jurisdiction with respect to proper legal disputes on the World Court[8]—a provision that would have meant a significant grant to an international body of power to decide substantive issues in a limited category—no corresponding debate took place concerning the powers of the political organs to pronounce upon international disputes. The reason was, of course, that no corresponding grant of decision-making power was proposed. Agreement was general that these organs should be limited to recommending solutions on the merits of the case. The absence of debate was a contributing factor to the obscurity surrounding the peaceful settlement function notwithstanding the great importance attached to it by governments and national populations.

A pattern of agreed-on and uniform restraints in the handling of disputes was thus provided in the Charter's provisions pertaining to the handling of disputes, and the restraints were regarded by the participants as very important. Their prospects of being applied in practice would seem logically to have been enhanced by the almost obvious fact that both the U.N. and the League of Nations must have been predicated on the existence of a consensus sufficient to permit the settlement of all disputes. They could not have been expected to succeed as mere paper organizations. There were, indeed, in the preparatory phase of establishing the U.N., a number of expressions of awareness that the organization could not succeed in the absence of adequate collaboration, particularly among the major powers. [9]

There appears to have been in the preparatory phase greater emphasis on the requirement for such collaboration than had been the case with the League, and it is ironic that once the United Nations began its operations there was less attention to building cooperation and greater reliance on the organizational structure per se than had been the case with the earlier organization. In fact, with proof that the hoped-for degree of collaboration did not exist, talk about it ceased and attention—as far as concerned the United Nations—turned to strengthening dispute-handling machinery and making the strongest possible use of it.

This turn of policy can, perhaps, be best accounted for by the fact that it really was no "turn" but a continuance of the traditional approach. It seems unlikely that officials ever contemplated what might be required to build the necessary degree of consensus. This view reflected resistance to change and may also have rested on tendencies to underestimate the degree of consensus required to achieve peace and security and to exaggerate the potential of dispute-handling institutions per se. Both views are illusory; in combination they produce an illusory view of the problem of world peace.

In regard to the possible underestimation of the required degree of consensus, the prevalent way of thought about the attainability of collaboration may have involved a sequence of ideas somewhat like this:

1. The United Nations must succeed in its major purpose, using force to this end if necessary.
2. The necessary degree of collaboration must exist.
3. If the United Nations is going to be able to handle severe disputes by using force, it will, a fortiori, be able to resolve lesser disputes.
4. The necessary degree of collaboration is therefore certain to emerge.

The other main component of the attitude under discussion placed unwarranted confidence in international institutions for dispute-handling per se. This view was fed by several streams, two of which were of particular importance. The first was the notion of law, with its sources long antedating both the League and the United Nations. Some observations on this factor, as it applies to the present thesis, will be ventured in Chapter 3. The second main stream, with its sources in the two world wars, was the expectation and determination that the United Nations contain strong and dynamic machinery capable of taking any actions necessary for the maintenance of international peace and security.

The tendency to view the U.N.'s "enforcement" function as the principal hope for peace in the immediate post-war world may also have resulted in part from the normal wartime trend toward material values and the preference for tangible means for solving problems over such intangibles as are involved in the molding of world opinion. This tendency was doubtless reflected in the emphasis placed on the tangible aspects of the United Nations and the downgrading of its capabilities for building world consensus.

As a consequence of such considerations, when it became evident, as it soon did, that the U.N. was unable to fulfill its function as planned, people were not inclined to see the failure as a result of the absence of a necessary underlying consensus; they did not turn to consideration of how to build such a substructure for an effective system. Rather, blame tended to be placed on the inherent difficulties of peace-making and, more particularly, on wrongful and aggressive attitudes and actions attributed to hostile powers. Hopes for peace continued to concentrate on the institutions and machinery of dispute-handling, and progress was seen as requiring their strengthening and their strongest possible use.

Among several efforts to strengthen international dispute-handling machinery, perhaps those of most lasting significance were

1. the Uniting for Peace resolution, discussed in Chapter 5
2. the "peace-keeping operation," discussed in Chapter 6
3. the conferral on regional security organizations of the right to employ force and other tangible pressures without the sanction of the United Nations, discussed in Chapter 12.

The second of the perceived solutions, the strong use of the organization, has been undertaken in a variety of cases with the effect that the U.N. has exceeded its mutually agreed-on powers. The first such case of importance will be briefly described here for illustrative purposes. A number of others will be considered in ensuing chapters.

In the first year of the United Nations began the series of cases in which the organization has apparently exceeded the basic limitations of its power to seek settlements on the merits of disputes. This occurred with the Spanish case, in 1946, in which the Assembly called on member states to withdraw their ambassadors and ministers from Spain, with the plainly indicated purpose of applying pressure for a change of regime in that country. If the Charter's limitations had been applied, the United Nations would have done no more than recommend a change of regime. In fact, the relevant resolution was phrased in the form of recommendations,[10] and in this and other ways members of the majority evidently convinced themselves that the organization was acting in accordance with its Charter. However, since measures of pressure were initiated with the plain purpose of enforcing a policy pronouncement, there was a clear implication that that pronouncement was, in fact, a binding decision.[11]

The responsible representatives were working within the traditional format of international relations by using an available means of pressure deemed useful in the circumstances. If any question had been raised about this causing the organization to exceed its powers, the answer might have been that in this way it might be enabled to produce a desirable result and that, in any event, the effort could do no harm.

Informed elements of the world public knew (if they thought about it) that the Charter of the U.N., adopted only the previous year, gave no authority to the organization to decide that states should change their governments. Here they saw the U.N. apparently doing exactly that and, moreover, undertaking to enforce the decision. The consequences of such contradictions will be considered below. The point to be made at this stage is that the world public will not usually notice or be impressed by legal or technical justifications brought forward in attempts to justify actions under the Charter. The impression made on that public is the important consideration, and the only one, in the perspective of the present thesis. The purpose of bringing the Spanish case into the U.N. was to mobilize world opinion against the Spanish regime. Such actions are flawed if the powers invoked exceed those agreed to.

We now consider the positive advantages of the course being proposed, which would entail bringing all significant disputes not otherwise promptly resolved into the United Nations and there dealing with them in accordance with relevant provisions of the Charter interpreted so as to be acceptable to all concerned. It will be ventured, to this end, to propose policy guidelines believed to embody such interpretations.

The first of these, as previously explained, is the following:

In proposing solutions or methods of solution of substantive issues of international disputes, non-judicial organs of the United Nations (usually the Security Council or the General Assembly) should neither exceed nor give the appearance of exceeding the powers of discussion or recommendation.

This is followed by a second guideline, corollary to the first, on the subject of collective measures:

When tangible pressures are applied by the United Nations in the handling of international disputes and situations, such measures should be visibly directed to the purposes laid down in the Charter for such measures (i.e., to deal with aggressions, other breaches of peace, or threats to peace). Such measures should not be given the appearance of being designed to enforce substantive decisions on the merits of disputes; all efforts should be made, when necessary, to avoid giving such an appearance.

To the extent that a visible effort might be made by one or more states capable of commanding attention to implement the relevant Charter provisions according to these interpretations, the people of the world would, for the first time in history, begin to see important states endeavoring to impose uniform and agreed-on restraints on international political activity, including the handling of

their own disputes. Their perceptions of the world would begin to
record the first faint glimmerings of an international constitutional
system. The principle was stated recently, with respect to the
United States Supreme Court, as follows:

> The power of the Supreme Court to command acceptance
> and support not only for its decisions but also for its
> role in government seems to depend upon a sufficiently
> widespread conviction that it is acting legitimately,
> that is, performing the functions assigned to it, and
> only those functions, in the manner assigned.[12]

The principle is even more important in the international
realm for the reason that here we still have to make a start. World
leaders have been largely indifferent to Charter limitations on U.N.
dispute-handling powers, apart from the matter of obtaining requisite majorities. The minimum requirement might be the formulation of sound interpretive guidelines on essential procedural points,
and rigid adherence to these. The requirement for rigid adherence
can be expected to be a major point of practical difficulty if the
search for world security is undertaken along the lines herein suggested.

In addition to the importance of basic constitutional principles,
we may also suggest some more detailed and pragmatic benefits to
be derived from adherence to agreed-on powers.

As just suggested, the Charter contains the faint blueprint of
a system that, if developed, would represent progress toward world
security. In effect, it suggests the desirability, in the interests of
a cooperative approach, of a limitation rather than an extension of
powers. It has incalculable value in indicating the outer limits of
powers generally acceptable, whether on the part of the world organization, other groups of states, individual states, or other political entities.

As one part of the system thus postulated, the majority in any
given case in a competent U.N. organ would be bound to limit the
organization to discussion and recommendations concerning the
merits of the controversy. The party or parties on the other side
would be bound to acquiesce in this procedure but would not be bound,
morally or legally, to comply with any resulting recommendations.[13]
The system would thus not be calculated to bring about immediate
solutions of disputes. Parties on both sides of a given case would,
however, be bound together in the debating process, as would the
other members of the competent organ. The debating atmosphere
would improve as the impression gained ground that disputes were
being handled in a forum in which parties would not be subjected to

the assertion of powers and pressures never agreed to. Debates would tend to have less of the character of political warfare, to become correspondingly full and free, and to be centered on the right issues. To the extent that international debates achieved this character, they would better fulfill the ideal role attributed to the debates of legislative bodies in domestic societies—the tendency, through full exploration and rational discussion of the truly relevant issues, to reach the solutions best calculated to preserve and strengthen the system. Starting from our present anarchic condition, they would in effect be a knitting machine that might be capable of gradually weaving a fabric of world consensus, albeit a loose one, and thereafter of preserving and strengthening it.

"Negative" advantages of the course being advocated would consist of the removal of obstacles to peace and security created by past practices. In this connection, our first proposition might be that the traditional anarchic approach suffices in itself to nullify any potential of the U.N. in the desired direction. The discontinuation of this approach would constitute the first and greatest "negative" advantage. Vis-a-vis the U.N. itself, the course here advocated would result in the removal of the following obstacles created by U.N. pressures beyond those authorized in the Charter:

1. Relations are strained when disputes are handled by one or more parties in ways perceived by others to be exceedingly relevant and agreed powers of dispute-handling, or that otherwise defeat expectations of equitable treatment. The level of tension in the international realm is thereby increased, and the environment for the productive conduct of relations is worsened.

2. Confusion is caused among informed elements of the public when the United Nations appears to act in ways inconsistent with the powers conferred on it in the Charter. This confusion has a greater significance than is suggested by its self-evident character, due to dichotomies between the U.N. and governments on one hand and world opinion on the other. The predominant public attitude toward the world organization—frustration because of its inability to achieve its primary purpose of maintaining world peace and security— is grounded in confusion and ignorance of the organization's chartered powers. It can hardly be said that confusion is brought about on a conscious level when people, knowing their own governments refuse to concede to the United Nations the power to decide issues of concern to them, see such powers of decision apparently being applied by the world organization against others, such as Spain in 1946. Apathy and lack of interest are too great for that. Such disparities must, however, have subconscious alienating effects contributing to the obvious tendency of people to concern themselves

with the ultimate successes and failures of the organization rather than with the power it possesses for the achievement of its objectives.

    3. People have tended to form an image of the powers asserted as a significant juridical structure forming the main alternative in the search for world security to the traditional approach, sometimes called the "balance of power."

    This supposed structure is illusory in that it lacks the substructure of consensus, which is essential to enable the successful application of such asserted powers and jurisdictions in all disputes. Instances appear throughout this study in which components of the structure have been employed by majorities as a means of pressuring the other side.

    The perceived structure is an obstacle to progress because its background and manner of employment draw attention to it as the key to peace, and thus distract attention from possibly more fruitful channels of progress. It grew naturally out of the willingness of officials to use the United Nations without regard to Charter limitations on its powers. This attitude was a continuation of the traditional approach to the conduct of relations, characterized by pressure and counter-pressure, leading to confrontations and a gradually deteriorating spiral of insecurity.

IMPLEMENTATION

    Efforts to implement the present proposal would concern only the method of handling disputes. They would have nothing to do with nationally felt requirements for security measures such as arms and alliances. Even where methods of dispute-handling are concerned, if a state dedicated to mutual and reciprocal observance of Charter provisions decided that its security needs in a given case required it to exceed the limitations of those provisions, it could only be expected to proceed accordingly. The successful implementation of this proposal would require at least a generation of peace plus some luck.

    If an attempt were made by one or more governments to take action along these lines, a possible first step could be the outlining, at the outset, of its basic elements. Taking as an illustration the set of guidelines proposed in this study (consolidated at the beginning of Chapter 13), this outline could be proposed as a resolution or, conceivably, as an addendum to the Charter. However, proponents should make it clear that the effort would continue on a case-by-case basis regardless of the fate of the formal proposal.

An alternative approach would be to proceed case by case, seeking first to bring significant disputes and situations before the appropriate U.N. political organ and then to ensure that they are there dealt with in conformity with Charter procedures properly interpreted.

Debates at all stages would be of the essence. At the first procedural stage, these could be said to have the goal of transforming U.N. dispute-handling procedures so that this forum might come to be recognized as one in which disputes could be considered dispassionately and from which no pressures or demands would emanate beyond those agreed to as acceptable to all. It might be some time before this goal could be achieved. However, the debates, even in this first stage, might have their most important effect on world thought patterns, which is the primary goal to be sought. For the world to see important states trying to impose limits in the handling of disputes, including disputes of concern to themselves, according to a uniform and agreed-on plan, would be something new in history. The appearance thus given would be that of the intrusion of something resembling law into a world format theretofore dominated by considerations of expediency. Such impressions, even if only impressions that efforts are being made, would represent change in the actual handling of disputes. With some significant change in prevalent thought patterns in such matters, new opportunities for further progress, previously unthought of, might be seen.

In effect, the resulting thought pattern would amount to the placing of international relations on a sound juridical basis. This familiar phrase would here be given a simple definition, namely the handling of international disputes in accordance with agreed-on and limited international procedures. This effect would be a revolutionary change, opening up new and unlimited possibilities of progress. By contrast, the present anarchic situation offers little such hope.

While procedural debates might constitute the first phase, they could have continuing importance because of the diversity of situations that might arise, and because of efforts that might be made to have the rules set aside for particular cases. At all stages of such debates, efforts should be made to emphasize the potential of the procedures advocated for contributing to long-range goals of peace and security.

The second main subject of debates, and the more important, would consist of the substantive issues of individual disputes. As the debating atmosphere gradually improved, these debates should correspondingly become more cogent, full and free, and capable of fulfilling the traditional consensus-building role of this process. Little need be said of the content of substantive debates. States will naturally continue to seek solutions conforming to their perceived interests, which are also usually perceived by them as conforming to the requirements of justice, peace, and security. As the debating process and environment improved, these attitudes could then be expected gradually to be modified in the direction of increased consensus among contending parties and bring about the degree of community sentiment necessary to ensure the successful settlement of all disputes.

Such an eventuality would by no means end the importance of the debating process, which can be said to have its principal significance not in the achieving of a particular pattern of international procedures and functions, nor in the achievement of agreements on certain issues or a broad range of issues, but rather in the continuous shaping of world opinion into patterns permitting the solutions of all disputes in the face of changing conditions. The process here conceived as suitable for establishing peace and security is seen as equally suitable and essential for maintaining it thereafter.

Turning to the plan of this study, Chapter 1 has undertaken to set forth its major thesis. Chapter 2 contains some necessary further detail concerning the role of collective measures. The remaining chapters are devoted to such matters as major trends entering into present concepts of the U.N.'s dispute-handling function and those of other organizations; functions and procedures devised in the search for solutions of past disputes; descriptions of how some past disputes were actually handled; and indications of how these disputes might have been handled in accordance with the guidelines outlined herein. Some indications may thus be given as to the kinds of problems that can be expected, and how they might be solved, if attempts are made to apply these provisions and interpretations in future cases.

The ensuing chapters will give difficulty to readers who assume that all efforts to strengthen the role of the U.N. in the political realm must seek to strengthen its authority, and thus enable it to solve the generality of disputes that arise pursuant to the traditional approach to the conduct of relations. This is true here only in a very indirect and long-range sense. States involved in disputes can only be expected to pursue their policy objectives as before, but, procedurally, representatives pursuing the approach advocated here should be seeking to lessen tensions and thus gradually build a degree of community that will ensure the manageability of all disputes. Governments involved in immediate disputes should be persuaded, if possible, to acquiesce in this approach on the grounds that their prospects of success would be at least as good as under the traditional approach of pressures and counter-pressures.

In the chapters that follow, a few additional guidelines are proposed consistent with, or in some cases subordinate to, those already suggested. These are all consolidated in the final chapter, which is largely devoted to questions of their practical implementation.

NOTES

1. Art. 4.

2. The reference here is to the peaceful separation of Norway from Sweden in 1905, the Aaland Island case of 1920-21 between Finland and Sweden, and the Eastern Greenland case between Denmark and Norway, settled by the World Court in 1933.

3. See the opening pages of this chapter, supra.

4. As to the view of President Franklin Roosevelt, see, inter alia, Foreign Relations of the U.S., 1941, vol. 1, at 363, 366-67; id. 1942, vol. 3, at 572-73; id. 1942, China, at 185-86; id. 1943, The Conferences at Cairo and Tehran, at 530-33; The Memoirs of Cordell Hull (New York: Macmillan, 1948), vol. 2, at 1642-43, 1646-47; J. M. Burns, Roosevelt: The Soldier of Freedom (New York: Harcourt Brace Jovanovich, 1970), at 358-59, 427-29, 560; D. Yergin, Shattered Peace: The Origins of the Cold War and the National Security State (Boston: Houghton Mifflin, 1977), at 42-48; C. Thorne, Allies of a Kind: The United States, Britain and the War against Japan, 1941-45 (New York: Oxford University Press, 1978), at 277; and M. Sherwin, A World Destroyed: The Atomic Bomb and the Grand Alliance (New York: Vintage Books, 1974), at 88-89, and authorities cited therein.

5. Foreign Relations of the U.S., 1945, vol. 1, at 418, 422.

6. Report of Committee III/2 to Commission III, Doc. 1027, III/2/31(1), 12 United Nations Conference on International Organization Documents (hereafter U.N.C.I.O. Docs.) 159, 162: The Conference committee that drafted the provisions of Chapter VII of the Charter, mainly on the collective measures function, also placed a note in the record stipulating that if peaceful settlement were undertaken by the Council with respect to the serious types of cases with which that Chapter was concerned—aggressions, other breaches of peace, and threats to peace—it was to have the same recommendatory power provided for the Council in Chapter VI. Report of Committee III/3 to Commission III on Chapter VIII, Section B; Doc. 881, III/3/46, id. at 502, 507. Committee III/3 proposed giving the Council greater power; however, the proposal was dismissed with little discussion. Summary Report of the 14th Meeting of Committee III/3, Doc. 628, III/3/33, id. at 379, 380-81.

7. Ch. 4, text at notes 1-8, infra.

8. Summary Report of the 14th Meeting of Committee IV/1, Doc. 661, IV/1/50; 13 U.N.C.I.O. Docs. 224; Report of Subcommittee D to Committee IV/1 on Art. 36 of the Statute of the International Court of Justice, Doc. 702, IV/1/55, id. at 557; Summary Report of the 17th Meeting of Committee IV/1, Doc. 759, IV/1/59; id. at 246.

9. Chairman of the United States Delegation, the Secretary of State, Charter of the United Nations: Report to the President on the Results of the San Francisco Conference, at 68 (1945) (55:30:83); minutes of the closing plenary session of the Conference, Doc. 1209, p. 19, 1 U.N.C.I.O. Docs. 658, 665, 669, and 684; L. Weiler and A. Simons, The United States and the United Nations: The Search for International Peace and Security (New York: Macmillan, 1967), at 39-49.

10. The relevant portion of the resolution (G.A. Resolution 39 [I] [1946]) provided as follows:

> The General Assembly . . .
> Recommends that if, within a reasonable time, there is not established a government which derives its authority from the consent of the governed, committed to respect freedom of speech, religion, and assembly and to the prompt holding of an election . . . the Security Council consider the adequate measures to be taken in order to remedy the situation;
> Recommends that all Members of the United Nations immediately recall from Madrid their ambassadors and ministers plenipotentiary accredited there.

11. The case is considered further in Ch. 6, text at notes 4-8, infra.

12. A. Cox, The Role of the Supreme Court in American Government (New York: Oxford University Press, 1976), at 104-105.

13. Some questions concerning the practicality of the present thesis (one or two of which may occur to some readers at this point) will be considered in the final pages of this study.

2

COLLECTIVE AND PROVISIONAL MEASURES

APPLICATION OF TANGIBLE PRESSURES BY THE UNITED NATIONS

Proper Role of Collective Measures

The collective measures function of the United Nations, as noted above, empowers the Security Council to apply tangible pressures—force or measures less than force, such as diplomatic and economic sanctions—when deemed necessary to deal with aggressions, other breaches of peace, or threats to peace. The relation of this function to that of peaceful settlement should, from the perspective of the present thesis, be similar to that between the police and the organs that seek solutions of disputes in individual democratic societies. It is, of course, the latter—courts and legislatures—that engage in the search for solutions and conduct debates on the issues, that contribute to the maintenance of requisite community sentiments as the underlying bases of the respective governments. The role of the police is residual, concerned with the maintenance of order. The establishment of this relationship between the major relevant U.N. functions would mean virtually a reversal of traditional roles. The general view has been that for the U.N. best to fulfill its major purpose it should be able to move with decisive force or other tangible pressure for the maintenance of peace when necessary. That this expectation is unrealistic is attested to by the history of the organization.

The second policy guideline suggested in Chapter 1 would require that collective measures be deployed only to deal with aggressions, other breaches of peace, and threats to peace and that when there is the possibility that such measures might appear to be enforcing substantive decisions in given disputes, all efforts should be made to dispel such impressions and to make clear the sole and real purpose of the measures. The reason for the latter rule would have nothing in it of hypocrisy. It would be simply that the consensus-building role of U.N. dispute-handling activities is not helped by giving the impression that the organization is exercising a power it was never given, namely the decision of disputes on their merits.[1]

While all applications of tangible pressure should thus conform to the Charter definition of collective measures, it is not always necessary to indicate such a designation. No harm was done by the absence of such an official categorization of the arms embargoes against Albania and Bulgaria in the Greek case, in 1948, and against the People's Republic of China in the Korean case, in 1951.[2] However, a desirable subsidiary guideline would be the following:

> Tangible pressures initiated by the United Nations in the handling of disputes and situations should never be placed in any legal category other than that of collective measures.

The reason for this proposal is that, while most people probably do not pay attention to the legalities brought forward to explain particular U.N. actions, statements to the effect that United Nations measures are not within the collective measures function must tend to build the impression that such measures can be employed for reasons other than those stipulated in the Charter.

Role of the General Assembly in Collective Measures

The above-proposed guidelines are intended to apply to measures initiated by the General Assembly as well as those initiated by the Security Council.

It was, of course, the intention of the framers of the Charter that the application of tangible pressures be the monopoly of the Council. In 1950, however, in the Uniting for Peace resolution, the Assembly asserted a residual authority to initiate collective measures when the Council was prevented by veto or other means from acting in cases of necessity.[3]

Meanwhile, the first actual instance of the initiation of tangible pressures by the Assembly took place during the organization's first year, in the Spanish case. The impression conveyed was, as indicated above,[4] that of diplomatic sanctions being applied for the purpose of forcing a change in the Spanish regime. The measure was, however, clearly not intended to be in the collective measures category. Measures of tangible pressure were subsequently initiated by the Assembly both before and after the adoption of the Uniting for Peace resolution. None, however, were designated collective measures, and with regard to some there were indications that they were not intended to be in that category. There have been signs that, notwithstanding the Uniting for Peace resolution, the basic supposition has continued to be that the Assembly has no authority to initiate such measures.

Some Assembly-initiated measures that were directed, and seen to be directed, to dealing with breaches of or threats to peace and therefore did not cause the kind of damage presently under discussion were the arms embargoes members were asked to apply in the Greek and Korean cases;[5] the Assembly's finding that the intervention of the People's Republic of China in the Korean case in 1950 was an act of aggression and its decision that the United Nations military measures already in progress be directed to meet the alleged aggression;[6] and the deployment of the United Nations Emergency Force in the Suez crisis of 1956.[7] Assembly-recommended measures taken by states that were seen not as being directed against breaches of or threats to peace but as attempts to enforce changes in internal or external relationships, or both, included, in addition to the Spanish case already mentioned, economic measures against South Africa and an arms embargo against Portugal, both in 1962.[8] The changes the Assembly apparently sought to enforce by these measures were the elimination of apartheid in South Africa and the elimination of colonialism in Portuguese territories in Africa. It is the latter kind of Assembly action that the proposed guidelines would be designed to eliminate.

It is immaterial, from the perspective of this discussion, whether or not tangible pressures are explicitly designated collective measures and whether they are initiated by the Council or by the Assembly.

"DEMANDS" OR "RECOMMENDATIONS" BY THE SECURITY COUNCIL?

Collective Measures

The Charter provision (Article 25) that members "agree to accept and carry out the decisions of the Security Council" was directed specifically to Council decisions to apply collective measures. While a modification of the rule with respect to military measures is also contained in the Charter, the general impression prevails that the Council is empowered to order member states to participate in the application of measures decided on.

The following contrary policy guideline is nevertheless proposed:

> In seeking the participation of member states in
> the application of collective measures, the Security
> Council should limit itself to recommendations.

The particular benefit to be derived from this policy would be elimination of the disillusioning effect that must ensue when member states that are not parties to a particular dispute and are, in Charter theory, supposed to be collaborating with the Council, refuse to do so.

As of the time of writing there have been three cases widely regarded as having involved the application of collective measures by the United Nations: those of Korea, Rhodesia, and South Africa. As far as the first two, at least, are concerned, it is clear that not all members of the United Nations took part in the sanctions. This fact did little damage in the Korean case, since the Council had merely recommended that members take part.[9] In the Rhodesian case it issued direct orders that members take the required measures. When some evidently refused to do so,[10] the damage to the organization must have been considerable.

One of the states refusing (for about six years) to comply with the Council's orders was the United States, which enacted a law authorizing the importation from Rhodesia of a commodity embargoed by the Security Council.[11] While it may well be considered that this action was unfortunate, the considerable criticism directed against the responsible authorities both within and without the United States represents a misdirected effort to support the United Nations.

In some particular cases mandatory sanctions might succeed. In most cases, however, efforts in this direction must tend to perpetuate illusions such as that the United Nations has the capacity to apply collective measures with any degree of consistency; that to this end it can effectively call upon states to participate; and that any states that fail to comply are merely occasional aberrants from the norm. In fact, as will be considered more fully in the next chapter, the world is far from possessing a rule of law in any way comparable to the capabilities of domestic legal systems, which are normally able to apply the police power dispassionately and consistently.

The guideline proposed above would have been dismissed out of hand at San Francisco as directly contrary to the prevailing concept of the collective measures function, according to which the Council was to be empowered to mobilize the world in order to deal with aggressions, other breaches of peace, and threats to peace and, to this end, to order the participation of states.

Precedents for the proposed guideline nevertheless go back to a contradiction that was manifested early on between the requirements of the Charter and the attitudes of states. According to Article 43, each member state was to conclude a separate agreement with the Security Council outlining the nature and the extent of assistance to be rendered by it in the event the Council should decide to apply military measures. It has proved impossible, up to the time of writing, to conclude any of these agreements. Evidently, however, it is only on the basis of the agreements that states can be held to be legally bound to participate in such measures. If it is held that collective measures must be mandatory in this sense, all such measures involving force have been legally impossible and will continue to be unless and until the agreements are concluded.

Such was apparently the view entertained in the Security Council with respect to the measures taken in the Korean case in 1950. Although the members appear to have considered that the Council could not initiate collective measures, they caused that organ to recommend that member states give military assistance to the Republic of Korea to meet the alleged aggression from the north.[12] The resulting military operation was considered, in this view, not as a collective measure by the United Nations but as one undertaken by the member states that responded to the recommendations, and on their responsibility. Following out this theory, the United Nations would have placed itself in a logically awkward position in initiating the measures by recommendation but denying responsibility for them. In fact, it can scarcely be said to have followed this course. It authorized the use of the United Nations flag and United Nations medals by the participating forces. The purpose was, obviously, to use the organization's prestige as a means of mobilizing world support for the operation. The pursuit of this precedent in future cases of the same kind, for the reason just indicated, was recommended in a report of the United Nations Collective Measures Committee, set up as a result of the Korean case to consider problems raised by it.[13]

It may have been a result of such considerations that Secretary-General Lie, at the time, and Secretary-General Thant, later, both categorized the Korean operation as a United Nations collective measure.[14] These authorities thus provide a direct precedent for the guideline here being advocated.

Other precedents of a different kind and more limited character also exist in the various cases in which either the Council or the Assembly has attempted to exert pressure by recommending that member states apply specified measures. These occurred in the cases of Spain,[15] apartheid in South Africa,[16] Portuguese overseas territories,[17] Rhodesia,[18] "peace-keeping operations" in the Middle

East, Zaire, and Cyprus,[19] and perhaps others. They were applications of pressure that were not designated collective measures, and some of them were ostensibly directed to ends other than those prescribed in the Charter for collective measures. In the latter respect they were contrary to one of our proposed guidelines. For present purposes, however, they have significance as indications of the willingness of both the Council and the Assembly to <u>recommend</u> that member states apply tangible pressures.

The sacrifice that would be entailed in adopting the proposed guideline would be slight or non-existent, since it is only an illusion that the Council has the power to order states to apply collective measures. When it attempts to apply this power and fails to receive the cooperation even of member states in applying the required measures, as in the Rhodesian case, the combined effects of illusion (resulting from the apparent elaborateness of the legal structure employed) and disillusionment must be detrimental to prospects for building the requisite base for world security.

Provisional Measures

Pursuant to Article 40 of the Charter, the Security Council may "call upon" the parties to a dispute to comply with "provisional measures" prescribed by that organ with the purpose of preventing deterioration of a dispute or situation. By definition such measures are not supposed to affect the permanent rights, claims, or positions of the parties. This measure is generally considered to be mandatory. Thus, when the Council calls upon the parties to a dispute to comply with the commonest form of provisional measure, a cease-fire, such calls are generally formulated as orders and considered to be legally binding.

The present proposal is as follows:

The Council should limit itself to recommendations in the exercise of the provisional measures function.

The basic reason for this proposal is the fact that, within the traditional and existing format of international relations, disputes arise in which the parties are too far apart to permit prompt and effective solutions. Demands that states comply with provisional measures might similarly prove unacceptable in some cases as entailing unacceptable sacrifices. It is self-evident that the states will not comply with such demands, however they might be phrased. Consequently, the idea that the Council exercises a binding power of decision in this function is illusory.[20]

With respect to long-range goals, implementation of this proposed guideline could be expected to merge with the effects of the others here proposed and thus to contribute to the building of world community, peace, and security. From a more immediate standpoint of practicality, recommendations that states accept provisional measures seem at least as likely of acquiescence as binding orders that they do so.

NOTES

1. Ch. 4, infra.
2. Respectively, G.A. Resolution 288 (IV) (1949) and G.A. Resolution 500 (V) (1951).
3. Ch. 5, n. 2 and accompanying text, infra. The present discussion is primarily concerned with the fact that the Assembly does, on occasion, initiate tangible pressures. The question of the desirability of its doing so is discussed in J. Halderman, The United Nations and the Rule of Law: Charter Development through the Handling of International Disputes and Situations (Dobbs Ferry: Oceana, 1967), at 149-62.
4. Ch. 1, n. 10 and accompanying text, supra.
5. N. 2 and accompanying text, supra.
6. G.A. Resolution 498 (V) (1951). See pp. 99-101, infra.
7. Ch. 6, text at n. 1 et seq., infra.
8. Respectively, G.A. Resolution 1761 (XVII) (1962) and G.A. Resolution 1807 (XVII) (1962).
9. Ch. 5, text at n. 9 et seq., infra.
10. Ch. 3, text at n. 36 et seq., infra.
11. Amendment to the Strategic and Critical Materials Stockpiling Act, Nov. 17, 1971, 85 U.S. Statutes at Large 427. This enactment was repealed in 1977 by Public Law 95-12, Mar. 18, 1977, 91 U.S. Statutes at Large 22.
12. N. 9 and accompanying text, supra.
13. Report of the Collective Measures Committee, U.N. General Assembly Official Records (hereafter U.N. GAOR), 6th Sess., Supp. 13, at 28 (1951).
14. "Introduction of the Annual Report of the Secretary-General on the Work of the Organization 1 July 1950-30 June 1951," id., Supp. 1A, at 3; "United Nations Stand-By Peace Force," address by U Thant, June 13, 1963, U.N. Review, vol. 10, no. 7, at 54 (July 1963). See, in accord, D. Bowett, United Nations Forces: A Legal Study (New York: Praeger, 1964), at 267.
15. N. 4 and accompanying text, supra.
16. N. 8 and accompanying text, supra.

17. Id.

18. Ch. 4, n. 26 and accompanying text, infra.

19. This concept is the subject of Ch. 6, infra.

20. Evidence is furnished by the history of Security Council demands for cease-fire in the Middle East war of June 1967. See, e.g., "Report of the Security Council 16 July 1966-15 July 1967," U.N. GAOR, 22d Sess., Supp. 2, at 36-47 (1967). Another illustration is found in the following passage from S.C. Res. 215 (1965), pertaining to the India-Pakistan Conflict of that year:

> The Security Council, Regretting the delay in the full achievement of a complete and effective cease-fire . . . as called for in its resolutions 209 . . ., 210 . . ., 211 . . ., and 214. . . .

3

STRUCTURE OF ILLUSION: THE LEGAL COMPONENT

This and several later chapters will endeavor to analyze some of the components of the structure of illusion discussed toward the end of Chapter 1.

Among these components, the concept of law is necessarily pervasive, since the structure consists of purported legal powers of international dispute-handling machinery, including, particularly, the idea that United Nations political organs have the power to make legally binding decisions on substantive issues in international disputes. The structure is given form and apparent substance by the importance of law per se. Some of the factors contributing to this role are independent of international security organizations and some, of course, go back to antiquity.

The word "law" is imprecise, being capable of several quite different meanings. As applied to domestic and international relations, for example, it means different things. The predominant meaning in the minds of most people is derived from domestic societies. Thus, when people hear the word "law," even in an international context, they tend to relate it to domestic, and thus to effective, law. Even if it is well understood that international law is not effective, the use of "law" in this context tends to build up the idea that it is potentially, and perhaps not far from, effective law. The tendency is to think of international law as an existing body of rules. The corresponding rules of domestic law may be widely seen as the central and focal point of domestic legal systems; thus the maintenance of order can be seen as deriving from the efforts of legislative, judicial, and executive authorities in formulating, modifying, repealing, interpreting, and applying the rules. This view, carried over to the international realm, can lead to the belief that efforts to build and strengthen law can by themselves ultimately make it effective.

However, what people generally regard as law, even in the domestic sphere, is superficial, since it must rest upon a more fundamental base. The crucial decision-making role of the authorities mentioned above is not in enacting, interpreting, and applying rules of law but in contributing to the continuation in a changing world of the necessary cohesion in the thought patterns of the people in the society; in effect, of the "real" constitution.

The concept of law in the sense of visible attributes can, however, be given a reasonably consistent definition as the aggregate of the rules and the institutions by which they are applied with the effect of maintaining peace and security. Law thus defined is a legal or constitutional system, a notion interchangeable with that of a system of order. [1]

An essential component is lacking in the international realm, namely the capability of maintaining order. [2] People tend, however, to regard rules, and supposed rules, in this area as rules of law. Thus, the aggregate of rules that apply for the amicable handling of the great mass of international disputes and situations is regarded as comprising a massive and nearly comprehensive body of rules of law. [3]

These include, among other things, the fact that West Irian is within the boundaries of Indonesia. This boundary is, of course, as "legal" as international boundaries generally are. No international border, however, is established by law in the predominant sense derived from domestic systems capable of maintaining order. The manner in which West Irian was included within the boundaries of Indonesia provides an illustration as to why this is so.

That case involved the claim of Indonesia to West Irian, which was under Netherlands government and control. Indonesia claimed that West Irian had always been part of its territory and that it should have been included in Indonesia when the latter country obtained independence from the Netherlands. [4] The dispute intensified in 1961 and was brought into the General Assembly, where Indonesia candidly threatened to use force if necessary to achieve its end. [5] Armed clashes in fact occurred. [6] The Netherlands indicated that it was prepared to relinquish control of the territory and turned the attention of the Assembly to the question of the right of self-determination of the inhabitants. Indonesia claimed that since it was the rightful sovereign of West Irian, the right of self-determination did not apply to that territory. [7] It also rejected a proposal that the question of sovereignty be referred to adjudication by the World Court, claiming that the Court would be prejudiced in favor of the colonial power. [8]

The "anti-colonialist" group in the Assembly supported the Indonesian position, resulting in the defeat of a resolution that would have recommended a solution that took account of the self-determination principle. [9] The dispute was then taken out of the General Assembly and to negotiations in which the parties were aided by a mediator suggested by the Secretary-General. The result was an agreed settlement[10] according to which the territory was to be handed over to Indonesia, after which the wishes of the inhabitants were to be consulted. When the Assembly expressed its appreciation of the settlement,[11] some members objected that it represented a yielding to the threat of force.[12]

This settlement has been regarded as an accomplishment of international law.[13] However, it can scarcely be so regarded in light of the prevalent notion of law, which, as indicated, appears to be derived from domestic law and to comprise systems capable of maintaining order. It is impossible to envision as part of such a system rules by which parties to a dispute can settle it by disposing of territory and its inhabitants without consulting the latter, or that permit the settlement of disputes by the use or threat of force.

These are not methods for building the community sentiment that is the underlying prerequisite of effective law and distinguishes such law from the reality of international law.

Another distinction between the two concepts of law is that effective domestic systems rest, to varying extents, on the police power in addition to community sentiment. Indeed, a semblance of order can be maintained if the necessary degree of cohesion exists among a dominant element of a given population to enable it to enforce its will on the rest. There is no prospect of such a dominant element achieving supremacy in the international realm, so as to be able to impose its kind of peace on the world. Thus the proposition again emerges that the only possible basis for world security is the achievement of a minimal requisite degree of community sentiment among the world's people generally.

Prevalent thinking, however, does not partake of this line of thought; rather, most people think of international law as a system in existence that can, by work and effort directed to law itself, be brought to a point of effectiveness.

People customarily regard their own countries' respective policies as being based on justice, a notion perhaps aided by a residual idea of a natural law pervading the world. Accompanying this preconception may well be an expectation that others should be readily persuaded to agree with these policies in particular situations.

This melioristic tendency finds further support in a number of factors. One that is important is that the great mass of international transactions and disputes are handled amicably.[14] Customs arise for handling different kinds of situations, and it seems easy and natural to equate these with law. It is particularly easy to extend this concept of common law to the notion that international law emerges out of international custom. Similarly, domestic concepts of contract encourage the belief that agreements entered into between nations carry legal obligations.

Indeed, it may be readily conceded that in terms of the predominant notion of law derived from domestic societies there is
justification for saying that many localized areas of international
relations are, in fact, governed by law. Law, in this context, has
been defined above as the aggregate of the rules and the institutions
by which the rules are applied with the effect of maintaining peace
and security. It would be difficult, on the basis of this definition,
to challenge assertions that there is a law of the European Economic
Community, or that there is a law of the International Civil Aviation
Organization. These areas—one functional and one regional—well
illustrate this idea, because they possess recognizable rules in the
form of constitutional treaties. They are rather extreme situations
supportive of the notion of law. Advocates of international law can,
however, easily argue that the definition is to be extended to all
areas of international activity where there is any possibility of conflict, except those actually the subject at the moment of intractable
disputes.

It is admittedly difficult to challenge the notion of law illustrated by this localized approach. The challenge must be based on
a broader view of the world problem of peace and security.

The crux of the definition of "law," in such a view, is the element of effectiveness. The problem of world law, in the sense of
effective law, is therefore not to be identified by considering only
areas in which it is possible to resolve all disputes and situations;
nor is it directly related to the characteristics customarily attributed
to law—rules and dispute-handling institutions. It is rather to be
found in the fact that the present and traditional environment of international relations[15] permits the emergence of intractable disputes.
While it may be argued that the great mass of disputes can be handled
amicably and in accordance with rules that bear some relationship to
law, the problem does not consist of closing a few identifiable gaps.
New intractable disputes may arise in the most unexpected quarters.
An example is the rule of inviolability of embassies, until recently
one of the best established rules of "international law." Among the
areas of general agreement a generation ago were the regimes of
territorial seas and the high seas. More recently these areas have
become subjects of disagreement and even violence. The world is
far from the degree of community necessary for peace and security,
farther perhaps than it was in the period preceding the dawn of the
modern state system.

By international agreement, international law is supposed to
consist of custom, treaties, the general principles of law recognized
by "civilized" nations, judicial decisions, and writings of jurists.[16]
Law as thus described may have utility when, at some future time,
the necessary consensus is established to prevent the emergence of
intractable disputes. However, in today's conditions, emphasis on

such notions of law can only divert attention from channels of endeavor that might prove fruitful.

Unfounded assertions that particular situations are governed by law are particularly liable to foster illusions because of the promise of law and order created in the minds of observers through their tendency to relate "law" with the role of domestic law. It has been said with respect to broken promises bearing on the public welfare that "each of them serves, in greater or less degree, to break down that mutual trust that makes cooperation possible and knits people together into a society."[17]

The illusory character of law in international relations is manifested by the fact that while governments customarily say that they adhere to it, they are generally unwilling to submit to third-party determinations of what the law means in particular situations they deem important to their interests. This is another aspect of the dichotomy, described above, involving the willingness of governments to have the United Nations enact decisions on substantive issues apparently directed against others, but not against themselves. Particular governments seem capable in some circumstances of upholding a variety of concepts of law while disavowing the same or similar concepts when seen from a different perspective, and to do this with complete sincerity, apparently unaware of the contradiction.

There was such a demonstration in favor of "law" at San Francisco when a clear majority of the participating governments strongly supported the proposal that the World Court should have general automatic jurisdiction over any proper legal dispute brought before it by any member of the United Nations.[18] Only the Soviet Union and members of the communist bloc overtly and adamantly opposed the proposal. Other states which opposed it, including the United States, indicated that they were largely motivated by apprehension that if the proposal were adopted ratification of the Charter would be jeopardized. The debate gave reason to suppose that the bulk of the world's governments had decided to espouse the law in the genuine sense of being willing to accept binding third-party adjudications of disputes over interpretation.

When this proposal failed, the Conference unanimously adopted a recommendation that all members of the United Nations accept the Court's jurisdiction under the optional procedure that had been provided.[19] Pursuant to this procedure, states desiring to do so can accept the Court's jurisdiction vis-a-vis other states making the same acceptance, on a basis of reciprocity. If all states accepted jurisdiction through this procedure, general jurisdiction would be achieved.

Thereafter, in the United States, in regard to an effort to have the country accept such jurisdiction, a favorable attitude toward law was manifested—until the issue reached the floor of the Senate. In initiating the debate, Senator Elbert Thomas could say that "rarely in my legislative experience have I encountered such an important measure with the people of the country so unanimously in support of it."[20] He pointed out that the President and Secretary of State supported the proposal, as did the American Bar Association and other organizations, and that all witnesses testifying to the Senate committee had been in favor. Yet a reservation introduced during the debate, with the potential effect of largely nullifying the proposed acceptance of jurisdiction, was easily adopted.[21] This reservation, the so-called Connally amendment, touched a sensitive nerve of the American public, being phrased in terms of preserving United States jurisdiction over its own domestic affairs. The Court has, by its nature, no jurisdiction in such matters. All agree that it should not have such jurisdiction. The amendment reserved to the United States the right to decide whether particular disputes were within or outside its jurisdiction. This action was deceptive, in that most laymen could view it as not interfering with the proper jurisdiction of the Court over international disputes although it served effectively to continue the traditional insistence of states on deciding for themselves, in the last resort, issues of concern to themselves. Its effect extended beyond the United States, since other parties to disputes submitted under the resulting declaration could claim its benefits pursuant to the principle of reciprocity.[22] Also, some governments copied this reservation in their declarations of acceptance.[23]

In 1960 a proposal originated in the Senate to repeal the reservation. Although this move had Presidential support, it provoked such strong resistance from elements of the population[24] that it was finally abandoned. The deceptive nature of the phrasing of the reservation was such that this proposed repeal could be interpreted as a proposal to invite the World Court to intervene in American domestic affairs.

More deceptive, however, than the phrasing of the reservation had been the original impression that the grant of jurisdiction to the Court enjoyed almost unanimous approval. A sudden relinquishment of such a significant portion of a traditional attribute of sovereignty as was here proposed—once the intended effect is widely understood— is unlikely to receive either public or governmental approval in the United States or anywhere else.

While the demonstration of this last-mentioned psychological trait by the American public received a great deal of publicity, it did not prevent the United States from supporting actions by the Security Council and the General Assembly by which these organs have given the appearance to the world public of handing down binding decisions without the consent of parties concerned. A power of decision on the merits of disputes exercised by the Council or the Assembly would be a more far-reaching power than one exercised by the Court. The latter would be limited to deciding proper legal issues on the basis of law, whereas the Assembly and Council would not be so limited and could thus demand changes in existing legal situations. [25]

In some of the cases just referred to, involving purported decisions of the Council and the Assembly, technicalities were brought forward to justify what was done. We are here less concerned with these legalities than with the impression made on world opinion, since it is here that the goal of world community must be realized. The cases range from that of Spain in the first year of the Organization to those of Namibia, and Israeli rights in Jerusalem, current at the time of writing. [26]

Of particular interest in the present context is a statement of the United States government made in reference to the Rhodesian case in 1966, since, with undoubted sincerity, it both upholds the right of the United Nations to decide that case with binding effect and reserves the right of the United States to be its own judge in the event the United Nations should ever propose to take similar action against it. [27]

The government of Rhodesia, which had been a self-governing British colony, declared Rhodesia's independence in 1965 in a dispute concerning the suppression of the rights of the country's black majority by the white minority. The Security Council in 1966 found the situation to constitute a threat to peace, and there ensued the first instance of formal United Nations sanctions, mandatory in the sense that member states were ordered by the Council, with legally binding effect, to apply the measures decided on. [28]

However, the overall impression given by the handling of the case was not of an effort to deal with a threat to peace but rather of an effort to bring about changes in the internal and external regimes of Rhodesia.

To illustrate, reference may be made to some Council resolutions after Rhodesia's declaration of independence on November 11, 1965. In a resolution passed the following day, that organ:

    1. Decides to condemn the unilateral declaration of independence made by a racist minority in Southern Rhodesia;

    2. Decides to call upon all States not to recognize this illegal racist minority regime in Southern Rhodesia and to refrain from rendering any assistance to this illegal regime. [29]

There was in this resolution no finding that the situation constituted a threat to or breach of international peace. One intended effect seems to have been to initiate, at the least, diplomatic sanctions against Rhodesia with the purpose of bringing pressure in favor of a change of regime. The Council's finding that the regime was illegal was the assertion of a judicial function.

A Council resolution of April 9, 1966,[30] which authorized the stoppage at sea of ships carrying oil for Rhodesia, contained the following preliminary provisions:

> Considering that such supplies will afford great assistance and encouragement to the illegal regime in Southern Rhodesia, thereby enabling it to remain longer in being,
>
> 1. Determines that the resulting situation constitutes a threat to the peace. . . .

The resolution then called upon the United Kingdom to apply the measure in question, which was evidently intended to be an exercise of the collective measures function authorized by the Charter.

Similar introductory phrases are found in the resolution of December 16, 1966,[31] which specifically ordered member states to apply a range of measures and is accordingly acclaimed as the first exercise of mandatory United Nations sanctions:

> The Security Council
>
>   * * * * *
>
> Deeply concerned that the Council's efforts so far and the measures taken by the administering Power have failed to bring the rebellion in Southern Rhodesia to an end,
>
>   * * * * *
>
> Acting in accordance with Articles 39 and 41 of the United Nations Charter,
>
> Determines that the present situation in Southern Rhodesia constitutes a threat to international peace and security. . . .

The effect of such statements is, of course, influenced by the over-all situation. Given one in which there was a more visible threat, the resolutions might have been read as directing action toward the threat. In fact, public opinion is believed to have regarded these findings of threats to peace as no more than an expedient affording the technical basis for allowing the institution of measures intended to force changes in the Rhodesian regime.

Such was also the effect of the debates and other discussions surrounding the Council actions, including the U.S. government statement presently under discussion, which said in part:

> Here we have witnessed an illegal seizure of power by a small minority bent on perpetuating the subjugation of the vast majority. . . .
>
> We in the United States learned over 100 years ago that any attempt to institutionalize and legitimize a political principle of racial superiority in a new state was unacceptable. The effort to do so created an inflammatory situation, and our nation had to rid itself of this false and hateful doctrine at great cost. What could not be accepted by the United States in the mid-19th century cannot be accepted by the international community in the late 20th century.

Here and elsewhere, the statement was careful to say that the situation constituted a threat to peace. At the same time, it confirmed the generally held impression that the primary purpose of the measures was to force changes in the Rhodesian regime.

The question of how the United States would react if it should become the target of similar action is implied and answered in the following paragraph:

> Because the Security Council considers the situation in Rhodesia, with its unique legal and factual elements, as constituting a threat to the peace requiring the application of mandatory sanctions, does not absolve it from the independent exercise of judgment in different situations. Moreover, each of the permanent members of the Security Council has the power to prevent the use of enforcement measures in other situations where it may deem them to be inappropriate.

In effect, it seemed to be saying, the United States could prevent similar action against itself by using its veto. No such recourse was, or could have been, recognized as available to Rhodesia to enable it to avoid United Nations sanctions.

This inequality of powers and remedies can be plausibly justified by Charter language. The Council has the power to apply col-

lective measures on the basis of finding the situation in question to
be a threat to peace, regardless of how the purpose may be perceived by the general public. In turn, permanent members of the
Council have the right to veto decisions to apply collective measures.

However, it is the impact on public opinion, and not the official
designation of a measure, that determines whether a given action advances or retards the building of community sentiment, and thus
what effect it will have on the ultimate prospects for permanent
world security.

The action in the Rhodesian case is believed to have been generally perceived as an attempt to enforce substantive decisions
against Rhodesia; the assertion on the part of the United States of a
right of veto in the event of similar action against itself in some
future case must have appeared, in this light, as an assertion of
"one law for us, another law for them." This assertion could be
expected to convey an impression of unjustified unequal treatment
in view of the proposition, incorporated into the Charter as Article
27(3), that in the exercise of the Council's peaceful settlement function a state may not vote in its own case.[32] This provision has the
effect of eliminating the veto in such matters, and it could have been
adopted by the permanent members only because it was understood
that the peaceful settlement function was limited to powers of discussion and recommendation. The framers of the Charter thus
solved the problem under discussion on a basis of equality.

For reasons discussed in Chapter 4 it is, perhaps, not unexpected that authorities concerned with this statement should have
assumed that the United Nations had the right to make a binding decision and to attempt to enforce it, as long as the Council had decided that the situation in question was a threat to peace.

The present discussion sees this question from a different perspective, one that results in insisting that every effort be made to
keep the collective measures and peaceful settlement functions
separate and distinct in the eyes of all concerned. This view will
also be considered in Chapter 4.

Another instance of differing perspectives seems to be involved in the invocation of the veto power by the United States in its
statement on the Rhodesian case. Here there seems to have been a
change of perspective on the part of the U.S. government itself,
since it had originally upheld the exception of Article 27(3) on the
grounds that the American people would not understand if a state
were allowed to vote in its own case.[33] There was evidently, in
1944, when this statement was made, a greater concern for public
reactions than in 1966.

No doubt it is also this latter perspective that accounts for
the fact that while the U.S. statement gave some explanation as to

why the situation in Rhodesia warranted collective measures, it did not explain on the basis of factual developments why this was so on April 9, 1966, but had not been the case on the preceding November 20.[34]

Neither did it explain why the Rhodesian case had come to warrant such measures, whereas the cases of Portuguese territories in Africa and of apartheid in South Africa did not.[35] The latter major disputes appear to have been like that of Rhodesia in their essential characteristic, namely that they involved the deprivation of the human rights and civil liberties, including the right of self-determination, of large majority populations by minority regimes. The failure to explain the apparent inconsistencies in the handling of these cases shows a disregard for the desirability of developing a consistent pattern of world thought in the interests of permanent world security.

Finally, this perspective did not entertain the suspicion, which might have been adduced from the Rhodesian case itself and from other intractable disputes that had arisen during the United Nations period, that the underlying consensus necessary to an effective system might not exist and that, consequently, there was no international regime of law such as would be required for the consistent and effective application of a police power.

It sufficed, evidently, to find sets of words and phrases in the Charter that could be combined to provide supposed legal justification for the program it was desired to carry out. They also, in this case, were employed to form the basis of the U.S. government statement under discussion, representing a rather elaborate undertaking to convince the informed public of the reality and value of international law in its prevailing concept.

The aftermath was deleterious for this concept in that for at least the first decade the economic sanctions against Rhodesia were not carried out with sufficient consistency to achieve their purpose, however assessed;[36] in that the British government, which had initiated the oil embargo that comprised the first formal sanctions in the case, later appeared to have been involved in violations thereof;[37] and in that for approximately six years the United States authorized, by law, trade with Rhodesia in an embargoed commodity.[38] While this law was protested in the United States on grounds of its being wrong and illegal, there was little disposition to attribute the difficulty to any deficiency in the notion of law itself as applied to international relations.

Another facet of United States governmental thinking is revealed by a comparison of its above-mentioned statement with a version revised for newspaper publication.[39] The latter lessened somewhat the emphasis on the finding of a threat to peace, while a new section stressed United States opposition to the racial policies of the Rhodesian regime. Since the statement continued to uphold the right of the United Nations to decide the issue and enforce the decision, the revised statement seemed to be saying that the organization had this right because, among other reasons, it was used in pursuit of United States policy goals. Thus, while that government was purporting to be upholding law per se, it was, perhaps unconsciously, indicating that law is really to be regarded as a tool of policy. [40]

I find it difficult to identify any cases in which settlements can be attributed to United Nations pressures short of force but purporting or appearing to exceed its powers of discussion and recommendation. Admitting that some cases may have been overlooked, and that the statement may be contradicted by dispute settlements of the future, it reflects a situation that generally holds true and is of considerable moment. As a rule, United Nations pressures for agreement to particular terms of settlement of particular disputes, when they exceed the powers of discussion and recommendation, give the appearance of deciding the issue with legally binding force. The result is that in a considerable and continuing series of disputes the United Nations has appeared to apply rules of law, and the rules have appeared to be defied. The impression has thus been given of rules of law that depart from the realm of reality and take up their existence in that of illusion.

A world environment capable of ensuring order would be under a "rule of law" that would normally acquire the visible attributes of law, i.e., rules and institutions. The present study therefore has as its goal the establishment of the rule of law in international relations.

From the perspective of law, a proposition ventured at the outset of this study comes more clearly into focus, namely that the world really needs to accept uniform restraints, according to an agreed plan, in the handling of disputes and situations. It is impossible to envision the growth of law without some such recognizable restraints of sufficient significance to have an effect on the conduct of relations. The world has been without such restraints in that governments have felt free to apply any available pressures they deem appropriate in the pursuit of their objectives. It is difficult to envision such a "system" evolving into effective law, and in fact this has not happened.

A "legal," as compared to a "political," approach is a way of describing the direction of desirable efforts to progress toward the goals under discussion. Such an approach has varying degrees of necessity as well as of practicality in varying situations. In regard to the need for uniform restraints in the handling of disputes,

I have advocated the application of dispute-handling procedures of the U.N. Charter within their agreed-to limitations. If this suggestion were taken up, a necessary legal approach would require rigid adherence to these limitations. Other attributes of a proper legal approach would be that disputes and situations would be dealt with on the basis of their facts and that the true nature and purpose of international powers being employed in particular cases would be made clear to the world.

There should be no inhibition against the use of such normal and law-related tools as rules, or assumed rules, of conduct; agreements; commitments; third-party procedures; and institutions for dispute-handling. To be avoided, on the other hand, is emphasis on the notion of law per se. [41] A moratorium on talk of law as an existing fact in international relations and on the use and strengthening of this concept as a channel to peace might hasten the day when, like a fresh spring appearing unexpectedly in the desert, something resembling effective law might appear in the international realm.

We have had in the past precisely the wrong combination: much talk about law per se, and little concern about identifying and applying correct legal approaches in the handling of disputes and situations.

Although this study does not adopt the monistic concept of a single law in existence and pertaining to all levels of human society, including the international, it is possible to conceive of this concept and then to attribute some of the world's troubles to the way in which the law has been misused.

Perhaps a more down-to-earth statement of the principle would be that policies that contravene basic principles of law cannot contribute to the growth of the rule of law; that is, to a system capable of maintaining order. [42]

NOTES

1. "Law matches government every inch of its course. The two are not different things, but the same thing." A. Bentley, The Process of Government: A Study of Social Pressures (Cambridge: Harvard University Press, 1967), at 272.

2. "To idealize an ineffective law is a dangerous practice." R. West, Conscience and Society: A Study in the Psychological Prerequisite of Law and Order (London: Methuen, 1942), at 41.

3. A recent comprehensive treatise upholding the reality of international law as customarily perceived and its potential for the future development of peace and security is L. Henkin, How Nations Behave: Law and Foreign Policy (New York: Columbia University Press, 1968, 2d ed. 1979).

4. U.N. GAOR, 16th Sess., Plenary, at 617-18 (1961).

5. Id. at 848-49.

6. "International Law and the United Nations," address by the Secretary-General to the International Bar Association, 5 U.N. Monthly Chronicle, Aug.-Sept. 1968, at 114, 117.

7. U.N. GAOR, 16th Sess., Plenary, at 848 (1961).

8. Id.

9. Id., Annexes, Agenda Items 88 and 22(a), at 26 (Doc. A/L 368); id., Plenary, at 874-75.

10. 437 U.N. Treaty Series 273; U.N. GAOR, 17th Sess., Annexes, Agenda Item 89, at 2 (Doc. A/5170) (1962).

11. G.A. Resolution 1752 (XVII) (1962).

12. U.N. GAOR, 17th Sess., Plenary, at 51, 54, 56, 57 (1962).

13. "International Law and the United Nations," 5 U.N. Monthly Chronicle, supra, at 117.

14. Henkin, How Nations Behave, supra, at 182; id. 2d ed. 320.

15. "Environment" as used here refers to the thinking of peoples, as distinguished from that of governments, on the theory that only through the development of a commonality of public thinking can governments be relied on to act in a way consistent with the requirements of permanent security. For this purpose "environment" is preferable to "public opinion" as having longer range and more basic connotations, although the latter phrase may be used in particular contexts herein where it is less awkward.

16. I.C.J. Statute, Art. 38.

17. S. I. Hayakawa, Language in Thought and Action, at 104 (1939). Emphasis in original.

18. Ch. 1, n. 8, supra.

19. Doc. 870, IV/1/73 (Annex 3 to Report of the Rapporteur of Committee IV/1, Doc. 913, IV/1/74 [1], 13 U.N.C.I.O. Docs. 381, 413 [1945]); Minutes of the Ninth Plenary Session, Doc. 1210, P/20, 1 U.N.C.I.O. Docs. 612, 627.

20. 92 Congressional Record 10617 (1946).

21. Id. at 10624, 10697. For the debate see id. at 10624-26, 10683-97. The text of the U.S. Declaration may be found in the International Court of Justice Yearbook, 1946-1947, at 217.

22. For some uses that have been made of the reservation, see Gross, "Bulgaria Invokes the Connally Amendment," 56 American Journal of International Law 357 (1962).

23. For some reservations evidently in force at the time of writing, see International Court of Justice Yearbook, 1969-1970, at 65 (Malawi), 75 (Sudan). Some states filed but later repealed similar reservations.

24. Compulsory Jurisdiction: International Court of Justice, Hearings before the Committee on Foreign Relations, United States Senate, on S. Res. 94, 86th Cong., 2d Sess. (1960). For a statement by the Secretary of State indicating presidential support see id. at 10.

25. See also Ch. 1, text at notes 7-9, supra.

26. The Spanish case is discussed in Ch. 1, text at n. 10 et seq., supra, and Ch. 5, n. 3 et seq., infra; that of Namibia in Namibia, Ch. 8, and Ch. 9, text following n. 1, infra. In regard to Jerusalem, a series of resolutions has asserted the illegality of certain Israeli actions in that city. See Ch. 8, n. 3 and accompanying text, infra.

27. "International Law in the United Nations," address by the U.S. Ambassador to the United Nations, Arthur J. Goldberg, to the Association of American Law Schools, 56 Department of State Bulletin 140, 142-44 (Jan. 23, 1967).

28. S.C. Resolution 232 (1966).

29. S.C. Resolution 216 (1965). The U.N. had probably already created, by virtue of a series of prior resolutions, the general impression of endeavoring to bring about a Rhodesian regime that would recognize democratic freedoms and political rights, including universal adult suffrage (e.g., G.A. Resolution 1889 [XVIII] [1963]). Comprising, for the most part, General Assembly resolutions cast in the form of recommendations, these resolutions were themselves proper in the view of this discussion and are mentioned only because they contributed background for the impression later created of a U.N. effort to enforce desired changes. (A change occurred when G.A. Resolution 2022 [XX] of Nov. 1965, recommended measures that appear to have represented an effort to enforce desired policies in view of the imminent Rhodesian declaration of independence.)

30. S.C. Resolution 221 (1966).

31. N. 28, supra.

32. Art. 27(3) of the Charter. See also Ch. 13, n. 10, infra.

33. Foreign Relations of the U.S., 1944, vol. 1, at 748 (1966). See Ch. 13, n. 10, infra.

34. S.C. Resolution 217 of this date called on states to withhold diplomatic, and to break economic, relations with Rhodesia but was plainly not intended to apply collective measures. See Halderman, "Some Legal Aspects of Sanctions in the Rhodesian Case," 17 International and Comparative Law Quarterly, at 672, 684-685, 691-694 (1968). This resolution, like the later resolutions of Apr. 9, 1966 (n. 30, supra), and Dec. 16, 1966 (n. 28, supra), which intentionally initiated collective measures, came subsequent to Rhodesia's declaration of independence on Nov. 11, 1965.

35. Ch. 5, text at n. 20 et seq., infra.

36. See, e.g., The Economist, vol. 244, July 29, 1972, at 36; N.Y. Times, Feb. 6, 1975, p. 7, col. 1. The greatly intensified movement toward democratic rule in Rhodesia, beginning in the mid-1970s, was obviously precipitated mainly by the collapse of the Portuguese empire in southern Africa.

37. T. H. Bingham and S. M. Gray, "Report on the Supply of Petroleum and Petroleum Products to Rhodesia," Sept. 1978, London, Foreign and Commonwealth Office.

38. Ch. 2, n. 11, supra.

39. Goldberg, "Rhodesia Is a Moral Issue," Washington Post, Jan. 8, 1967, Sec. E, p. 3, col. 3.

40. The U.N. sanctions seemed to be regarded mainly as a tool of U.S. policy in the statement by President Carter when signing a repeal of the law referred to in the text at n. 38, supra, authorizing an exception to those measures:

> This measure [i.e., the repeal] is a central
> element in our African policy. . . .
>
> *   *   *   *   *
>
> With the cooperation of the Congress, we
> have taken a step of great importance in our
> southern African policy. . . . 76 Department of
> State Bulletin 333 (Apr. 11, 1977).

41. National courts would not be hampered, in following this suggestion, in basing opinions on such international criteria as international agreements, custom, decisions of international tribunals, or the writings of authorities on relevant matters. They would be inhibited only from referring to these sources or their own resulting decisions as "international law."

42. The undesirability of "institutionalizing" law is discussed in Ch. 12, infra.

4

ENFORCEMENT OF
SUBSTANTIVE SOLUTIONS

This and several of the following chapters will attempt to analyze in the light of this study's major thesis some of the international
dispute-handling structures that are brought forward to support
United Nations actions purporting to decide international disputes on
their merits.

The most important and legitimate of these structures finds
its base in the juxtaposition, in some cases, of elements of the "enforcement" function and the peaceful settlement function.

Let us consider, first, the case in which the United Nations
has indicates its preferred solution, in which there has been a finding of a threat to peace, and in which sanctions are directed against
the party deemed the wrongdoer. Such actions are likely to appear
to be intended to enforce United Nations decisions on the merits of
the case.

The guidelines proposed in Chapter 1 of this study would require that the two functions be clearly delineated and that it be made
clear that measures of enforcement are directed solely to the threat
to peace and not to enforcement of the decision.

The question then suggests itself of whether this course of action would not appear hypocritical, since all concerned could see
that the effect of the measures, if successful, would be to enforce a
particular solution.

The question arose during the drafting of the Charter. Indeed,
it arose then in much sharper form than it did later in practice,
since at the earlier stage officials were more concerned with limitations on the grants of power their own governments were willing to
make to the United Nations. By reason of this consideration, it was
made clear by the Conference committees concerned respectively
with collective measures and with peaceful settlement that the Security Council's recommendations of terms of settlement of disputes
would not carry any binding force.[1]

A somewhat different question was whether the Council should have the power to force a change in an existing situation if it deemed that to be the only way to maintain peace and security. That it might have had this power was indicated in the first paragraph of Chapter VIII, Section B, of the Dumbarton Oaks Proposals:

> 1. Should the Security Council deem that a failure to settle a dispute in accordance with procedures indicated in paragraph 3 of Section A, [2] or in accordance with its recommendations made under paragraph 5 of Section A, constitutes a threat to the maintenance of international peace and security, it should take any measures necessary for the maintenance of international peace and security in accordance with the purposes and principles of the Organization.

At the 18th meeting of the United States Delegation to the San Francisco Conference, Mr. Pasvolsky said that under the Dumbarton Oaks Proposals the Council could do anything and take any steps if peace and security were affected; in his view, a possible interpretation of Chapter VIII, Section B, paragraph 1, was that the Council could even impose terms of settlement. [3]

As indicated in Chapter 1 of this study, this statement represented a view of collective measures probably prevalent both at that time and subsequently. However, in the process of formulating the Charter this view obviously came into conflict with the right of states to be their own judges in their own disputes. Fears were expressed that it might give rise to settlements similar to that of Munich, and to possible U.N. intervention in the internal affairs of the states. A solution was proposed by Mr. Dulles entailing the removal of the phrase "any measures" in the above-quoted paragraph and the insertion of language that would make it clear that Council action would be limited to the sanctions specifically provided for in that section. [4] Ultimately, the paragraph in question was eliminated and the following paragraph amended to form the present Article 39 of the Charter: [5]

> The Security Council shall determine the existence of any threat to the peace, breach of the peace, or act of aggression and shall make recommendations, or decide what measures shall be taken in accordance with Articles 41 and 42, to maintain or restore international peace and security.

Articles 41 and 42, corresponding to paragraphs 3 and 4 of Chapter VIII, Section B of the Dumbarton Oaks Proposals, authorize, respectively, non-military and military measures.

In the hearings on the Charter before the Foreign Relations Committee of the United States Senate, reference was made to the following passage, having reference to the U.N.'s peaceful settlement function, in the Report to the President of the U.S. Delegation to the San Francisco Conference:

> The parties are not obligated at this stage of a dispute to accept the terms of settlement recommended by the Security Council, any more than they are obligated to accept the Council's other recommendations. If, however, their failure to do so results in a threat to the peace, then the enforcement provisions of Chapter VII come into play. [6]

Senator Warren Austin[7] suggested that it was undesirable thus to link the enforcement power with the power of the Council to recommend particular solutions. The spokesman for the Department of State said that the two ideas were not to be linked, and agreed with the following formulation by Senator Austin:

> Can you say, then, that the use of military authority which is granted by Chapter VII, is not intended by this treaty to be used to enforce in this indirect way, that is spoken of here on page 84 [of the Report to the President], the recommendation of the Security Council, but is used only for the purpose of preventing hostilities?[8]

The answer was in the affirmative.

This statement, like the Charter's language defining the collective measures function, leaves open the possibility that such measures might result in the enforcement of a particular solution if that were the only means of maintaining peace and security.

A logical basis has thus been provided for hypothetical elaborations, which may have contributed substantially to the structure of illusion under discussion. Steps through which these elaborations may have passed might have been somewhat as follows:

First, as provided in the Charter, the United Nations may make recommendations on substantive issues and may apply collective measures to deal with breaches of peace and threats to peace.

Second, also as provided by the Charter, the United Nations may enforce a particular solution of a controversy if that is the only means of maintaining or restoring peace in the given situation.

Third, when a threat to peace is deemed to be caused by the refusal of a party to accept a United Nations proposal made pursuant to its peaceful settlement function, the United Nations proposal, as such, may be enforced.[9] It is at this point that jurisprudence departs from the powers agreed to as generally acceptable to all member states.

Fourth, on the basis of a finding that a threat to peace exists, the United Nations may proceed to make and enforce a decision on the controversy. Under this rule—as exemplified by the Rhodesia case—the finding of the threat (or breach) is a technicality enabling the United Nations to proceed to the application of measures for the primary purpose not of dealing with the threat, but of enforcing the United Nations-prescribed solution.

Fifth, even without a threat to peace, the United Nations may proceed to initiate measures designed to enforce its desired solution of a given dispute.

Sixth, without any effort at enforcement or any finding of a threat to peace, the United Nations may simply decree purportedly binding decisions of disputed situations.

Such a progression of ideas, if it contributed, for example, to the handling of the Spanish case of 1946, must have run its course quickly, since that case occurred in the first year of the United Nations and would fall in the fifth category. The sixth stage was achieved in practice by at least 1950, when the general impression was conveyed that, without any gesture toward enforcement, the Security Council made a legally binding demand on Egypt to cease interfering with Israeli-connected shipping in the Suez Canal.[10]

The suggestion is not that the thought processes of dominant decision-makers went through any such evolutionary process, but only that the genuine dilemma that was considered at San Francisco may have put in train a thought process in the world public that brought about easier acceptance that certain uses made of the United Nations involving elements connected with that dilemma were right.[11]

A careful analysis of the problem under discussion might be thought to rule out use of the word "dilemma," since the resulting rules are rather clear. The political organs of the U.N. would be entitled to decide on the issues when enforcement of a particular solution would be the only apparent means of solving the given dispute. In other cases, pronouncements on the merits would be limited to recommendations.

The word "dilemma" is still appropriate, however, in view of the essentially political world in which the rules have to operate. Majorities have been all too ready in the past to cause the U.N. to appear to decide issues, notwithstanding the Charter's broad prohibition of such decisions. Any serious attempt to apply this limitation would probably be undermined by adoption of an explicit exception

allowing substantive decisions to be made and enforced when the resulting changes were deemed the only means of maintaining or restoring peace. It is to be noted that such an exception was not stated
in the Charter; nor was it allowed for in the accompanying record of
the drafting committee. A similar result ensued when this question
was taken up by the Foreign Relations Committee of the U.S. Senate.

The relevant guidelines herein proposed in Chapter 1 are likewise without such an exception. The important consideration as
here perceived is a corollary of the apparent concerns of the governments that drafted the Charter. Whereas they were concerned with
protecting traditional attributes of sovereignty, we are here concerned with the certainty that perceived invasions of those attributes
of sovereignty would result in strained relations and possibly other
setbacks to the realization of the potential role of the U.N. in the
pursuit of peace and security.

The dilemma accordingly continues to exist, and it is not possible to suggest any more detailed guidelines for its solution.

It may be illuminated, however, by a consideration of some
past cases, and suggestions as to how relevant Charter provisions
might have been applied to them. This writer believes that in no
case have they been properly applied, from the perspective of this
discussion.

The early Spanish case[12] involved the initiation of tangible
pressures for the indicated purpose of forcing a change of regime
in the target country. There was no finding of a threat to peace and
thus no possibility of directing the measure to dealing with such a
threat. The U.N., in these circumstances, should have done nothing
more than recommend a solution.

In the Palestine case of 1947-48, the United Nations conveyed
the impression of deciding the future of Palestine by virtue of the
Plan of Partition with Economic Union adopted by General Assembly
Resolution 181 (II) of November 29, 1947. The case presented an
evident threat to peace at the time and an actual breach in mid-1948.
The possibility of enforcing the "decision" was incorporated in the
resolution and was a frequent subject of discussion. However, tangible pressures to this end were not applied.

In its language, the resolution in question did no more than
recommend the partition plan. However, it went on to embrace the
idea that the "recommendation" might be enforced:

The General Assembly . . . requests that

* * * * *

(b) The Security Council consider, if circumstances
during the transitional period require such considera-

tion, whether the situation in Palestine constitutes a threat to the peace. If it decides that such a threat exists, and in order to maintain international peace and security, the Security Council should supplement the authorization of the General Assembly by taking measures, under Articles 39 and 41 of the Charter, to empower the United Nations Commission, as provided in this resolution, to exercise in Palestine the functions which are assigned to it by this resolution.

(c) The Security Council determine as a threat to the peace, breach of the peace or act of aggression, in accordance with Article 39 of the Charter, any attempt to alter by force the settlement envisaged by this resolution.

In the discussion of these paragraphs, the United States insisted that the Council, acting under paragraph (c), should decide on its own responsibility whether a threat to peace had come into existence. However, paragraph (b) indicates that if enforcement measures were applied, the purpose would be to enforce the Plan. The United Nations Commission referred to in paragraph (b) was the Palestine Commission, charged by the resolution, to which the Plan was annexed, with assisting in the implementation of the Plan. Accordingly, the import of this paragraph is that, if necessary, measures should be applied to enforce the Plan.

Surrounding debates indicated that such was the intent of these paragraphs and that a number of governments simply assumed that the United Nations had the power to enforce the Plan. These included New Zealand,[13] Denmark[14] (whose delegation introduced paragraphs [b] and [c]), and Canada, whose delegation said on this point:

If . . . [the Security Council thought that the situation constituted a threat to peace], then the powers of the United Nations commission to act under the General Assembly resolution would be supplemented by authority from the Security Council. . . .

With regard to sub-paragraph (c), Mr. Pearson felt that the wording proposed by Denmark would remove or lessen some of the doubts concerning the strength behind the provisions for implementation and enforcement.[15]

While the United States delegation did not state flatly that the United Nations was legally entitled to enforce the Plan, it supported paragraphs (b) and (c) and gave other indications that it supported the power in question. Such a power of enforcement, of course, implies that in the given case a binding decision on the merits had been made. On this point the United States delegation said that "recommendations of the General Assembly . . . had virtually the force of law."[16] Later the U.S. Representative in the Security Council said that:

> Attempts to frustrate the General Assembly's recommendation by the threat or use or force, or by incitement to force, on the part of States or people outside Palestine, are contrary to the Charter.[17]

In the first place, such statements, with their emphasis on legal obligation, may be compared with the decisive refusal, only two to three years earlier, of the governments participating at San Francisco to confer any third-party authority to determine the proper interpretation of law in particular situations. They refused, after extensive debate, to confer such authority on the World Court and refrained without discussion from doing so with respect to the Security Council and the General Assembly. In the second place, such statements should be compared with the consensus expressed during the hearings on the Charter before the U.S. Senate Committee on Foreign Relations, exemplified by the statement of the Committee's chairman[18] that in the U.N.'s exercise of the peaceful settlement function "the recommendation carries no compulsion whatever."[19]

The earlier discussions on the Palestine case were in the context of the Plan of Partition with Economic Union and were no doubt intended to apply pressure against the Arabs of Palestine, and against the surrounding Arab states, in the hope of inducing them to accept the Plan.

Only when it became clear that this could not be done, and when the situation was deteriorating into violence, was attention turned to the possibility of actually applying enforcement measures.

Had such measures been applied, the case might have presented a good illustration in practive of the theoretical juxtaposition of functions that is believed to lie at the root of the problem discussed in this chapter. There was an obvious threat to peace in the case, justifying the application of measures under the Charter. Even without the strong indications given by some governments, and by the United Nations, of intent to enforce the Plan, the application of such measures in this case would by itself have tended to give the

appearance of enforcing the partition of Palestine. This was because the Arab countries neighboring Palestine, acting in defense
of what they considered to be Arab rights, invaded Palestine in an
effort to prevent the establishment of the Jewish state. Collective
measures ostensibly directed simply to the maintenance of peace
would, in the circumstances, have had to be directed against the
Arabs; it would thus have assisted the Jewish population in proceeding to set up its state and would have been seen by the world as intended to enforce this essential part of the partition plan.

The case thus illustrates the difficulty of applying the guidelines recommended in this study, which would aim at having it generally understood that the collective measures were designed only to
deal with threats to peace, while the terms of settlement advocated
by the United Nations were recommendatory only.

Explaining the respective roles of the functions employed
would be one course of action to this end. The United States Representative in the Security Council in fact undertook this task as part
of his successful role of leadership in the Council's decision not to
apply collective measures. He said in part:

> The Security Council is authorized to take force-
> ful measures with respect to Palestine to remove a
> threat to international peace. The Charter of the
> United Nations does not empower the Security Council
> to enforce a political settlement whether it is pursuant
> to a recommendation of the General Assembly or of the
> Security Council itself.

> What this means is this: The Security Council
> under the Charter can take action to prevent aggres-
> sion against Palestine from outside. The Security
> Council, by these same powers, can take action to
> prevent a threat to international peace and security
> from inside Palestine. But this action must be
> directed solely to the maintenance of international
> peace. The Security Council's action, in other words,
> is directed to keeping the peace and not to enforcing
> partition. [20]

A desirable corollary step would have been to emphasize that
the proposed terms of settlement were recommendations only.

Another possible recourse, taken unintentionally to some extent in this case, was the consideration of the two functions under
separate agenda items. They were also considered in different organs and at different times. The effect was diminished by the fact

that the functions had been merged and confused in the earlier resolution recommending partition and in the surrounding debates, with
the effect that world opinion was already fixed in regarding "enforcement" in this case as intended to enforce the United Nations-proposed
solution.

The next case to be considered is that of Korea, in 1950.

Following the attack from North Korea against South Korea in
June 1950, military assistance to the latter country was mobilized
under United States leadership. In turn, the whole operation was
placed under United Nations sponsorship and the United Nations
flag. [21] The conflict became a major war in which the United Nations
was, in effect, a party.

Because of the circumstances of the case, the world public is
believed to have naturally viewed the purpose of the U.N. measures
as primarily to deal with a breach of peace. As to political goals,
the organization had previously sought to bring about the unification
of Korea under a democratic regime; however, this issue probably
did not become prominent in world thinking.

In October 1950, however, it appeared that the United Nations
forces would be victorious and would take over the whole of Korea.
The General Assembly then "recommended" that its military command in Korea take all steps to ensure conditions of stability throughout the country and that it proceed toward the holding of elections and
the installation of a unified, democratic, and independent government. [22]

This resolution outlining the desired future organization of
Korea and providing for use of the U.N. military force for its implementation probably appeared to most observers to be a definitive
decision. [23] It may have seemed to many a reasonable course in
view of the U.N.'s earlier efforts to bring about a unified and democratic Korea and, particularly, in view of its participation in the
Korean War. This view might have been strengthened had the victory anticipated in October 1950 eventuated. Its best justification
might have been that the collective measures, together with the decision to eliminate the North Korean regime, the decision to establish a democratic government for the whole of Korea, and the carrying out of the decisions, constituted the only way of dealing with the
threat to peace and breach of peace that had brought about the U.N.
intervention. The subsequent history of the country tends to bear
out this analysis. Moreover, the substantive decision in this case
would not have strained relations with any substantial regime or fac-
tion in competition with the South Korean regime for control of the
country—the only such regime would have been eliminated if the anticipated victory had come about.

On the other hand are the simple fact that the framers of the Charter and the participating states refrained from endowing the organization with any such decision-making powers and the further strong probability that pretensions of exercising such a power tend to build up confusion and illusions bound to be detrimental in terms of the long-range potential of the organization. Indeed, the more reasonable such an action may appear in a given case, the more invincible it may cause these obstacles to become against efforts to demolish them.

The Katanga case of 1961-63 is of importance to the present discussion, since in it the U.N. was generally perceived to employ military force deliberately to carry out a U.N. decision on a substantive issue, namely the suppression of the secessionist regime of Katanga Province in the Congo (now Zaire). The U.N. adopted a resolution that, at the least, strongly disapproved of this secession and that, in retrospect, could readily be interpreted as calling for its suppression. The regime collapsed after fighting between its forces and the U.N. force (ONUC). According to the guidelines proposed here, such an application of tangible U.N. pressures should be confined to dealing with a visible threat to peace or breach of peace. It should, in other words, conform to the Charter authorization for the use of such pressure: the collective measures function. The use of this force, however, was designated as a "peace-keeping operation," a category said to fall within the peaceful settlement function and distinctly outside the collective measures function. In keeping with this categorization, the role of this operation in dealing with a threat to peace was de-emphasized, though the Zairean case in its larger context had earlier been said to constitute such a threat.

The idea of a "peace-keeping operation" amounts to an important, if tacit, amendment of the Charter permitting the application of tangible pressures for purposes other than those specified in the written Charter. The operation in Katanga has been the most important precedent for the proposition that measures so categorized can legally be employed to enforce U.N. decisions on substantive issues. It is accordingly discussed more fully below in Chapter 6 on the "peace-keeping operation."[24]

We will consider finally, in this chapter, the case of Rhodesia. As indicated in Chapter 3, the regime of that country in 1965 proclaimed its independence from Great Britain, of which it had been a colony. What precipitated the secession was a dispute concerning the human rights of the black majority, including the right of participation in government. A series of U.N. resolutions over a period of several years prior to the secession had deplored the deprivation of these rights and urged that the situation be remedied.[25] Shortly before, as well as after, the declaration of independence, resolutions became more condemnatory and recommended that member states apply certain measures of tangible pressure with the evident purpose of furthering desired solutions. [26] The general effect was, accordingly, equivalent to that of United Nations decisions on the merits of the dispute and of efforts to enforce these decisions.

The initiation of resolutions for collective measures in April 1966, [27] and for "formal," mandatory, measures in this category in December of that year, [28] did not serve to change this view of the United Nations' purpose in Rhodesia. Both resolutions found the situation to be a threat to international peace, and the second specifically ordered member states to apply the measures. Both also, however, deplored the continuance of the secessionist regime, so that these resolutions, taken together with previous resolutions, surrounding debates, and the absence of a clearly discernible threat to peace, probably produced a general view that the finding of a threat to peace was a technicality providing the legal basis to enable the Council to proceed to apply measures having the real purpose of forcing changes in the regime.

The power of deciding on the existence of breaches of peace is explicitly conferred on the Council, and it is sometimes maintained that its decisions on this point are conclusive. [29] However, in the perspective of this discussion, tangible pressures on the part of the organization should not be applied unless they are directed to dealing with visible threats to peace or actual breaches. When such a threat is not apparent, such pressures may be seen by the world as having a different purpose entirely, such as appears to have been the case regarding the Rhodesian sanctions, at least during their first decade. It is true that thereafter a threat to peace became clearly visible, as well as breaches of peace. The outcome was a war, which, at the time of writing, seems to have had a desirable outcome in the creation of a democratic Zimbabwe. This outcome was scarcely advanced by the appearance the U.N. gave of attempting to enforce a decision on the merits of the case. This appearance must, on the other hand, have had the undesirable effect of contributing to confusion and illusions concerning the proper powers of the organization in relation to the building of peace and security.

The cases discussed in this chapter have contributed in various degrees to the embedding in world opinion of the idea that the U.N. has the legal capacity to decide issues in dispute. How can such an impression be avoided in situations where the organization must both pronounce on the disputed issue and apply tangible pressures to deal with a breach of, or a threat to, international peace?

A possible recourse, mentioned above in connection with the Palestine case and employed in several cases (though probably not with any such purpose as is here in mind), would involve the use of separate resolutions for the two functions of peaceful settlement and collective measures. Careful explanations in the resolutions and accompanying debates as to which Charter powers are being employed would similarly be helpful.

Believed to be of overriding importance, however, are the intentions of the parties. It is doubtful that the real intent of decision-makers can be concealed and that they can thus convince the public that they have any other purposes than their real ones.

Thus, in the original application of sanctions in the Korean case, the economic sanctions (arms embargo) against the People's Republic of China in 1951,[30] and the similar measure against Albania and Bulgaria in the Greek case in 1949,[31] the measures were all initiated by recommendation that member states take the indicated action on their own decision and responsibility, with an apparent denial that the measures were collective measures. The application of U.N. military pressures in the Middle East, Zairean and Cyprus cases, by their designation as "peace-keeping operations," also involved implied or explicit denials that they were collective measures.[32] These denials are here considered to have been incorrect; however, they did little damage to the goals herein being pursued, since the measures were seen by the world public as being directed to proper U.N. purposes, namely the handling of threats to, or breaches of, international peace.

Conversely, if authorities should make serious efforts to conceal the real intent of a majority of members to cause the U.N. to enforce decisions on substantive issues, it seems probable that the true intent of the measures would nevertheless be readily discerned by the world public. No doubts on this score are likely to have been created in the Spanish case by the attempt to shift responsibility to member states, or in the Rhodesian case by the fact that the U.N. action was placed in the formal category of collective measures.

Thie study's conclusions on this subject are, then, a mere reiteration of the applicable guidelines it proposes: Political organs of the U.N. should not go beyond recommendations in pronouncing upon issues in dispute and should not apply tangible pressures unless these can readily be seen to be reasonable and bona fide efforts to deal with visible threats to peace or actual breaches of peace.

NOTES

1. Ch. 1, n. 6, supra.

2. Ch. VIII, Sec. A of the Dumbarton Oaks Proposals was the forerunner of Ch. VI of the Charter, which defines the Council's peaceful settlement function. Sec. B was the forerunner of the Charter's Ch. VII on collective and provisional measures.

3. Foreign Relations of the U.S., 1945, vol. 1, at 418-19 (1967). Pasvolsky was a special assistant to the Secretary of State who had directed preparatory work on the Charter in the U.S. Department of State.

4. Foreign Relations of the U.S., 1945, vol. 1, at 420 (1967). See also Ch. 1, text at notes 5 and 6, supra. Dulles was an adviser to the U.S. Delegation.

5. Apparently instrumental in carrying this suggestion into the Charter were Doc. 478, III/3/B/1, 12 U.N.C.I.O. Docs. 657, and Doc. 628, III/3/33, id. at 379.

6. Charter of the United Nations: Report to the President, supra, at 84.

7. In 1946 Austin became the second U.S. Ambassador to the U.N.

8. Hearings before the Committee on Foreign Relations, U.S. Senate, 79th Cong., 1st Sess., on the Charter of the United Nations, at 279 (1945), (y4. F76/2: C38/rev.).

9. Kelsen upholds this view. H. Kelsen, The Law of the United Nations: A Critical Analysis of Its Fundamental Problems (New York: Praeger, 1950), at 293-94, 444-50.

10. S.C. Resolution 95 (1951). This case is discussed in terms of the present thesis in Halderman, The United Nations and the Rule of Law, supra, at 16-19, 67.

11. Two competing views on this matter are reflected in the Charter. One tends to merge peaceful settlement and collective measures into a single integrated function. Exemplifying this view, the voting formula presented by the four sponsoring powers at San Francisco states that

> "[D]ecisions and actions by the Security Council may well have major political consequences and may even initiate a chain of events which might, in the end, require . . . measures of enforcement. . . ." Doc. 852, III/1/37(1), 11 U.N.C.I.O. Doc. 710, 712 (1945).

This view is reflected in the application of the rule of unanimity to Council actions pursuant to the peaceful settlement function. The second view places more emphasis on the distinct and separate nature of the two functions and is reflected in the exception to the unanimity rule by which states are forbidden to vote in disputes to which they are party. The two views were debated in the 53d meeting of the U.S. delegation at San Francisco. Foreign Relations of the U.S., 1945, vol. 1, at 873, 874-75. The latter view is here considered the preferable one: that a proper view of the peaceful settlement function would result in the conclusion that the veto should not be applied to this function in any case.

12. Ch. 1, text at n. 10 et seq., supra, and Ch. 5, text at n. 3 et seq., infra.

13. U.N. GAOR, 2d Sess., Ad Hoc Comm. on the Palestine Question, at 166 (1947).

14. Id. at 170, 266.

15. Id. at 221.

16. Id. at 221.

17. U.N. Security Council Official Records, hereafter SCOR, 3d Year, 253d meeting, at 265 (1948).

18. Senator Tom Connally, at that time a recent delegate to the San Francisco Conference.

19. Hearings before the Committee on Foreign Relations, 79th Cong., 1st Sess., supra, at 275.

20. U.N. SCOR, 3d Year, 253d meeting at 265 (1948).

21. S.C. Resolutions 82, 83, and 84 (1950). Statement of President Truman, 23 Department of State Bulletin 83 (1950).

22. G.A. Resolution 376 (V) (1950).

23. The U.N., for which the Assembly was speaking, was naturally superior to the military force, which was its instrument. The U.N. was caused to "recommend" that the force carry out the resolution in misplaced deference to a supposed general limitation of the Assembly to that power in its dispute-handling activity. A comparable use of "recommendation" is mentioned below in Ch. 6, text at n. 59.

24. Ch. 6, text at n. 19 et seq., infra.

25. Ch. 3, text at n. 29, supra.

26. E.g., G. A. Resolution 2022 (XX) of Nov. 5, 1965 (cited at Ch. 3, n. 29, supra), and S.C. Resolution 217 (1965), discussed in Ch. 5, n. 33, infra.

27. Ch. 3, text at n. 30, supra.

28. Ch. 3, text at n. 28, supra.

29. Goldberg, "International Law in the United Nations," supra, at 143.

30. G.A. Resolution 500 (V) (1951).

31. G.A. Resolution 288 (IV) (1949).

32. These operations are discussed in Ch. 6, infra.

5

RECOMMENDATIONS THAT
MEMBER STATES APPLY
TANGIBLE PRESSURES

This chapter, like Chapter 4, is concerned with uses of tangible pressures by the United Nations as a means of causing the organization to appear to be making binding decisions on substantive issues in dispute. The discussion now moves away from applications of pressure grounded on the Charter function of collective measures and takes up some devices designed to take measures out of that category.

This entails moving into a large area in which the power of recommendation given to the Security Council and the General Assembly as part of their peaceful settlement function has been employed in various ways as Charter authority for the application of tangible pressures. I have previously discussed in detail some of these uses of "recommendation" and will not endeavor to repeat what has been said.[1] My present purpose is primarily to show how the proposed guidelines would cut through the confusing maze of practices that has developed and place relevant United Nations practice on a foundation that is solid in the sense of being generally agreed to by all concerned. In this chapter the concern will be with recommendations by the Council and the Assembly that member states apply desired pressures on their own responsibility. Chapter 6 is concerned with pressures clearly understood to be applied by the United Nations or other international organizations, but placed outside the collective measures category in whole or in part through application of the supposed power of recommendation. Chapter 7 discusses a further leap in the same general chain of thought, moving from the proposition that "merely" recommendatory action cannot be interventionist to the proposition that as long as an action, decision, or other procedure is not wrongfully interventionist it is permitted under the Charter. A further channel is thus opened to various propositions holding that binding decisions can be made that are entirely unrelated to applications of tangible pressure.

Of principal concern in the present phase of the discussion is the practice of attempting to take measures out of the collective measures category, thus freeing them from Charter limitations surrounding this function, by the use of "recommendation."

In some cases, notwithstanding the intent of responsible authorities that given actions should not be in the collective measures category, those actions are plainly seen by the public as dealing with breaches of or threats to peace. The problem arising from such situations is relatively slight. In other cases, however, the actions are generally seen as being intended to force compliance with decisions on the merits of disputes. There thus emerges the problem that forms the main subject of the present discussion, which the proposed guidelines are intended to solve.

The guideline proposed in Chapter 1 would require that all tangible pressures initiated by the United Nations, whether by binding orders or by recommendations to member states and whether initiated by the Council or by the Assembly, should be seen by all concerned as being directed to purposes for which such pressures are authorized by the Charter, i.e., to deal with aggressions, other breaches of peace, or threats to peace.

The relevant proposed guidelines would be consistent with the Uniting for Peace resolution of 1950,[2] where, in its relevant operative paragraph, it provides:

> that if the Security Council, because of lack of unanimity of the permanent members, fails to exercise its primary responsibility for the maintenance of international peace and security in any case where there appears to be a threat to the peace, breach of the peace, or act of aggression, the General Assembly shall consider the matter immediately with a view to making appropriate recommendations to Members for collective measures. . . .

The motive for this resolution came from the Korean case, in which, a few months earlier, the Council had initiated military measures to deal with the breach of peace that had occurred in that country. The Council had been able to act only because of the temporary absence of the Soviet Representative, who would undoubtedly have vetoed the resolutions had he been present. He shortly returned and did, in fact, veto subsequent proposals of the majority in this case.

The primary motivation of the Uniting for Peace resolution was, then, the desire to assert for the General Assembly a power to act in the event that action is deemed to be required and the Council is prevented from fulfilling its primary responsibility.

A basis in the Charter for this juxtaposition of responsibilities is found in Article 24, in which members "confer on the Security Council primary responsibility for the maintenance of international peace and security." The word "primary" is interpreted in the Uniting for Peace resolution as connoting that the Council's responsibility is primary but not exclusive. This theory is enunciated in a series of paragraphs in the preamble:

> Reaffirming the importance of the exercise by the Security Council of its primary responsibility for the maintenance of international peace and security. . . .

* * * * *

> Conscious that failure of the Security Council to discharge its responsibilities on behalf of all the Member States . . . does not relieve Member States of their obligations or the United Nations of its responsibility under the Charter to maintain international peace and security.

> Recognizing in particular that such failure does not deprive the General Assembly of its rights or relieve it of its responsibilities under the Charter in regard to the maintenance of international peace and security. . . .

Thus is laid a basis in logic for the ensuing operative paragraph, quoted above, in which the Assembly asserts its residual power to initiate collective measures by recommendation to member states, in situations of the kind for which such measures are authorized by the Charter.

A crucial question in light of the present thesis is whether the resulting measures may be deemed to be taken by the organization or by the member states that comply with the recommendation.

It seems possible that the drafters of the resolution intended the former, while the majority of governments supporting the resolution envisioned the latter result.

That the drafters of the resolution intended to assert a residual power in the Assembly to apply collective measures is indicated by the reference to this function in the operative and preamble paragraphs quoted above, and by the incorporation at the beginning of the preamble, as embodying the first-stated purposes of the United Nations, of paragraphs (1) and (2) of Article 1 of the Charter, whose introductory lines are:

> 1. To maintain international peace and security,
> and to that end: to take effective collective measures
> for the prevention and removal of threats to the peace,
> and for the suppression of acts of aggression or other
> breaches of the peace. . . .

It is thus stressed at the outset of the resolution that collective measures are a function of the United Nations, not just of the Council, and that they are to be effective. The preamble then follows a logical sequence of ideas in asserting that while the Council has the primary responsibility for applying this function when necessary, the Assembly has a residual authority to act when the Council is prevented by the veto from doing so.

While a consistent theory of the power of the Assembly is thus embodied in the resolution, a quite different concept was brought forward by the majority in the debate and proceeded to dominate the public view of the purpose of the resolution. This was the concept that had already been brought forward in the Spanish case and had been given a further and more modest exposition in the Korean case of June 1950.

This predominant view holds that the Assembly's power in the premises derives from the power of recommendation embodied in Articles 10, 11(2), and 14 of the Charter, which authorize the Assembly to discuss and make recommendations concerning any questions "within the scope of the present Charter," "relating to the maintenance of international peace and security," or "for the peaceful adjustment of any situation, regardless of origin, which it deems likely to impair the general welfare or friendly relations among nations." It was, of course, originally intended that these recommendations relate to solutions of problems; there was no thought that they could be used to initiate measures for tangible pressure. Measures of the latter kind are provided for in the Charter exclusively in the provisions defining collective measures. The idea that this power of recommendation could have been used as a means for enforcing decisions on substantive issues would have been unthinkable as a general grant of power capable of being directed by the U.N. against any of its members.

Nevertheless, the Spanish case, in the first year of United Nations operations, conveyed the impression that these provisions were being employed for just such a purpose.[3] A subcommittee of the Security Council found that there was no threat to peace in the Spanish situation and thus no basis for United Nations collective measures against Spain.[4] The Soviet Union and like-minded delegations continued to maintain that there was such a threat; however, there was no proposal that either the Council or the Assembly

should overrule the subcommittee's finding. The subcommittee
went on to say that the Assembly had the power to recommend that
member states withdraw their diplomatic representatives from
Spain as a means of pressure in favor of the desired change in the
regime of Spain:

> The General Assembly has power under Article 14 to
> make recommendations as to the peaceful adjustment
> of any situation. . . . Furthermore, the General
> Assembly's powers of recommendation under Article
> 10 cover all matters within the scope of the Charter,
> including the purpose of the Charter set out in para-
> graph 2 of Article 1, which is to take appropriate mea-
> sures to strengthen universal peace.[5]

This statement was influential in setting the tone for part of the debate in the Assembly, in which some members were of the view
that if states carried out the Assembly's recommendations by withdrawing diplomatic representation from Spain, the action would
be taken by the states on their own responsibility and not by the
United Nations.[6] The fallacy involved in this approach has been
discussed in Chapter 1.[7]

The United States and other western delegations may have
supported this Assembly action in the hope that by "going along"
with the Soviet Union they could contribute to the possibility, which
was then still considered to exist, of establishing the degree of
collaboration required to enable the United Nations to function effectively. This view is supported to some degree by the fact that
the United States abstained from the vote in the committee stage,[8]
apparently because of apprehension that the action would be an unwarranted intervention in an issue properly within Spanish domestic
jurisdiction.

The Korean case of 1950 marked the collapse, for the time
being, of hopes for effective great-power collaboration. It also
provided several opportunities (including the Uniting for Peace
resolution) to rectify the mistake, in terms of the thesis presently
under discussion, represented by the Spanish case.

The first opportunity was in June 1950, when the Security
Council recommended that member states go to the assistance of
the Republic of Korea in dealing with the attack on that country
from the north.[9] The Council did not consider that it could order
the participation of states in collective measures, since the agreements contemplated in Article 43 of the Charter had not been concluded.[10] These agreements were to specify the general quantity
and nature of troops and other resources to be made available by

the individual states. The Council, it is here believed, made a proper use of Charter power in <u>recommending</u> that states apply measures but was in error in its attempt to explain the action as something other than collective measures.

However, the Council apparently felt that it could not legally initiate collective measures by the organization except by issuing binding orders. The view that appeared to be prevalent was expressed by the British representative as follows:

> [H]ad the agreements provided for in Article 43 of the Charter been concluded . . . the action . . . would no doubt have been founded on Article 42. As it is, however, the Council can naturally act only under Article 39, which enables the Security Council to recommend what measures should be taken to restore international peace and security.[11]

The damage done by this allocation of Charter authority was minimal, since the ensuing action was intended to deal with an alleged aggression and was seen by the non-communist world as being a proper exercise of the United Nations enforcement power. Indeed, the Secretary-General at the time categorized this operation as a collective measure, a view subsequently endorsed by Secretary-General Thant.[12]

The Council's view of the matter at the time nevertheless did some damage, since it affirmed the proposition that measures to apply tangible pressure can have a basis in the Charter other than the provisions that authorize collective measures. This supposed basis was the phrase "shall make recommendations" in Article 39:

> The Security Council shall determine the existence of any threat to the peace, breach of the peace, or act of aggression and shall make recommendations, or decide what measures shall be taken in accordance with Articles 41 and 42, to maintain or restore international peace and security.

The phrase in question was originally intended to have the same general purpose as the recommendatory power found in Articles 10, 11(2), and 14 with respect to the General Assembly and in Article 37 with respect to the Security Council, namely that of defining the power to recommend substantive solutions. Its purpose here is to specify that the Council's peaceful settlement function, defined in detail in Chapter VI, is available for use in regard to the more serious class of cases dealt with in Chapter VII.[13]

The problem under discussion, of course, is not caused by the simple fact of initiating measures by recommendation. This is usually the only way in which such action can be taken under present conditions. The relevant problem in the Korean case was caused by the fact that the Council indicated, as the source of authority for the action, a Charter power other than that of collective measures and resorted to this supposed authority for the precise purpose of taking the action out of the collective measures category.

Our discussion is thus brought again to the Uniting for Peace resolution, and particularly to the view, which prevailed among the Assembly majority, that the Assembly derived its power to initiate measures from Articles 10, 11(2), and 14 of the Charter.[14] It thus followed the precedent of the Spanish case, here considered to be erroneous.

The Soviet Union, which had strongly advocated the Assembly action in the Spanish case, opposed the Uniting for Peace resolution on the grounds that the Security Council had the monopoly on United Nations action in the nature of collective measures. That resolution, as already observed, strongly suggests that such was not the case, indicating that the Assembly has a residual power that it may implement by recommendations to member states. The overall effect of the debate on the resolution was different, however, conveying the impression that the Council did indeed have the monopoly of power to apply collective measures, whereas the Assembly has a separate power to initiate tangible pressures, based on Articles 10, 11(2), and 14 of the Charter. This debate must also have conveyed the impression that Assembly measures under the resolution would not be limited to dealing with aggression, other breaches of peace, and threats to peace.

The United States delegation, in fact, said that the Assembly had the power to recommend measures that only the Council had the power to command, citing the case of Spain as a precedent.[15] The source of the power was in Article 10, it said, and the Soviet Union was said to have resisted at San Francisco the grant of such an extensive power in that provision because it "then realized that the broad scope [of the Article] meant that in reality their veto in the Security Council would not necessarily be the final word in behalf of this organization."[16] The delegation said that the General Assembly is empowered to make recommendations to the members on any matters "within the scope of the present Charter," except in regard to matters being dealt with at the time by the Council. By citing the Spanish case with approval, it indicated that this power could be aimed at the enforcement of a particular solution, and thus implicitly embraced an underlying power of decision.

Unlike the debate of the Spanish case, that concerning the Uniting for Peace resolution did not involve an immediate dispute. It asserted a general power of the Assembly, applicable to all, and its discussion was thus on a plane with that which had taken place at San Francisco in regard to the Charter itself. It is difficult to credit that the United States, and indeed other countries, could here take a position so contrary to their refusal five years earlier at San Francisco to confer any general power of decision on either the Assembly or the Council with respect to the merits of disputes. As a subsidiary point, it is difficult to credit that delegations could speak of such broad—in fact practically unlimited—powers of recommendation without making any distinction between recommended solutions to substantive issues and recommendations for action by member states, or of awareness that measures taken pursuant to the latter kind of recommendation, if directed toward enforcement of a particular solution, would in effect mean a decision as to what that solution should be.

Part of the explanation might be that the east-west struggle, reaching a climax in the Korean case, had erased from people's minds any Charter limitations on the free use of dispute-handling resources as a means of applying pressure. The resolution itself emerged directly out of the Korean case, and its consideration by the majority may have been dominated by sentiments of hostility engendered by that conflict. The measures contemplated were seen, as had been the "enforcement" power at San Francisco, as intended only for use against wrong-doers; in the minds of those supporting the resolution, this meant countries other than their own.

The power asserted by the General Assembly in the Uniting for Peace resolution was shortly put to use when the People's Republic of China intervened with military force against the United Nations operation in Korea. On February 1, 1951, the Assembly found in its Resolution 498(V), that the Chinese government had committed aggression and affirmed the determination of the United Nations to continue its action in Korea to meet the aggression. In keeping with the Uniting for Peace resolution, the preamble of Resolution 498(V) recited that the Security Council, because of lack of unanimity among the permanent members, had failed to exercise its primary responsibility for the maintenance of international peace and security.

It is of interest to this discussion that, whereas the Uniting for Peace resolution authorizes the Assembly to "recommend" to member states that they apply collective measures, the language of recommendation was not used in Resolution 498(V); nor was it appropriate to the case. The United States delegation, however, in proposing the resolution, said that the Assembly had the responsibility for recommending collective measures, since the Council had been prevented from acting.[17] Indeed, it seems certain that the prevalent theory, which had recently been applied to the Uniting for Peace resolution, was also applied here and that governments supporting Resolution 498(V) considered that they were acting pursuant to a power of recommendation.

The Assembly wished in this case to make certain decisions, and the word "recommends" was inappropriate in the circumstances. It may be observed, however, that whenever the United Nations initiates tangible pressures, a decision to this effect is unavoidable. A recommendation that member states apply measures implies inescapably a United Nations decision that the measures should be applied. Moreover, the purpose of leaders in causing the organization to act in this way is to mobilize world opinion in favor of taking and supporting the desired action. There appears to be an inconsistency, in these circumstances, in the claim that the organization does not make basic decisions or that it does not share substantially in responsibility for what is done.

What the Assembly desired to do through Resolution 498(V) required it to use language appropriate to the exercise of the collective measures function in accordance with the basic criteria defining that function in the Charter. It decided that the People's Republic of China had engaged in aggression and, further, that the measures already in progress in Korea should be continued for the purpose, in part, of dealing with that aggression.

This was proper; all applications of tangible pressures by the United Nations should, similarly, not only conform to these criteria but be seen by all concerned as conforming to them.

Notwithstanding that the responsible authorities considered themselves to be acting pursuant to other, much less clearly defined, authority,[18] Resolution 498(V) has potential value as a precedent if such authorities should ever wish to assert that a given Assembly action is an exercise of the collective measures function. They could point to this resolution and say that here was a clear exercise of that power, both in word and in deed.

The Spanish and Korean cases and the Uniting for Peace resolution tend to illustrate the proposition that states are not concerned with using international dispute-handling powers so as to build them into a system capable of functioning effectively, but rather are inclined to use them as instruments for applying pressures in the traditional conduct of relations.[19]

The establishment of the proposition that the Council and Assembly may initiate measures of tangible pressure that are not subject to the Charter restrictions on collective measures has greatly increased the usability of the United Nations as a means of furthering national policies in the traditional approach to international relations. In effect, it frees such measures for whatever use majorities may wish to make of them.

The range of possibilities thus made available may be suggested by reference to a resolution of the Assembly and one of the Council, in 1962 and 1963 respectively, dealing with apartheid in South Africa, and to two parallel resolutions passed at approximately the same time pertaining to alleged deprivations of certain rights of the inhabitants of Portuguese territories in Africa.

The earlier of the two Assembly resolutions, dated November 6, 1962,[20] deplored South Africa's policy of apartheid, its refusal to comply with previous United Nations resolutions on the subject, its disregard of its Charter obligations, and its aggravation of racial discord. Then, reaffirming earlier declarations that these policies seriously endangered international peace and security, it proceeded to request that member states apply diplomatic and certain specified economic measures against South Africa. It concluded by requesting the Council, if necessary, to apply sanctions to secure compliance. It was thus clear that the measures recommended by this resolution, and any future sanctions applied by the Council, were to have the purpose of forcing compliance with decisions on the merits of the dispute.

The Assembly resolution of December 14, 1962,[21] directed against Portuguese policies in regard to its African territories, was similar with respect to the points relevant to the present phase of this discussion. The policy change demanded was the granting of self-determination and independence to the peoples of the territories. The existing situation was said to be a threat to international peace. The only specific measure it was recommended that member states take against Portugal was the denial of arms and military equipment. The Council was asked to take "appropriate measures," if necessary, to secure compliance with this and other United Nations resolutions on the subject.[22]

In the first of these cases to come before the Council—concerning Portuguese territories—a resolution was proposed that, if adopted, would have declared the situation in question to constitute a threat to peace and would have decided, with binding effect, that an arms embargo should be put into effect against Portugal.[23] Its language was weakened in both respects, however, so that the final resolution declared the situation to be "seriously disturbing" to peace and security in Africa and recommended (instead of decided) that states institute the arms embargo.[24]

Revisions to similar effect were made in the subsequent Council resolution concerning apartheid in South Africa.[25]

Considering the Assembly resolutions from the standpoint of the responsible authorities, they demonstrated, as means of applying pressure, certain "advances" over the corresponding Assembly resolution in the Spanish case in that they declared the situations in question to be threats to peace. Those situations were thus forthrightly said to be of the kind that warranted the application of collective measures. However, the resolutions were not intended to apply such measures, because of the general supposition that the Assembly had no power under the Charter to do so.

When the cases came to the Council, the advocates of strong action had a different problem. The Council has the power to apply collective measures, but such action was opposed by some major western powers—France, Great Britain, and the United States—which were capable of preventing the adoption of any resolution they, or any of them, opposed. The same factual situation that had been described by the Assembly as constituting a threat to peace was described by the Council as "disturbing" the peace—language designed to avoid the Charter formula for describing situations warranting collective measures; this was done to indicate to the initiated that the resolutions were not intended to apply collective measures.[26] The resulting resolutions were designed to give the impression of applying the strongest possible pressure consistent with that understanding.

The resolutions in question illustrate the flexible interpretations that can be given Charter concepts and Charter language to employ them in the pursuit of the traditional approach to the conduct of relations. While they might appear to be rather extreme examples, the officials responsible for them gave no evidence in the record of considering them anything but routine applications of that approach. An impact must nevertheless have been made on world opinion, and this fact is of concern from the perspective of this discussion. For example, the three adverse effects discussed in Chapter 1—straining of relations, confusion, and the fostering of illusion—must all have resulted to some extent. In particular, it appears that officials could scarcely have devised a better demonstration of the illusion/disillusion syndrome, since they carefully constructed the language of pressure with the knowledge that the target states were fully aware that the pressure was more rhetorical than real.

Another use may be noted of the proposition that measures initiated by recommendation are not collective measures. The Charter requires that regional enforcement measures have the approval of the United Nations Security Council.[27] A competent authority of the United States government has argued that if a measure is initiated by recommendation of a regional organization, it is not in the enforcement category and so does not require such authorization.[28] The regional organization then under discussion was the Organization of American States (OAS), which in effect is limited by its charter to the power of recommendation when measures of force are at issue.[29] Such measures by this organization would, accordingly, never require United Nations authorization. This is one of the devices mentioned in Chapter 12, by which it was attempted at one time to give the OAS a virtual monopoly of authority, to the exclusion of the United Nations, in western hemisphere disputes and situations.

In addition to "recommendation," officials have also employed the phrase "calls upon" in their search for flexibility and options. It is employed in the Council resolution on the case of South Africa, referred to above in this chapter,[30] in which connection the United States Representative observed that it is a phrase found in the Charter and is not considered mandatory.[31] However, it has been given both mandatory and non-mandatory connotations and appears to have been used to avoid stating into which category a measure was intended to fall.[32] In the Security Council's resolution of November 20, 1965, on the Rhodesian case, states were "called upon" to apply diplomatic and economic measures against that country with the intent that these be something other than collective measures and be non-mandatory.[33] The same phrase was employed in the Council's resolution of April 8, 1966,[34] in the same case, but here with the purpose, generally understood, of authorizing collective measures, to be applied by Great Britain in detaining vessels carrying oil for Rhodesia. In these cases it was evidently the intent, not the language employed, that determined the "legal" nature of what was being done.

In regard to matters discussed in this chapter, responsible officials evidently have a clear and uncluttered view of, and belief in, their right to use international dispute-handling resources in any manner they may deem useful for the advancement of their national interests. The resulting practices represent a logical—though not the worst—result of an approach that seeks to keep all options open.

On the other hand, from the perspective of the need to build consistent world patterns of thought as the basis for peace and security these uses of the resources in question present a scene of confusion.

The relevant guidelines proposed in Chapters 1 and 2 would have the effect of cutting through this maze of confusion by simply requiring that all applications of tangible pressure by the United Nations be clearly visible to all concerned as directed to purposes for which such measures are authorized by the Charter—namely, to deal with aggressions, other breaches of peace, or threats to peace. Their more basic purpose is to ensure that such measures are not seen as attempts to enforce decisions on the issues of disputes. Immaterial, in a relative sense, are the questions of whether resolutions are mandatory or non-mandatory, whether they are initiated by the Council or the Assembly, and whether the measures proposed by such resolutions are formally designated collective measures.

While the present thesis thus holds that the Charter permits the initiation of tangible pressures by recommendation of the Council or the Assembly, it also insists that the authority to do so derives from the basic collective measures function. It is not to be confused with the power of recommendation that forms an integral part of the Charter definitions of the peaceful settlement function as found in Chapters IV and VI (and in Article 39 of Chapter VII) of the Charter. This requirement is essential to maintaining the distinction between the collective measures and peaceful settlement functions, a distinction basic to the thesis.

NOTES

1. Halderman, The United Nations and the Rule of Law, supra, at 167-89; Halderman, "Some Legal Aspects," supra, at 672, 684-98.

2. G.A. Resolution 377 (V).

3. Ch. 1, text at n. 10 et seq., supra.

4. "Report of the Sub-Committee on the Spanish Question," U.N. SCOR, 1st Year, 1st Ser., Special Supp., Rev. Ed. at 8 (1946).

5. Id. at 10. Art. 10 of the Charter provides:

The General Assembly may discuss any questions or any matters within the scope of the present Charter or relating to the powers and functions of any organs provided for in the present Charter, and, except as provided in Article 12, may make recommendations to the Members of the United Nations or to the Security Council or to both on any such questions or matters.

6. See, e.g., statements of France and Panama, U.N. GAOR, 1st Sess., pt. 2, Plenary, at 1192-93, 1220 (1946). See also the proposal introduced in committee by Chile and certain other delegations, id., 1st Comm., at 358, (U.N. Doc. A/C.1/108).

7. Ch. 1, text at n. 10 et seq., supra.

8. U.N. GAOR, 1st Sess., pt. 2, 1st Comm., at 298-99. The resolution under consideration at that stage would have recommended that states make a complete break of diplomatic relations with Spain. The final resolution, G.A. Resolution 39 (I), quoted in part in Ch. 1, n. 10, supra, for which the U.S. delegation voted, recommended only the withdrawal of ambassadors and ministers. Id., Plenary, at 1217-18, 1221-22. The U.S. delegation had earlier proposed a resolution that would have barred the Franco regime from participation in United Nations and related international organization activity and recommended to the Spanish people that they adopt a democratic form of government. Id., 1st Comm., at 354-55, (U.N. Doc. A/C.1/100).

9. S.C. Resolution 83 (1950).

10. Pp. 32-33, supra.

11. U.N. SCOR, 5th Year, 476th meeting, at 3 (1950). The reference to Art. 42 was supposed to indicate collective measures of the U.N.

12. Ch. 2, n. 14, supra.

13. Ch. 1, n. 6 and accompanying text, supra.

14. See, e.g., statements by delegations of the United States, Chile, France, Peru, and Cuba during the debate on the resolution. U.N. GAOR, 5th Sess., 1st Comm., at 64, 67, 70, 75, 79-80 (1950).

15. Id. at 117-18. The passages quoted in the text are from a verbatim text of the statement in 23 Department of State Bulletin 687 (Oct. 30, 1950).

16. The text of Art. 10 is set forth in n. 5, supra. The Soviet delegation seems, in fact, to have accepted that article at San Francisco as a means of avoiding an authorization to the Assembly to discuss and make recommendations on any matter within the sphere of international relations. The Soviets' motivation in raising this issue toward the end of the Conference, when it had already accepted Art. 14, which is generally considered to grant a broader authorization to the Assembly than does Art. 10, has been a subject of speculation. For a brief history of the controversy and a discussion of possible Soviet motives see R. Russell, A History of the United Nations Charter: The Role of the United States 1940-1945 (Washington: The Brookings Institution, 1958), at 761-64, 770-75 (1958).

17. U.N. GAOR, 5th Sess., 1st Comm., at 517 (1951).

18. Vallat finds the authority for the resolution in the prevalent theory as to the nature of the Uniting for Peace resolution. He holds that the Assembly had the power to recommend the measures in question and accordingly, that it had the power to determine

the existence of breaches of peace and threats to peace. He also insists that the action in the Korean case was taken by the states and not by the organization. F. Vallat, "The Competence of the United Nations General Assembly," 97 Académie de Droit International, Recueil des Cours 203, 267-70 (1959-II).

19. The Soviet Union opposed the Uniting for Peace resolution on the grounds that the Security Council had the monopoly on the collective measures function. See U.N. GAOR, 5th Sess., Plenary, at 324-35 (1950). Charged with inconsistency on the basis of its previous support of Assembly action in the Spanish case, it made an argument that presents some problems of analysis but suggests that measures not involving force should not be counted as in the enforcement category. Id. at 334. A decade later, however, it maintained that certain non-military measures taken by the Organization of American States against the Dominican Republic were enforcement measures requiring Security Council authorization under Art. 53 of the U.N. Charter. U.N. SCOR, 15th Year, 894th meeting, at 11-12 (1960). See also Ch. 12, text at n. 57, infra.

20. G.A. Resolution 1761 (XVII) (1962).

21. G.A. Resolution 1807 (XVII) (1962).

22. Later the Assembly called upon "all states to sever all relations with South Africa, Portugal, and the illegal minority regime in Southern Rhodesia and to refrain scrupulously from giving any military or economic assistance to these regimes." G.A. Resolution 2446 (XXIII) (1963).

23. U.N. SCOR, 18th Year, 1044th meeting, at 3-4 (1963).

24. S.C. Resolution 180 (1963).

25. S.C. Resolution 181 (1963).

26. For the debate concerning the language of the resolution on Portuguese territories, see U.N. SCOR, 18th Year, 1048th meeting, at 6-7; id., 1049th meeting, at 6. With respect to the resolution on apartheid, see the statement of the U.S. delegation, id., 1056th meeting, at 5-7. Dugard concludes from the language of the resolutions that they find their constitutional base in Ch. VI of the Charter. Dugard, "The Legal Effect of United Nations Resolutions on Apartheid," 83 South African Law Journal 44, 49-50 (1966).

27. Art. 53.

28. Meeker, "Defensive Quarantine and the Law," 57 American Journal of International Law 515, 521 (1963). This use of "recommendation" is considered further in Halderman, The United Nations and the Rule of Law, supra, at 201-205.

29. Inter-American Treaty of Reciprocal Assistance, Art. 20, OAS Treaty Series at 8; 21 U.N. Treaty Series at 77. This

provision is, in effect, incorporated by reference into the charter of the OAS by virtue of Art. 25 of that instrument. OAS Treaty Series at 1; 119 U.N. Treaty Series at 3.

30. N. 25 and accompanying text, supra.

31. U.N. SCOR, 18th Year, 1056th meeting, at 7 (1963).

32. Such, it appears, might have been the purpose of employing the phrase in S.C. Resolution 95 (1951), calling upon Egypt to permit Israeli-connected ships and cargoes to transit the Suez Canal. Some governments interpreted the resolution as constituting a binding order on Egypt. U.N. SCOR, 9th Year, 663d meeting, at 3-4, 7-9 (1954).

33. S.C. Resolution 217 (1965). One of the sponsors explained that this resolution would "not take any position on" the use of Ch. VII of the Charter or on the use of force. He said, similarly, that no position was necessarily implied on the use of Ch. VI as a basis for the resolution. U.N. SCOR, 20th Year, 1264th meeting, at 3 (165). No other possible Charter authority being mentioned, the question of the basis in the Charter for the resolution was left uncertain.

34. S.C. Resolution 221 (1966). Aspects of this resolution, as well as of S.C. Resolution 217 (cited at n. 33) and others in the Rhodesian case, together with surrounding debates and other circumstances relevant to the present discussion, are considered in Halderman, "Some Legal Aspects," supra, at 684-94.

6

THE "PEACE-KEEPING OPERATION"

Consideration of tangible pressures for which supposed powers of recommendation are invoked continues in this chapter. Such pressures are considered to be outside the collective measures function and its restrictions and may accordingly be considered available for the enforcement of substantive decisions. The particular subject of this chapter, the military component of the United Nations "peace-keeping operations," fits this description. The chapter is largely concerned with how this concept evolved to form a precedent for the enforcement of decisions on the merits of disputes.

The prototype of such operations was the United Nations Emergency Force (UNEF), deployed in the Suez crisis of 1956. This military force was set up by the General Assembly after the case had been transferred to it from the Security Council as the result of the French and British veto, which prevented the latter organ from acting. The purpose of the operation was originally said to be "to secure and supervise" the cease-fire agreed to between the parties to the conflict.[1] This was subsequently expanded by an Assembly resolution of February 2, 1957, providing that:

> [T]he scrupulous maintenance of the Armistice Agreement requires the placing of the United Nations Emergency Force on the Egyptian-Israel armistice demarcation line . . . with a view to assist in achieving situations conducive to the maintenance of peaceful conditions in the area.[2]

The force served as an observer corps, but its primary role, as indicated by the above-mentioned Assembly resolutions, was that of a military force applying military pressure. Its right to use force was restricted but not negligible, as will be indicated below. Its basic purpose may be said to have been to discourage by its presence, and its military potentiality, further resort to violence by the parties. It seems to have fulfilled the objective criteria of the collective measures function as these are defined in the Charter, namely the application by the United Nations of tangible pressure to deal with threats to, or breaches of, international peace and security. However, the competent authorities apparently never considered placing the operation in that Charter category. They categorized it instead as an exercise of the peaceful settlement function, and some official descriptions of it seemed calculated to convey the impression that it was not a military force with military functions. [3]

The category of the "peace-keeping operation" should, in the view of this discussion, be eliminated. Such would be the effect of the subsidiary guideline proposed in Application of Tangible Pressures by the United Nations, Chapter 2. The guideline would not, of course, eliminate applications of pressure intended to deal with breaches of, or threats to, international peace. Such was the initial purpose of all the military "peace-keeping operations" deployed by the United Nations as a primary means of handling international disputes and situations up to the time of writing. [4] The guidelines would only require that such measures be restricted to those purposes and that they not be attributed to any source of authority other·than the United Nations collective measures function. The latter requirement would eliminate the "peace-keeping operation," except possibly as a useful means of designating a distinct subsidiary category of collective measures.

UNEF contained the seed of the problem under discussion. Perhaps of decisive importance in the exclusion of this operation from the collective measures category was the fact that it was deployed by the General Assembly. That organ continued to maintain the view, which had prevailed among the majority that supported the Uniting for Peace resolution, that while it might initiate measures of tangible pressure, these could not be within the collective measures category.

Unavailable in this case was the device employed by the majority in support of its concept of the Uniting for Peace resolution, and by some governments in the earlier Spanish case, by which the Assembly is caused to recommend desired measures, with the resulting action said to be taken by the member states on their own decisions and responsibility. Needed in the Suez case was a United Nations force directly under United Nations command and control. [5]

Collective measures having been ruled out by the competent authorities as the Charter basis for UNEF, these authorities turned

to the peaceful settlement function. The force had certain characteristics that facilitated its placement in this category: the Assembly,
of course, merely recommended, rather than ordered, that member
states supply troop contingents, and the planned operation would not
entail coercion of states or other political entities. It was accordingly decided that it could be placed within the Assembly's power of
recommendation; a tenuous reason was thus furnished for the further
step of assimilating it with the peaceful settlement function, since
the latter is a power of recommendation. [6] Ignored was the fact
that the peaceful settlement function is concerned not with the deployment of military forces but with efforts to bring about substantive
solutions of international disputes.

In a well-known official description of UNEF, it was said by
the Secretary-General:

> While the General Assembly is enabled to establish the
> Force with the consent of those parties which contrib-
> ute units to the Force, it could not request the Force to
> be stationed or operate on the territory of a given coun-
> try without the consent of the Government of that coun-
> try. . . .
>
> *   *   *   *   *
>
> The Force obviously should have no rights other than
> those necessary for the execution of its functions, in
> cooperation with local authorities. It would be more
> than an observers' corps, but in no way a military
> force temporarily controlling the territory in which it
> is stationed; nor, moreover, should the Force have
> military functions exceeding those necessary to secure
> peaceful conditions on the assumption that the parties
> to the conflict take all necessary steps for compliance
> with the recommendations of the General Assembly. [7]

The Constitutional nature of the operation was thus described in the
Secretary-General's annual report for 1957-58:

> It should, of course, be clear that any such Force,
> unless it were to be called into being by the Security
> Council under Chapter VII of the Charter, must consti-
> tutionally be a non-fighting force, operating on the ter-
> ritories of the countries concerned only with their
> consent and utilized only after a decision of the Security
> Council or the General Assembly, regarding a specific

case, for those clearly international purposes relating
to the pacific settlement of disputes which are authorized
by the Charter. . . .[8]

Parallel with these indications of the nature of the force were
others that suggested an essentially different role. First, it will be
recalled that the operation was deployed in the Suez crisis of 1956,
almost before the hostilities had ended, with the mission of securing the cease-fire which had been agreed to and of securing the
boundary between Egypt and Israel. Such were hardly appropriate
tasks for a military operation under instructions to refrain from
all military pressures.[9] Its basic purpose might be said to have
been to stabilize the situation through its presence by discouraging
further resort to force by the parties. Consistent with this role
was the recognition by competent authorities that:

> [M]en engaged in the operation may never take the ini-
> tiative in the use of armed force but are entitled to
> respond with force to an attack with arms, including
> attempts to use force to make them withdraw from
> positions which they occupy under orders. . . .[10]

This definition of UNEF's role may have had its origins with a
United States proposal that a United Nations force be deployed in
the Lebanese crisis of 1958. Its purpose would have been to deal
with an alleged threat to the security of Lebanon, manifested in
part by alleged infiltration into that country of personnel and arms
from outside. On account of the latter allegations, the United
Nations had deployed an observer corps. Subsequently, following
the forcible overthrow of the regime of Iraq, the United States
deployed troops in Lebanon. The United States Representative in
the Security Council then proposed the deployment in that country
of a United Nations force, whose powers would include the following:

> They would not be there to fight unless they are at-
> tacked, but it should be fully clear also that they will
> have the authority to fire in self-defense in perfor-
> mance of their duties to . . . protect the integrity of
> Lebanon.[11]

The proposal was not adopted, but the foregoing statement may
have influenced the development of the "peace-keeping operation,"
as may the following statement of the Secretary-General, opposing
the proposal, later in the debate:

> This makes it clear that the representative [of
> the United States] had in mind a force with limited
> rights along the lines of the United Nations Emergency
> Force. . . . This Emergency Force has been granted
> only a limited right of self-defense.

> The definition of the authority, here quoted,
> makes it clear that the representative of the United
> States did not intend that a United Nations force in
> Lebanon, if established, should take military ini-
> tiative against opposition or dissident groups. On
> this assumption, such a force at present would find
> it quite difficult to operate outside Government-held
> territory if . . . such operations were to meet with
> armed resistance. In these circumstances, and re-
> maining as it must strictly within the terms of the
> Charter, it seems probable that a force would find
> itself restricted on the whole to a fairly passive role
> in Government-controlled territory—a role which, if
> it has to be filled, could be provided for by simpler
> means. [12]

A force in Lebanon in these circumstances, and with these
suggested powers, would have been an application of tangible pressure by the United Nations to deal with a threat to peace, and could
thus have been readily described as a collective measure. The
perceived inhibition against so designating UNEF, namely that it was
being established by the Assembly, which was supposed not to have
the power to initiate collective measures, was not applicable to the
proposed force in Lebanon, since this force was proposed to be set
up by the Council. Another logical reason for favoring the "collective measures" designation over that of "peaceful settlement,"
of course, lies in the nature of the two concepts under the Charter.
The latter has to be stretched—to say the least—to embrace military
forces deployed as means of handling disputes. The competent
authorities were clearly aware of the problem in defining UNEF,
and the Secretary-General further evidenced awareness toward the
end of the last- quoted passage, where he says that "remaining as it
must strictly within the terms of the Charter, it seems probable
that a force would find itself restricted . . . to a fairly passive
role. . . ." But who can say in advance what a force deployed in
such situations might be called on to do? Who is to decide whether
or not it is remaining within the terms of the Charter? The latter
question might become difficult and controversial even if the given
force applied itself single-mindedly to dealing with a breach of, or

threat to, peace. However, no such question would arise if the use of the force were designated a collective measure, since under such authority tangible pressure may be applied to any extent necessary to the maintenance of peace.

Since authorities were clearly aware of these problems attendant on the "peace-keeping operation," why was the use of a force in Lebanon not proposed as a collective measure? The reason may well have been anticipation of a Soviet veto. In order to proceed, in that contingency, it would have been necessary to turn to the Assembly. In view of the prevailing presupposition that the General Assembly was without power to initiate collective measures, it was logical to place the proposed force in the same category as UNEF.

If such was the Secretary-General's perception of the problem, it seems certain that he recognized simultaneously that while the need to use overt force was more likely to arise in the Lebanese situation, the same possibility could not be ruled out in the Suez case. He may therefore have been motivated to promulgate his above-quoted definition of the authority of UNEF to employ force. [13]

The authority thus recognized goes beyond the right of self-defense against wrongful attack, which is generally accorded to any individual or group. The holding of ground by force is clearly an exercise of tangible pressure. Later there was more explicit recognition of the right of UNEF to apply military pressure. [14]

In July 1962 the World Court handed down its advisory opinion concerning the obligation of member states of the United Nations to pay assessments for this operation and the one instituted in the Congo (Zaire) in 1960. In this opinion the Court undertook to pass upon the legality of both operations under the Charter.

Upheld in this opinion was the Secretary-General's characterization of the deployment of UNEF as an exercise of the peaceful settlement function. The Court undertook, moreover, to identify the specific Charter authorization for the force[15] and found it in the provisions, herein referred to generically as Articles 10, 11(2), and 14, that authorize the Assembly to discuss and to make recommendations concerning the solutions of international disputes and situations. They thus comprise the basis for that organ's peaceful settlement function.

The Court then proceeded to find a power to act, subsidiary to the basic power of discussion and recommendation provided in these articles. In its view, this power of action is distinguished from the kind of action authorized under the collective measures function, which is generally considered the monopoly of the Security Council. The kind of action said to be authorized by the peaceful settlement function is described thus:

> Whether the General Assembly proceeds under Article
> 11 or under Article 14, the implementation of its
> recommendations for setting up commissions or other
> bodies involves organizational activity—action—in con-
> nection with the maintenance of international peace and
> security. . . . Such committees, commissions or other
> bodies or individuals, constitute, in some cases, sub-
> sidiary organs established under the authority of Article
> 22 of the Charter.[16]

It seems undeniably correct that the Assembly, in the exercise of its peaceful settlement function, may set up subsidiary
organs to assist in carrying out its functions. A conciliation commission is an example of such an organ relevant to the peaceful
settlement function. UNEF, however, was a body of basically
different character under the Charter. Its purpose was to apply
military pressure in a situation constituting a breach of, and later
a threat to, international peace. Authority to act in this way is
found exclusively in the provisions defining the collective measures
function. It is basic to our present thesis that the collective measures and peaceful settlement functions should be maintained as
distinct, if interrelated, powers.

If it is true, as appears to be the case, that the competent
authorities did not consider placing UNEF in the collective measures category because it was initiated by the Assembly, and
because that organ is supposed to be lacking in such powers, it is
pertinent to recall the Assembly's action in February 1951 in
broadening and redirecting (against the People's Republic of China)
the military measures it was already applying against the North
Korean regime.[17] In everything but name that Assembly action
seems to have been a precedent for regarding the deployment of
UNEF as an application of collective measures.[18]

The force in Zaire[19] (ONUC) was established and deployed
shortly after that country's independence in 1960, to help maintain
order until the Zairean security forces were ready to fulfill their
responsibilities.[20] In a statement by the Secretary-General describing the nature of the operation, he said that "it was the breakdown of those instruments [for the maintenance of order] which had
created a situation which through its consequences represented a
threat to peace and security justifying United Nations intervention
on the basis of the explicit request of the Government of the Republic
of the Congo."[21] Thus, in one sentence, are found indications that
the operation was a collective measure, since it was being deployed
to deal with a threat to peace, and also was an exercise of the peaceful settlement function. The intent to place ONUC within the latter

category may be inferred from the suggestion that the deployment of the force in Zaire was legally justified by the request of that country's government. The description of ONUC here touches common ground with that of UNEF, with resulting inferences that ONUC was to operate with the consent of the host state and was to be non-coercive.

Another indication of the character being attributed to ONUC under the Charter was the duplication, mutatis mutandis, of the above-quoted statement in the official description of the force, to the effect that while UNEF could not take the initiative in the use of force, men engaged in the operation were entitled to respond with force when attacked, "including attempts to use force to make them withdraw from positions occupied under orders" of the competent United Nations authority. [22] The repetition of this language seems clearly to have been a signal that ONUC belonged in the same Charter category as did UNEF.

Early in the history of ONUC, the government of Zaire undertook to place its operations and movements in the town of Matadi under severe limitations. The Secretary-General, responding to this attempt, referred to both of the bases mentioned for the deployment of the force and went on to declare, in effect, that it was primarily a collective measure. [23] Inter alia, he said that:

> The considerations ruling the relationship between the Republic of the Congo and the United Nations, therefore, should not be seen solely in the light of the request of the Government and what flows from that request. The status, rights and functions of the United Nations are basically determined by the fact that the action was taken in order to counteract an international threat to peace. [24]

He went on to insist that it was the United Nations, not the host government, that had the authority to determine how such measures should be carried out. [25]

A military operation that had been officially placed in the same Charter category as UNEF was thus described in terms applicable to an exercise of the collective measures function. According to the view of this discussion, it would have been desirable to locate both operations within this function, since the use of UNEF was properly to have been regarded as an application of military pressure to deal with a bona fide threat to peace, and thus as a fulfillment of the Charter requirements for such measures.

Instead, after Matadi, it was officially and uniformly denied that ONUC was a collective measure. [26]

Since the denial of collective measure status to the deployment of UNEF is believed to have been motivated largely by the fact that it was initiated by the Assembly, the reason for the denial in the case of ONUC was necessarily different. It seems to have been the belief of competent authorities that governments and peoples of United Nations member states would be unwilling, or at least hesitant, to contribute troop contingents to the force if it were designated a collective measure. This unwillingness was thought to result from a supposed tendency to associate collective measures with "enforcement" and with coercive force, and thus with possible combat action and war. [27]

In light of this belief, the authorities may have seen UNEF as furnishing a convenient precedent for keeping an operation like ONUC, which it was also hoped would not use overt force, out of the collective measures category. They may have decided both to utilize this precedent and to take advantage of the Council's capability to initiate collective measures, by devising a formula that suggested ONUC was wholly or partly within both the peaceful settlement and the collective measures categories.

However, ONUC was soon called on to apply overt force. The first such instance, in 1960, could readily be accounted for as fulfillment of ONUC's mission of assisting in the maintenance of order in Zaire. [28] Since that situation was widely seen as a potential source of great-power conflict, this application of force was doubtless perceived by informed individuals as necessary to deal with a threat to international peace, and thus as a legitimate exercise of the collective measures function.

In 1961 and 1962, however, the operation gradually came to be seen as having the additional purpose of suppressing the secession from Zaire of Katanga Province. This impression resulted from a combination of Security Council pronouncements hostile to the secession and a series of clashes between United Nations forces and those of Katanga.

The first relevant resolution authorized the use of force if necessary, and in the last resort, to prevent civil war in Zaire. [29] It also authorized United Nations officials to remove mercenary soldiers in the employ of regimes other than the central government. A resolution of November 24, 1961, [30] aimed directly at the Katanga secession, declared the regime to be illegal and the resulting entity not to be a sovereign state; urged member states not to give it any support but to support the central government; and authorized the Secretary-General to take vigorous action to deport the mercenary soldiers on whom the military strength of the secessionist regime was largely dependent.

Military clashes occurred between forces of the United Nations and Katanga Province, culminating in hostilities in the winter of 1962-63, following which the secessionist regime collapsed.[31] The impression given to the world must have been that the United Nations had deliberately employed force to suppress the regime.

In July 1962, in the midst of these developments, the International Court of Justice handed down its advisory opinion in the Certain Expenses case. As already observed, it passed upon the legality of both UNEF and ONUC in answering the question presented to it concerning the duty of member states of the United Nations to pay assessments to defray the costs of their operations. The Court found that both were legally constituted and that neither was a collective measure. It seems possible that the finding regarding ONUC in the latter respect might have been influenced in several respects by the precedent of UNEF.

In the first place, and most important for the present thesis, the Court was faced, in the case of ONUC, with the collapse of the "peace-keeping operation" as that concept had been defined in relation to UNEF. That definition, it will be recalled, specified that the operation was not supposed to have "military functions exceeding those necessary to secure peaceful conditions on the assumption that the parties to the conflict take all necessary steps for compliance with the recommendations" of the competent United Nations organ.[32] The secessionist regime of Katanga Province had breached this assumption, and ONUC was engaging in hostilities. The assumption was thus proved to be hardly adequate as a means of defining the scope of military forces deployed to apply military pressure in sensitive international situations.

This development might well have encouraged the Court to find that the deployment of ONUC was a collective measure. Its operation was established by the Council, which is universally recognized as authorized to apply collective measures; it was deployed at least in part to deal with a threat to peace; and the Council had indeed, in the Matadi case, indicated that it was a collective measure. On the other hand, the Secretary-General and some other authorities had firmly denied that ONUC was in that category and, moreover, had indicated that it was in the same Charter category as UNEF. Judges of the Court, if they felt any inclination to rule that either or both operations were collective measures, may have been discouraged from doing so on the grounds that it would be unwise to controvert a course of action being pursued by political authorities and involving issues of major world importance.[33] If they took a relatively modest view of the role law and the Court should play in such a matter, they had a certain justification. Certainly these institutions were not remotely comparable to the status that had, for example, enabled the United States Supreme Court, in 1954, to challenge the deeply rooted—in both law and custom—system of racially segregated schools that existed in some parts of the country.[34]

The Court, in finding that the use of ONUC was not a collective measure, also avoided saying that it was a "peace-keeping operation":

> It is not necessary for the Court to express an opinion as to which article or articles of the Charter were the basis for the resolutions of the Security Council, but it can be said that the operations of ONUC did not include a use of armed force against a State which the Security Council, under Article 39, determined to have committed an act of aggression or to have breached the peace. The armed forces which were utilized in the Congo were not authorized to take military action against any State. The operation did not involve "preventive or enforcement measures" against any State under Chapter VII and therefore did not constitute "action" as that term is used in Article 11.[35]

This description of collective measures contains no indication that the Charter definition of the function authorizes the application of United Nations force to deal with "mere" threats to peace, nor that such applications of pressure need not be directed against states. In effect, the Court here rewrote the definition of collective measures so as to exclude all applications of pressure designed to deal with threats to peace falling short of actual breaches, and measures that, like ONUC and UNEF, are directed against situations as such. Also, it excluded measures directed against entities other than states.

According to this definition, it was wrong for the United Nations subsequently to direct sanctions against Rhodesia, since that situation was not alleged to be more than a threat to peace and since it was part of the United Nations position that Rhodesia continued to be a British colony and was not a state. Nevertheless, the measures in this case were officially regarded as formal collective measures under the Charter.

A year after the Court opinion, the Secretary-General undertook to fill the gap left by the opinion concerning the proper categorization of ONUC under the Charter. In an address on June 13, 1963, he referred to ONUC as a peace-keeping force. As to the Charter authorization for the operation, he indicated that it was an exercise of the peaceful settlement function; however, he did not stress this point. Nor did he say, as the Court had in reference to UNEF, that this kind of operation is initiated by recommendation. He was, perhaps, still inhibited, as the Court may have been, by the fact that ONUC had engaged in hostilities and was generally seen as having suppressed the Katanga regime by force. Stress was placed on the contention that such military forces operated with the consent of the parties directly concerned. Thus, he said:

> The nature of these developments is sometimes confused, wittingly or unwittingly, by an attempt to relate them to the use of force to counter aggression by the Security Council provided for in Chapter VII of the Charter. In fact, the peace-keeping forces I am about to describe are of a very different kind and have little in common with the forces foreseen in Chapter VII, but their existence is not in conflict with Chapter VII. They are essentially peace and not fighting forces, and they operate only with the consent of the parties directly concerned. [36]

In a later passage, the statement evidently undertook to make a more comprehensive recital of assorted constitutional bases of such operations, as well as to subsume ONUC into a category containing at least two other military operations:

> All three were improvised and called into the field at very short notice; all three were severely limited in their right to use force; all three were designed solely for the maintenance of peace and not for fighting in the military sense; all three were recruited from the smaller powers and with special reference to their acceptability in the area in which they were to serve; all three operated with the express consent and cooperation of the States or territories where they were stationed, as well as of any other parties directly concerned in the situation; and all three were under the direction and control of the Secretary-General acting on behalf of the organs of the United Nations. [37]

As to the justification for ONUC's engaging in hostilities and seeming to suppress the Katanga regime by force, the Secretary-General appears to have simply ignored the possibility that any such events had occurred.

This statement, like the Court's opinion in Certain Expenses, evidently represented an effort to vindicate ONUC as a legally authorized operation and to place the seal of approval on its action, which was generally perceived to have forced a change in the internal regime of Zaire. The question of how these actions could be reconciled with the original definition of the "peace-keeping operation" was austerely avoided in these high-level statements.[38]

The effect of the combined efforts of Court and Secretary-General was to continue the existence of a concept labeled "peace-keeping operation" but having a different essential meaning from the original concept bearing that name. The concept they brought to life had the appearance, conferred on it by the precedent of ONUC, of embracing military operations designed to enforce decisions on substantive issues in dispute. The Council resolution of November 24, 1961, had conveyed the impression of a United Nations decision that the secessionist regime of Katanga Province should be suppressed; the military events of December 1962-January 1963 apparently enforced that decision. The advisory opinion validated this use of force by raising no objection to what had been done; it also provided the corollary that ONUC was not a collective measure and thus, by implication, that it was not bound by the Charter limitations on operations falling within that category.

The Secretary-General's statement of June 13, 1963, represents a notable part of an effort to gain acceptance of the new concept of the "peace-keeping operation" as a part of the peaceful settlement function, by forcing it into the category of activities that are clearly components of that function. Thus, he suggested at one point that peace-keeping operations belong in the same category as mediation and other uses of the Secretary-General's office for the peaceful settlement of disputes.[39]

Also lumped together were peace-keeping operations designed to apply military pressure and military units performing other types of functions. This makes it possible to assert that there are but two categories of military units: those engaged in the "enforcement" function and those engaged in "peace-keeping operations." The Secretary-General likened the former category to war.[40] The latter would include on one hand military operations such as UNEF, ONUC, and the force in Cyprus, designed to apply military pressures in the handling of disputes and situations, and on the other units composed of military personnel performing essentially nonmilitary functions, such as observer corps.[41]

This lumping together of quite different functions[42] was apparently resorted to as a device for avoiding the clear and basic limitations on the grants of power agreed to at San Francisco and incorporated into the Charter definitions of the peaceful settlement and collective measures functions. By undertaking to remove some applications of military pressure from the latter major category and lump them with such bodies as observer corps in a category subsidiary to the peaceful settlement function, the concept of the "peace-keeping operation" has the evident purpose and effect of confusing the two functions. United Nations forces are relieved of the limitations of the collective measures function and enabled to be applied to enforce substantive decisions. They thus became means of pressure available to states forming <u>ad hoc</u> majorities on particular issues, in the pursuit of the traditional approach to the conduct of international relations. These concepts were given reality in the public's perceptions by the Katanga case.

When, in May 1967, the Secretary-General withdrew UNEF from Egypt on its demand, he justified his action in part by the statement that:

> It was thus a basic legal principle arising from the nature of the Force, and clearly understood by all concerned, that the consent of Egypt was a prerequisite to the stationing of UNEF on Egyptian territory. . . .[43]

This statement seems to represent an attempt to revive the original concept of the "peace-keeping operation." However, it is accompanied by, and indeed subordinated to, other statements to the effect that the only practical recourse in the circumstances was the withdrawal of the force;[44] it was thus suggested that had it been practical to do so, UNEF might have used force to maintain its positions.

The principal purpose of this reassertion of the original definition of the force may have been the maintenance of the dual role of "peace-keeping operations," which has been asserted from the beginning—namely that they both are and are not applications of military pressure.[45] With the resources thus made available, it would have been possible for the competent authorities to have justified both the removal of ONUC in the Katanga situation and the defiance by UNEF of the Egyptian demand for its withdrawal in 1967. In the latter case, for example, they could have asserted the force's right to defend itself, or its right to take necessary steps to ensure its freedom of movement, which were reasons that had been advanced for ONUC's military activity against the troops of Katanga Province.[46] In the latter case, the withdrawal of the force, had it been decided on, might have been justified by the rule that such forces may operate only with the consent of the parties to the dispute.[47]

It is tempting to conclude that the only consistent reason for maintaining ONUC in position and for withdrawing UNEF is that the former was strong enough to deal with Katanga Province, whereas the latter was not strong enough successfully to defy Egypt.

The use made of ONUC against Katanga Province must have contributed to the dissatisfaction and protests that resulted from the decision to withdraw UNEF from Egypt in 1967 as a prelude to the "Six-Day War" in June of that year.[48] It is doubtful that many of the protesters were aware of the original limitations supposed to have been imposed on UNEF by the Charter. Their reassertion by the Secretary-General was overshadowed by his parallel argument that withdrawal was the only practical course in the circumstances. The principal consideration affecting public opinion was probably the view that the deployment of UNEF was an exercise of the "enforcement" function and that it therefore had the power to apply coercion if necessary for the preservation of peace.

The protests, in their turn, contributed to the prevalence of the general impression that forces like UNEF and ONUC may be ordered to remain at their stations notwithstanding demands for their withdrawal by parties concerned in relevant disputes. They apparently stimulated the proposal of a panel of the United Nations Association of the U.S.A., in 1971, to the effect that it should be made clear at the time of deployment that forces in "peace-keeping operations" "should" not be withdrawn except on the approval of the organ responsible for their deployment.[49] The reason for the proposal was said to be that the withdrawal of UNEF in 1967 had had the unfortunate effect of undermining confidence in the United Nations "as a peacekeeper;"[50] the proposal was evidently intended to provide safeguards against such future withdrawals. One effect of its adoption would be to terminate the situation in which the United Nations authorities would have at their disposal two definitions of such operations, one of which would require them to withdraw a force at the demand of the host state or other party and the other of which would not. Adoption of the proposal would clearly imply that such decisions were for the United Nations; a decision that a force should remain in defiance of a demand for its withdrawal would presumably place it under a duty to use force if necessary to that end.

Not only does the present discussion find no objection to this location of authority for the application of United Nations tangible pressures, it considers it the only proper location. The difference between the present view and the one just described lies in the fact that the collective measures function is here considered the framework within which such measures should be contained in the interests of the long-range goals of world community, peace, and security. The "peace-keeping operation" is, by definition, apart from this function. (Aside from this aspect, the concept is virtually undefinable.[51])

The only requirement under the relevant proposed guideline is that tangible pressures be seen by all concerned as directed to dealing with aggressions, other breaches of peace, or threats to peace. The United Nations would have been perfectly capable, pursuant to this guideline, of instructing UNEF to operate strictly in cooperation with Egypt. It would necessarily be understood by all concerned that, in accordance with the Charter, the instructions of the force could be changed to a more active role if the threat were to intensify or a breach of peace were to develop. Also, a force sent to apply positive enforcement measures might have its instructions changed to adopt a "peace-keeping" role to meet changed circumstances of the given case. The phrase "peace-keeping operation" might thus serve a useful purpose as applied to military forces, but only if understood as a sub-category of the collective measures function.

Thus, under a proper Charter interpretation, UNEF might have been deployed in 1956 under the limitation that it operate with the consent of Egypt. In 1967 its instructions might have been altered, with the effect of defying, or even resisting, the host state's demand for its withdrawal. In both cases the operation would have been seen as directed to a proper purpose under the Charter, namely, that of dealing with a threat to peace. The important consideration is that operations so limited should not be seen as attempts to enforce substantive decisions on the merits of disputes.

The most important disadvantage of the "peace-keeping operation" is that, being outside the collective measures function, it can be employed so as to give the impression of such an attempt. It is true that in only one case as of the time of writing—that of ONUC in the Katanga episode—has such an operation been used in this way. It has, for this reason, been the only such operation to cause more than minimal damage to prospects for world peace and security.

The three forces deployed in the Middle East area;[52] ONUC, in its original aspect; and the operation deployed in Cyprus in 1964[53] all had the bona fide purpose of dealing with threats to peace or breaches of peace. They were no doubt seen as carrying out proper purposes of the United Nations. Such damage as was done by these operations, or by some of them, may have stemmed from denials that they were collective measures—denials which were particularly explicit in the case of ONUC after the Matadi incident.[54] They must have caused some confusion in the minds of observers sufficiently informed to know that the collective measures function constituted the only Charter authorization for the use of force in the direct handling of disputes. Also, denials in the cases of UNEF and ONUC must have contributed to a frame of mind tending to accept the later use of ONUC in such a way as to convey the impression that it was enforcing a substantive decision in the case of Katanga Province.

The last-mentioned case probably contributed to all three of the disadvantages listed in Chapter 1 as likely to result from pretensions of United Nations powers to make binding decisions, as well as of apparent attempts to enforce such decisions.

Relations were strained and tensions increased not only with respect to relations with the secessionist regime but, on a wider scale, inasmuch as the United Nations and its relevant majority were seen by some interests as seeking to deprive them of their property in Katanga Province.[55]

Confusion must have been an unavoidable result of the apparent action of the United Nations in suppressing a secessionist regime by force. Where in the Charter is the United Nations given such a power?[56]

The third damaging effect under discussion is the fostering of the illusion that a legal structure comparable to those of domestic systems exists in the international realm. Such an effect must have been created by the appearance—indeed, perhaps, the fact—that the United Nations was able in this case to decide on the suppression of a secessionist regime and then to proceed to carry out the decision by military force. This result contributed to the illusion, notwithstanding the success of the measure, because of the very small number of cases in which such success is possible. The most basic reason is, of course, that the member states have never conferred on the organization powers of this kind with the understanding that they are legal in the sense of being equally applicable to all.

Perhaps none of these inhibitory effects would have been entirely eliminated if the guidelines herein advocated had been pursued in this case. In such a contingency it may be assumed that the organization would have applied force that would have contributed to the downfall of the secessionist regime. Action pursuant to the guidelines would then have differed from the actual case in that, first, the relevant resolutions would have made it clear that two distinct functions were being pursued: (1) a recommended solution of the dispute, and (2) a use of force for the sole purpose of dealing with the threat to peace which the world apparently recognized in the Zairean situation. Given all the circumstances of the case—including the newly independent status of Zaire, the alleged intervention of European financial interests to preserve their interests

in Katanga, the agitation the case was causing in Africa and elsewhere—it might have been reasonable and proper for the United
Nations to maintain that the suppression of this particular secession
was required in the interests of maintaining international peace.
Granted that the case was a difficult one for the application of correct principles of the Charter, its handling could have been improved
by holding before the world public the fact that this was a threat to
peace, and that force was being employed to deal with it, in accordance with the Charter.

Turning to certain broader questions of practicality, UNEF
and ONUC were operations of which certain explanations would have
been necessary had it been undertaken to designate them collective
measures.

With regard to UNEF, the principal explanation would have
concerned the fact that this operation was initiated by the General
Assembly, contrary to the official view that it is without Charter
authority to take such action. The correct line of explanation, in
the perspective of this study, has been indicated in Chapters 2[57]
and 5.[58]

In the case of ONUC, the required explanations would have
had to do with the question of how the powers of such operations
can be effectively limited. As has been indicated, this problem
arose because of apprehensions that some governments tended to
equate "collective measures" with combat operations and would be
reluctant to provide troops for operations so designated. It was
evidently to overcome such apprehensions that the use of ONUC
was officially categorized an exercise of the peaceful settlement
function. It seems logical to assume that any further reliance on
this form of protection was dissipated by the experience of ONUC
itself. Moreover, it seems unlikely that governments were ever
inclined to rely on anything other than their own efforts to assess,
as realistically as possible, the true nature of the situations in
which they were asked to contribute troops.

Subsequent manifestations of the military "peace-keeping
operation" up to the time of writing have not significantly altered
the basic elements of concern to this discussion. Examples are the
force in Cyprus established in 1964 and the forces deployed in the
Egyptian-Israeli situation in 1973, in the Israeli-Syrian situation
in 1974, and in southern Lebanon in 1978. All were established by
the Security Council, all were to function with the consent of the
parties involved, and none has had any visible purpose other than
to deal with breaches of, or threats to, international peace.

The Council resolution that set up the United Nations force
deployed in Cyprus in 1964 did so by recommending the establishment of the force and without indicating to whom the recommendation

was directed.[59] This course appears to have been a rather extreme attempt to ensure that the operation would be considered to come under the peaceful settlement function in accordance with the analysis of the World Court in its advisory opinion in <u>Certain Expenses</u>. The "recommendation" could, in the circumstances, have been directed only to the Secretary-General, and the ensuing Council resolution made it clear that this was indeed the case.[60] This use of "recommendation" was a distortion of the correct relationship, since in such an important matter as the deployment of a United Nations armed force, the correct role of the Secretary-General, as "the chief administrative officer of the Organization,"[61] would be to carry out the Council's decision to establish the force.

While the damage caused by this particular case has probably not been great, since the purpose of the force was and has been seen to be the proper one, under the Charter, of dealing with a threat to peace, it constitutes a precedent for pervasive and damaging uses of the notion of "recommendation" as a means of arguing that applications of tangible pressures by the United Nations are outside the collective measures category.[62]

The constitutive documents of the Middle East force of 1973 contain the ambiguities characteristic of the "peace-keeping operation" but can be said to represent a swing back in the direction of the collective measures function. One such indication is that the Council categorically "decided" to establish the force.[63] The Secretary-General's report,[64] which constitutes the most important definition of the nature of the operation, states that:

> The Force will proceed on the assumption that the
> parties to the conflict will take all the necessary
> steps for compliance with the decisions of the
> Security Council.

This language is clearly derived from that of a report of 1956 on UNEF, but the important introductory phrase of the earlier document is omitted:

> . . . nor . . . should the Force have military func-
> tions exceeding those necessary to secure peaceful
> conditions on the assumption that the parties to the
> conflict take all necessary steps for compliance with
> the recommendations of the General Assembly.[65]

Instead, the sentences preceding the passage from the 1973 report have to do with the force's right of self-defense. Like the earlier UNEF, this operation was limited in its use of force to self-defense;

however, the scope of this right was somewhat more broadly defined. Whereas it had been described, in the earlier case, as including the right to respond to "attempts to use force to make them
withdraw from positions which they occupy under orders," the 1973
report states that the right of self-defense shall include "attempts
by forceful means to prevent it from discharging its duties under
the mandate of the Security Council." The report also specifies
the force's right of freedom of movement.[66] Most important in
this connection is the statement that:

> All matters which may affect the nature or the con-
> tinued effective functioning of the Force will be
> referred to the Council for its decision.

This statement was said by the United States Representative to mean
that the force was to be withdrawn only upon the decision of the
Security Council.[67] In view of the controversy that ensued from
the withdrawal of the earlier Middle East operation, the Secretary-
General's statement of 1973 seems to suggest that the force could
be ordered by the Council to remain even without the consent of one
or more of the parties.

The tendency of these operations toward a more central role
for the Security Council was consistent with Soviet wishes and was
forecast by a statement of the U.S. Secretary of State, shortly before the re-establishment of UNEF in 1973, indicating that his
government favored such a trend.[68] The trend was continued in the
decision to terminate UNEF in 1979 after the Soviet Union had made
known its intention to veto its continuance, notwithstanding that the
operation was desired to play a role in the process, which was
being assisted by the United States, of establishing peace between
Israel and Egypt.[69]

Insofar as the trend in question brings measures of tangible
pressure directed to handling breaches of, or threats to, international peace into conformity with the Charter definition of collective
measures, it is desirable if it represents a move to integrate all
such measures with the collective measures function. The same
would be true in relation to the role of the Assembly if this trend
were to be considered in relation to the collective measures function and the Uniting for Peace resolution. However, a tendency to
eliminate the role of the Assembly as to "peace-keeping operations"
seems to add to the confusion surrounding this concept, since such
measures are supposed to be manifestations of the peaceful settlement function and the Assembly has undoubted competence in regard to such measures under the Charter. The tendency is undesirable insofar as it might result in an increase in the proportion

of peaceful settlement measures brought within the exclusive competence of the Security Council and thus subject to the veto.

It might be argued that the "peace-keeping operation" has become an established part of United Nations activity, while the Assembly has been downgraded and virtually eliminated as a source of authority for such measures, and consequently that the detailed history of that concept contained in this Chapter, including the important role of the Assembly, is outmoded and out of place. To the contrary, I have considered it important to include this history in order to relate the concept to the thesis of the study.

As to the role of the Assembly, the decision of the United States and the Soviet Union virtually to write it off vis-a-vis this type of operation stands in striking contrast to the fact that UNEF, the first such measure, was established by the Assembly and the further fact that had it not been deemed necessary to resort to that organ the "peace-keeping operation" might never have been invented. Eliminating the Assembly might thus be read as eliminating a substantial reason for continuing the concept. On the other hand, the present downgrading of the role of the Assembly by no means precludes the possibility that a requisite majority in the future might, as has occurred in the past, decide to utilize it, with or without the assent of either the U.S. or the U.S.S.R., to activate new operations or continue existing ones.

In opening a session of the U.N. Special Committee on Peace-Keeping Operations, the chairman said that issues confronting the Committee involved profound constitutional questions and that "if the United Nations failed completely in its crucial task of maintaining international peace and security, many of its other impressive achievements might be lost."[70] "Peace-keeping" thus seems to be accorded a role similar to those of such concepts as "international law" and "arms control," which, according to the Charter, are to be developed separately as means of progress toward peace and security.[71] In the view of this discussion, no such concepts can be developed significantly in the absence of broader developments along lines suggested herein. The peaceful settlement and collective measures functions could, in this view, become constitutional pillars indispensable to the building of a system capable of maintaining peace and security. The constitutional questions involved in the concept of the "peace-keeping operation" are, in this perspective, insoluble. The concept represents a mixture and confusion of the two functions, amounting to institutionalized anarchy at a crucial point in the structure of international relations.[72]

NOTES

1. G.A. Resolution 1000 (ES-I) (1956).
2. G.A. Resolution 1125 (XI) (1957).
3. E.g., the passage quoted in the text at n. 7 infra. Some theories that have been advanced as to the Charter basis for UNEF are reviewed in Bowett, United Nations Armed Forces, supra, at 93 et seq.; and in R. Higgins, United Nations Peacekeeping 1946-1967: Documents and Commentary (London: Oxford University Press, 1969), vol. 1, at 260 et seq.
4. This formulation is intended to recall that this chapter's discussion is concerned with the use of force as a primary means of handling disputes. Official definitions of the "peace-keeping operation" are broader than this. We are not, for example, here concerned with the military force deployed by the U.N. in West Irian in 1962, although it was placed in that category by Secretary-General U Thant (see n. 37 and accompanying text, infra). The primary U.N. dispute-handling function in that case was the temporary administration of the territory, and the military force in question was merely the police arm of that administration. See Halderman, The United Nations and the Rule of Law, supra, at 33-35, 110, n. 41.
5. The relevant resolutions are in the form of decisions appointing the commanding officer, authorizing him to recruit an officer corps and to proceed with the organization of the force, etc. G.A. Resolutions 1000 and 1001 (ES(I)) (1956).
6. This device was further developed in 1964 when the Council recommended the establishment of a U.N. force to be deployed in Cyprus. See text at n. 59, infra.
7. "Second and Final Report of the Secretary-General on the plan for an emergency international United Nations Force . . .," U.N. GAOR, 1st Emergency Special Sess., Plenary Meetings and Annexes: Annexes, Agenda Item 5, at 19, 20-21 (1956).
8. "Introduction to the Annual Report of the Secretary-General on the Work of the Organization, 16 June 1957-15 June 1958," id., 13th Sess., Supp. 1A, at 2 (1958).
9. The International Court of Justice said in this connection:

The verb "secure" as applied to such matters as
halting the movement of military forces and arms
into the area and the conclusion of a cease-fire might
suggest measures of enforcement, were it not that
the Force was to be set up "with the consent of the

nations concerned." [Certain Expenses of the United
Nations (Article 17, paragraph 2, of the Charter),
Advisory Opinion of July 20, 1962 (1962), I.C.J. 151,
170.]

It is submitted that the Court was here pointing out the same irrec-
oncilable contradiction that is discussed in the principal text of this
book. In holding that the operation was, in fact, an exercise of the
peaceful settlement function and that UNEF was not authorized to
use force (see text at n. 15, infra), it was stating, in effect, that
in the event of a situation requiring the use of force to "secure" the
border, UNEF would be unable to fulfill its prescribed duty.

10. "Summary Study of the experience derived from the establishment of the Force . . . ," U.N. GAOR, 13th Sess., Annexes,
Agenda Item 65, at 8, 31 (U.N. Doc. 3943) (1958). See text at n.
22, infra.

11. U.N. SCOR, 13th year, 829th meeting, at 4. For the
U.S. proposal see id., Supp. July-Sept. 1958, at 31 (U.N. Doc.
S/4050/Rev. 1).

12. Id., 835th meeting, at 8. The Secretary-General was
discussing a Japanese proposal similar to the U.S. proposal but
incorporating some amendments. Id., Supp. July-Sept. 1958 at 38
(U.N. Doc. S/4055/Rev. 1).

13. Text at n. 10, supra.

14. UNEF's authority to use force is indicated by such statements as the following:

> If UNEF is to be expected to continue to discharge suc-
> cessfully its present mandate, it must have a certain
> minimum military capacity to prevent violation of the
> Line by civilians or small military parties from es-
> calating. . . . ["Survey of the United Nations Emergency
> Force: Report of the Secretary-General," U.N. GAOR,
> 20th Sess., Annexes, Agenda Item 21, at 22, 26 (U.N.
> Doc. A/C.5/1049) (1965).]

A similar indication is given in D. Wainhouse, International Peace-
keeping at the Crossroads: National Support—Experience and Prospects (Baltimore: Johns Hopkins University, 1973), at 201 (1973).
The existence of the authority was recognized in 1963 by the Director
of the General Legal Division of the Legal Department of the United
Nations, writing in his personal capacity: O. Schachter, "The
Relation of Law, Politics and Action in the United Nations," 109
Académie de Droit International, Recueil des Cours 165, 210
(1963-II).

15. Certain Expenses, supra, at 164-65.

16. Id. at 165.

17. G.A. Resolution 498 (V) (1951).

18. See discussion in Ch. 5, supra.

19. The Democratic Republic of the Congo changed its name to the Republic of Zaire on Oct. 27, 1971.

20. S.C. Resolution 143 (1960). The Charter basis for this operation is discussed in Bowett, United Nations Armed Forces, supra, especially at 175 et seq., 274-85.

21. "First Report by the Secretary-General on the implementation of Security Council Resolution S/4387 of 14 July 1960," U.N. SCOR, 15th Year, Supp. July-Sept. 1960, at 16-17 (U.N. Doc. S/4389). This report was specifically endorsed by the Council in S.C. Resolution 145 (1960); however, in view of the broad mandate of the Council, the pronouncements of the Secretary-General on this operation should be regarded as authentic statements of United Nations positions unless specifically disavowed.

22. Id. at 19-20. The statement pertaining to UNEF is quoted in the text at n. 10, supra.

23. Id. 16th Year, Supp. Jan.-Mar. 1961, at 220-22, 262-63 (1961).

24. Id. at 262.

25. Id. at 263.

26. An early instance of such denials was the Secretary-General's statement to the 839th meeting of the General Assembly's Fifth Committee on Apr. 17, 1961. For the full text see U.N. GAOR, 15th Sess., Annexes, Agenda Items 49-50, at 35-37 (U.N. Doc. A/C.5/864) (1961).

27. ". . . Message dated 24 February 1961 from the Secretary-General to certain African States concerning the need for troops and the function of the Force," U.N. SCOR, 16th Year, Supp. Jan.-Mar. 1961, at 187-89 (1961), Annex VII to U.N. Doc. S/4752. Schachter, "The Relation of Law," supra, at 219-23. This position is upheld by legal argumentation, id. at 215-28. For an opposing view see Halderman, The United Nations and the Rule of Law, supra, at 104-108. This consideration seems not to have entered into initial thinking about UNEF. It is conceivable that it may have done so with respect to the proposed force in Lebanon and in later thinking about UNEF, discussed as a possibility in the text at n. 13, supra.

28. ONUC took over major airports and the Kinshasa (then Leopoldville) radio station for the stated reason of preventing a breakdown of law and order. "Annual Report of the Secretary-General on the Work of the Organization 16 June 1960-15 June 1961," U.N. GAOR, 16th Sess., Supp. 1, at 10.

29. S.C. Resolution 161 (1961).

30. S.C. Resolution 169 (1961).

31. These events are summarized in "Annual Report of the Secretary-General on the Work of the Organization 16 June 1962-15 June 1963," U.N. GAOR, 18th Sess., Supp. 1, at 8-11.

32. Text at n. 7, supra.

33. After referring to several resolutions of the Council and the Assembly tending to endorse the setting up of ONUC, and emphasizing that they were adopted unanimously or without dissent, the Court said:

> In the light of such a record of reiterated consideration, confirmation, approval and ratification by the Security Council and by the General Assembly of the actions of the Secretary-General in implementing the resolution of 14 July 1960, it is impossible to reach the conclusion that the operation in question usurped or impinged upon the prerogatives conferred by the Charter on the Security Council. [Certain Expenses, supra, at 176-77.]

34. Ch. 11, n. 18, infra.

35. Certain Expenses, supra, at 177.

36. Thant, "United Nations Stand-By Peace Force," supra, at 54-55.

37. Id. at 56. UNEF was certainly one of the other two operations here referred to; the third was evidently the force deployed in the West Irian case. The latter is here believed to belong in a basically different category from the other two. See n. 4, supra.

38. It could not, of course, be avoided in all contexts. The Secretary-General's annual report on the work of the organization in the year of the collapse of the Katanga regime recounted the relevant military events but asserted that United Nations Headquarters had been unaware of them due to a communications failure. "Annual Report . . . 16 June 1962-15 June 1963," supra, at 9. While this report denied that the U.N. had intervened in the case (id. at 13), the Introduction to the corresponding report for the following year admitted that there had been such intervention and that "the United Nations operation thwarted the Katanga secessionist effort." Id., 19th Sess., Supp. 1A, at 7 (1964). The legal justification for these actions seems to have been mainly that the force was entitled to provide for its defense and to ensure its freedom of movement. See n. 46 and accompanying text, infra. In an article published in the U.N. Chronicle in 1979 a high U.N.

official said that "ONUC carried out what some may call the enforcement action during the battle of Kolwezi that ended the secession of
Katanga." J. Jonah, "Importance of U.N. Peace-Keeping Operations Emphasized," 16 U.N. Monthly Chronicle, July 1979, at 78.

39. Thant, "United Nations Stand-By Peace Force" supra,
at 56.

40. Id. at 54.

41. For another exposition of these categories as main com-
ponents of the "peace-keeping operation" concept, see "Report of
the Secretary-General and the President of the General Assembly,"
Annex II to the "Report of the Special Committee on Peace Keeping
Operations," U.N. GAOR, 19th Sess., Annex 21, at 26, 79 (U.N.
Doc. A/5915 and Add.1) (1965).

42. The reality of the difference was evidently attested to
privately by Hammarskjold when, following the deployment of the
U.N. observer corps in Lebanon in 1958, he objected to sending a
U.N. military force to protect the observers. His biographer,
Urquhart, records that "Hammarskjold had emphasized from the
beginning that the Observer Group in Lebanon was not a police force
like UNEF" and that his reaction to the proposed military force was
to rule it out immediately "because it would completely change the
nature of the operation required by the Security Council. . . ."
B. Urquhart, Hammarskjold (New York: Knopf, 1972), at 265 (1972).

43. "Report of the Secretary-General on the withdrawal of
the United Nations Emergency Force," U.N. GAOR, 5th Emergency
Special Sess., Annexes, Agenda Item 5, at 4, 16 (U.N. Doc. A/6730)
(1967). For the final report (Doc. A/6730/Add. 3), see also 4 U.N.
Monthly Chronicle, July 1967, at 135, 151.

44. Documents cited in previous footnote at, respectively,
p. 15 and pp. 147-49.

45. Text at notes 7-14, supra.

46. The right to freedom of movement for the respective
operations was provided for in the agreements between the United
Nations and the host states of the two forces, Egypt and Zaire. The
freedom of movement agreed to was countrywide in the case of
ONUC (U.N. SCOR, 15th Year, Supp. July-Sept. 1960, at 27-28
(Doc. S/4389/Add. 5)) and limited to certain areas in the case of
UNEF (U.N. GAOR, 11th Sess., Annexes, Agenda Item 66, at 52,
56 (Doc. A/3526) (1957)). However, viewing these agreements in
context, it is clear that they were not intended to authorize the use
of force against the host states to ensure freedom of movement of
the operations.

47. The Secretary-General, in the passage quoted in the
text at n. 43, supra, refers only to the necessity of the consent of
Egypt, the host state. If this were the extent of the requirement, the

military force would not be impeded from engaging in combat with parties to the particular situation other than the host state. However, the original concept of the "peace-keeping operation" forbade such forces to use any force in excess of that required to maintain peaceful conditions on the assumption that the parties to the conflict would comply with relevant resolutions (text at n. 7, supra). All combat operations seem thus to have been forbidden. In his address of July 1963, the Secretary-General had said that ONUC and other "peace-keeping operation" forces had carried out their functions with the consent and cooperation of all the parties directly concerned, indicating that this was a prerequisite to the functioning of such forces (text at n. 37, supra). To similar effect see Jonah, "Importance of U.N. Peace-Keeping Operations Emphasized," supra, at 78.

48. The Secretary-General spoke of some of the protests as "very damaging to the United Nations and to its peace-keeping role in particular." "Report of the Secretary-General on the Withdrawal of UNEF," supra, at p. 10; 4 U.N. Monthly Chronicle, supra, at 135. One of the protesters was the President of the United States, who expressed dismay at the withdrawal. 56 Department of State Bulletin 870 (1967).

49. The United Nations in the 1970s: A Report of a National Policy Panel established by the United Nations Association of the United States of America (New York: U.N. Association, 1971), at 24.

50. Id.

51. A high official of the U.N., writing in the U.N. Chronicle in 1979, touched on this definition in asserting that the main difference between "peace-keeping" and "enforcement" is that the former function is subject to the Charter clause prohibiting U.N. intervention in domestic affairs, while the latter is not. Jonah, "Importance of U.N. Peace-Keeping Operations Emphasized," supra, at 78. This definition has to do with the usual assertion that peace-keeping operations require the consent of the parties to the case. It would be wrongful intervention in this view, and violative of the non-intervention clause of the Charter, to introduce an agency onto the territory of a state without its consent. On the other hand, the clause in question specifically exempts "enforcement" measures from its scope; presumably, consent is not required in such cases. Reliance on the non-intervention clause for the definition of the "peace-keeping operation" is, however, rather implausible. One reason is that, as will be discussed in Chapter 7, its use in particular cases has come to be based on subjective rather than objective considerations. (See Ch. 7, text at n. 14, infra.) Another is that states, as a rule, continue to assert the traditional attribute

of sovereignty by which they decide, on the basis of their perceived interests, whether or not to admit particular agencies to their respective territories. Whether or not a given agency were within the Charter's "enforcement" category would hardly be a relevant consideration in this context.

This view is consistent with that expressed in Ch. 7, to the effect that the non-intervention clause is both unnecessary and counter-productive in the search for peace and security.

52. These operations are considered in n. 63 and accompanying text, infra.

53. Text at n. 59, infra.

54. Text at n. 26 et seq., supra; see also Halderman, The United Nations and the Rule of Law, supra, at 104-108.

55. See, e.g., C. Hoskyns, The Congo Since Independence: January 1960-December 1961 (New York: Oxford University Press, 1965), at 473.

56. Considering that the United States began with secession, it is rather noteworthy that no concern about such an apparent assertion of United Nations power was expressed by individuals or groups that had protested the grant of much more limited power by that country to the World Court. The organizations included the Daughters of the American Revolution and the Sons of the American Revolution (Compulsory Jurisdiction, Hearings on S. Res. 94, supra, at 154, 454), which, along with others, would certainly have denied that the U.N., had it existed at the time, had any right to undertake to suppress the secession of the American colonies.

57. Role of the General Assembly in Collective Measures, Ch. 2, supra.

58. Ch. 2, text at notes 14-19, supra.

59. S.C. Resolution 186 (1964).

60. S.C. Resolution 187 (1964).

61. See U.N. Charter, Art. 97, on the relevant role of the Secretary-General. The correct relationship, as indicated above, had apparently been determined by the Security Council in connection with the proposed deployment of an observer corps in Yemen, in 1963. Whereas the Council there "requested" that the Secretary-General take the desired action (S.C. Resolution 179 (1963)), the discussion preceding the request indicated that the operation should not be initiated without the Council's acquiescence. U.N. SCOR, 18th year, 1037-1039th meetings (1963).

62. Another facet of this approach is found in L. Meeker, "Defensive Quarantine and the Law," 57 American Journal of International Law 515 (1963), in which the Deputy Legal Adviser of the U.S. Department of State argued that no international measures of tangible pressure are to be regarded as collective, or "enforcement,"

measures if initiated by recommendation. The purpose of the argument was, specifically, to explain that the "quarantine" measure in the Cuban missile crisis of 1962 was not a regional "enforcement action" requiring U.N. authorization. Ch. 12, text at n. 51, infra.

63. S.C. Resolution 340 (1973). This operation is frequently referred to as UNEF II. A second operation, the United Nations Disengagement Observer Force (UNDOF), was established by S.C. Resolution 350 on May 31, 1974. UNEF II was to assist in maintaining a cease-fire between Egyptian and Israeli forces, while UNDOF was to perform a similar function as between Israeli and Syrian forces. The Secretary-General's Report containing the broad terms of reference of this UNEF operation (U.N. SCOR, 28th Year, Supp. Oct.-Dec. 1973, at 91 (U.N. Doc. S/11052/Rev. 1 (1973)) was also made applicable to UNDOF. See S.C. meetings of May 30 and May 31, 1974, U.N. Docs. S/PV. 1773 and S/PV 1774. (S/PV refers to provisional records of Security Council meetings.) An essentially similar Report of the Secretary-General (U.N. SCOR, 33rd Year, Supp. Jun.-Mar. 1978, at 61 (U.N. Doc. S/12611, Mar. 19, 1978)) was made applicable to a third force in the area, the United Nations Interim Force in Lebanon (UNIFIL), established pursuant to S.C. Resolution 425 (1978) of the same date. Variations between this and the earlier Report, attributable largely to differences in terms of reference of UNIFIL, are not significant for our present discussion.

64. U.N. SCOR, 28th Year, Supp. Oct.-Dec. 1973, at 91 (U.N. Doc. 5/11052/Rev. 1 (1973)).

65. Text at n. 7, supra.

66. See n. 46 and accompanying text, supra.

67. U.N. SCOR, 28th Year, 1752d Meeting at 6 (1973).

68. Address by Secretary of State Kissinger to the General Assembly, Sept. 24, 1973, 69 Department of State Bulletin 469, 472 (1973).

69. N.Y. Times, July 25, 1979, p. 1, col. 1 and p. 8, col. 1.

70. Special Committee on Peace-Keeping Operations, 69th meeting, Feb. 14, 1977 (U.N. Doc. A/AC. 121/SR.69), at 2.

71. Arts. 13(1)(a) and 11(1).

72. In addition to the inherent importance of various measures embraced by the concept, including use of military force, it is also thought of as a very important part of the "structure" referred to in the text above. Thus, Ch. 1 of the United Nations Yearbook of 1965 is devoted to a "Review of the Question of Peace-Keeping Operations," and comparable manifestations of interest and acknowledgment of importance were evidenced in ensuing volumes until mitigated by the realization that agreement on basic issues was beyond reach. In 1970 the United States delegation to the General

Assembly, in a statement on objectives for that organ in the 25th
anniversary year of the U.N., said that:

> [T]he United States will offer proposals, or support the
> proposals of others, with these objectives among others:
> first, to put United Nations peacekeeping operations on
> a firmer and more reliable basis. [U.N. GAOR, 25th
> Sess., Plenary, 1854th meeting; 63 Department of
> State Bulletin 437, 438 (1970).]

Second place on the list was given to improving the peaceful settlement function. There is thus indicated a possible continuation of
the basic order of priorities that prevailed at the time of the San
Francisco conference. The concept of the "peace-keeping operation"
has merely replaced that of collective measures, or "enforcement,"
as the function of first importance.

7

NON-INTERVENTION AND
U.N. COMPETENCE

Chapters 4 through 8 deal with a structure of illusion consisting of supposedly binding decision-making powers of U.N. political organs. Chapters 4-6 have sought to deal with components of this structure that link substantive decision-making with the application of tangible pressures, either real or potential. Chapter 8 will be concerned with purported decision-making powers unrelated to tangible pressures.

This chapter will briefly consider a device, which might or might not be associated with tangible pressures, available to majorities as a basis—though here considered an improper one—for initiating substantive decisions. It consists of the proposition that if U.N. consideration of a dispute or situation is not barred by the Charter prohibition against intervention in domestic affairs of states, the organization may proceed to take whatever action it sees fit to bring about a settlement. Actions thus permitted would include the making of decisions on the merits of disputes.

The Charter provision that bars intervention in domestic affairs is Article 2(7), which reads as follows:

> Nothing contained in the present Charter shall
> authorize the United Nations to intervene in matters
> which are essentially within the domestic jurisdiction
> of any state or shall require the Members to submit
> such matters to settlement under the present Charter;
> but this principle shall not prejudice the application of
> enforcement measures under Chapter VII.

This provision was really not necessary, inasmuch as the United Nations is an international organization with defined powers limited to dealing with international problems. Domestic matters are not international; consequently the organization would be forbidden to consider them, regardless of the existence or non-existence of the clause in question. The jealous concern of states, throughout history, with perceived attributes of sovereignty made it certain that participants would regard the U.N. as an organization of defined and limited powers, and the present study has already considered how this supposition was borne out by the careful delimitation of its powers in the area of dispute-handling. Yet the assumption is believed to be widely held—in terms of various specific cases—that if U.N. consideration is not barred by the domestic jurisdiction clause the organization may proceed to apply such measures as it may see fit, regardless of these limitations. There is at least one explicit statement of this view, found in the U.S. government statement on the Rhodesian case discussed above in Chapters 3 and 4. This statement, it will be recalled, upheld not only the application of collective measures but also the making and enforcement of decisions on the merits of the dispute.[1] The following portion is relevant to this chapter:

> A number of individuals . . . have attacked, on both legal and policy grounds, this action of the Security Council and the support which the United States has given it.

> * * * * *

> Second, it is argued that the action of the Security Council involves a violation of article 2, paragraph 7, of the U.N. Charter. . . .

> The fallacy of this argument can be seen when the facts of the case are tested against the provisions [of the paragraph].

> —Rhodesia is not a "state" and has not been recognized as such by a single government or international organization.

> —The situation in Rhodesia is not "domestic," since it involves the international responsibilities of the United Kingdom under Chapter XI of the Charter relating to non-self-governing territories.

> —The action of the Security Council does not constitute "intervention," since the Council has acted at the request and with the concurrence of the legitimate sovereign, the United Kingdom.

—Article 2, paragraph 7, by its own terms, does
not apply to the application of enforcement measures
such as the mandatory economic sanctions imposed by
the Council in this case. [2]

Because of its negative formulation, it might be argued that this
statement was not intended to set forth affirmative grounds for
United Nations competence but only to answer an argument that had
been raised against such competence. However, forming as it does
part of an important statement entitled "International Law in the
United Nations," having as one evident purpose the upholding of the
legality of United Nations measures in the Rhodesian case, its intended import may reasonably be assumed to have been to set forth
affirmative legal bases for what was done. Although it was not employed by the United Nations on such a basis, the particular argument here under discussion, having been propounded by an important
government, became available for citation in further cases of the
kind. As far as its negative formulation is concerned, this was also
the case for some of the other arguments advanced in the statement.
The purpose here might have been to make it relatively easy to rebut
possible future uses of the statement as a precedent for unwanted
actions.

Sufficient to rule out this wrongful use of the non-intervention
clause would be the guideline advanced in Chapter 1, which would
limit to recommendations all General Assembly and Security Council pronouncements on the merits of disputes, and its corollary,
which would require that all applications of tangible pressure be
manifestly directed to purposes for which collective measures are
authorized by the Charter.

However, the broad problem posed by the non-intervention
clause, in terms of this discussion, cannot be so easily disposed of.
It has grown roots and branches and now forms part of the structure
of illusion mentioned above, demolition of which is here perceived
as essential to progress toward world peace and security. It may
therefore be useful to consider the clause from a corresponding perspective.

Fears of wrongful intervention in domestic affairs developed
emotional content as the structure of international institutions and
their supposed powers developed. The Covenant of the League of
Nations excepted from the dispute-handling activities of that organization all matters that, by international law, were solely within the
domestic jurisdiction of a party to a given situation. [3] This formulation was followed in the Dumbarton Oaks Proposals. [4] The changes
carried out at San Francisco were motivated by the decision to incorporate in the Charter authority for United Nations activity directed

to the improvement of economic and social conditions, the observance of human rights, and related matters. One change was in the
location of the non-intervention clause, to make clear that it applied
to the whole Charter and not just to dispute-handling activities. The
legal criterion for what constituted domestic jurisdiction was deleted, and United Nations competence was barred as to matters "essentially" within domestic jurisdiction instead of just those "solely"
within that jurisdiction.

The reason for the changes was explained thus by the United
States delegation, which played a leading role in bringing it about:

> To extend this principle [i.e., non-intervention
> in domestic matters] to the activities of the Organiza-
> tion as a whole, instead of limiting it to the pacific
> settlement of disputes as had been proposed at Dum-
> barton Oaks, seemed desirable because of the amplifi-
> cation of the power and authority given to the Assembly
> and, particularly, to the Economic and Social Council.
> Without this general limitation, which now flows from
> the statement of the principle in Chapter I, it might
> have been supposed that the Economic and Social Coun-
> cil could interfere directly in the domestic economy,
> social structure, or cultural or educational arrange-
> ments of the member states. Such a possibility is now
> definitely excluded.[5]

The Conference committee that drafted the provision similarly indicated in its report that, in view of the inclusion in the Charter of
functions in the economic, social, and cultural fields, it was necessary to frame the non-intervention clause so as to make sure that
the organization would not "go beyond acceptable limits."[6]

Naturally, the framers of the Charter did not intend to incorporate affirmative grants of power unacceptable to their governments. The impression was conveyed by the above statements, however, that the non-intervention clause was written to prevent wrongful incursions into domestic affairs that were being authorized in
various parts of the Charter.[7]

Corollary propositions might readily be seen as being (1) that
no action is wrongful if found not to be barred by that provision and
(2) that such a finding is, in fact, a determination that the proposed
action is legal. Indeed, the Conference committee report just referred to stated explicitly that the problem there under discussion
called for the non-intervention clause "as an instrument to determine the scope of the attributes of the Organization and to regulate
its functioning in matters at issue."[8]

The intent to set up dual criteria of competence—affirmative grants of power on the one hand, the non-intervention clause on the other—was again made clear in the drafting of the final clause of Article 2(7), providing that the principle of non-intervention "shall not prejudice the application of enforcement measures under Chapter VII." As originally proposed by the sponsoring powers, the clause would have excepted from the non-intervention clause all measures under Chapter VII. [9] The modification, limiting the exception to enforcement measures, was intended to remove from the exception the "peaceful settlement" portion of Chapter VII, and thus to link it with the major exposition of this function in Chapter VI as subject to the rule of Article 2(7). The intent seemed to be to fortify that rule, making it clear that even though a situation might be suitable for the exercise of the peaceful settlement function under affirmative Charter grants of power, its exercise would be barred as to matters falling within the domestic jurisdiction of a party. [10]

Two fallacies were contained in this approach, from the perspective of this discussion. The first was embodied in the hope that these dual bases of United Nations competence could be effectively coordinated. The second was the belief, which continued after the first fallacy was exposed, that legal grounds are provided for the taking of any proposed action by a finding that the action is not barred by the non-intervention clause. The above-quoted argument of the United States government in the Rhodesian case can be traced directly to this fallacy.

The first fallacy was quickly exposed after the United Nations began to function. In the Spanish case, in the organization's first year, a view inimical to the hope of effective correlation was proposed by the Subcommittee of the Security Council and foreshadowed the Assembly's tacit decision that the case in question was not essentially domestic. [11] The view of the Subcommittee was perhaps stated best by its chairman in a statement to the Council[12] in which he said that:

> [Y]ou start off with the postulate that it is no business
> of any other nation to concern itself with how the
> people of that country govern themselves. This is
> prima facie, primarily a matter of domestic concern.

and then went on immediately to say:

> . . . but if the facts indicate that that regime by its
> nature, by its conduct, by its operations, is likely
> to interfere in international peace and likely to be
> a menace to its neighbors, then the existence of

that regime is no longer a matter of essentially
domestic concern.

The Subcommittee, in its report, argued to similar effect, concluding that:

> There can be no question that the situation in
> Spain is of international concern. . . .
>
> . . . The allegations against the Franco regime
> involve matters which travel far beyond domestic
> jurisdiction and which concern the maintenance of
> international peace and security and the smooth and
> efficient working of the United Nations as the instru-
> ment mainly responsible for performing this duty.[13]

There is probably no question more strongly held to be within
domestic jurisdiction than that of how countries should be governed;
the Spanish case can thus be said to have represented a breakdown
of the whole concept that matters of essentially domestic concern
can be defined by objective standards. Its role in this respect has
been thus indicated:

> The argument of the Australian delegate [i.e., the
> statement of the Subcommittee Chairman, quoted
> above] was repeated by other delegates. Once the idea
> was accepted, it was another short step to a definition
> of matters within domestic jurisdiction, or domestic
> questions, as those which were not of international
> concern, and the development of a subjective, or politi-
> cal, concept of domestic jurisdiction was complete.[14]

International law doctrine has attempted to protect the rule of
non-intervention in regard to attempts by the people of a country to
overthrow their regime, the general "rule" here being that outside
intervention in such matters is wrongful, even on the request of the
recognized government, when a revolt has achieved such a degree of
support as to render the outcome in doubt.[15] It would certainly be
the view of the United States, Algeria, and other countries that third
parties would have had no right to interfere with their own struggles
for freedom. Yet the United States, in the above-quoted statement,[16]
asserts that the Rhodesian secession was not essentially domestic
within the meaning of the non-intervention clause, because it continued to have "non-self-governing" status under the Charter and
because Great Britain had requested the intervention of the Council.

The latter country was obviously considered still to be the rightful
sovereign, notwithstanding the secession. In the case of Katanga
Province, the United Nations was perceived by most people as using
force deliberately to suppress a secession.[17] On the other hand,
the organization has given its support to several secessionist movements.[18]

The United Nations has also intervened (within the original
meaning of Article 2[7]) in the area of activity concerned with economic and social matters, observance of human rights, etc. Mention may be made of the series of resolutions incorporating pronouncements of varying force on South Africa's policy of apartheid,
condemning that country for its refusal to change that policy, and
recommending that member states apply tangible pressure to encourage such change.[19] It seems most probable that at the time the
Charter was formulated participating governments considered such
matters to be within the domestic jurisdiction of states concerned;
their purpose in modifying the proposed non-intervention clause was
to proscribe even discussion of them by the organization.[20]

There are thus several subjects that states felt were legiti-
mately within their domestic jurisdictions, and as to which intervention on the part of the U.N. would be barred. These subjects
are generally closely linked with the jealous regard of states for
their perceived rights of national sovereignty. Encroachment on
these rights is correspondingly likely to provoke resistance, strain
relations, and otherwise bring about the kinds of damage, though in
varying degrees, already discussed as arising from U.N. measures
perceived by target states as exceeding its powers as agreed to.
There are, however, no apparent means of preventing such intervention.

Damage is, of course, exacerbated in such cases when the
U.N. is caused to exceed the limits prescribed by the Charter for
the handling of disputes within U.N. competence. This practice is
facilitated by the second fallacy under consideration, namely the use
of the Charter non-intervention clause—specifically, finding that it
is not applicable to a particular situation—as the sole criterion of
competence. Use of this device enables majorities to cause the U.N.
to avoid the limitations attached to affirmative grants of power.

Such is the nature of the above-quoted argument of the United
States government in the Rhodesian case. Of particular concern to
this discussion was the purpose and effect of the argument in upholding the legal authority of the United Nations to decide substantive
issues in the Rhodesian case and to enforce such decisions. Adverse
consequences held in this study to flow from such assertions of
authority were discussed in Chapter 1.[21]

In addition to the portions of the statement already noted in this chapter, one that deserves attention is a statement to the effect that the United Nations could legally undertake to deal with matters essentially within the domestic jurisdiction of a political entity on the grounds that the entity in question was not a state in international law. [22] This statement most clearly indicates that the United Nations is not an organization of defined powers or an international organization limited to international powers but, on the contrary, has virtually unlimited powers of intervention in domestic affairs, provided only that the non-intervention clause is, for any reason, found not to be applicable to the given situation.

This role for the non-intervention clause may have received an impetus even during its drafting. Indications were given then that it was to be the principal criterion of United Nations competence, and even that it formed the only limitation on the powers of the organization. [23] Later, in a large number of cases, the non-intervention rule was interposed as the principal or only defense against proposed United Nations actions. Even though it was frequently overruled, and the principal criterion was proved to be not this rule but the politically motivated desires of ad hoc majorities in United Nations organs, its prominence in the debates may have served to bring it to the public mind as the principal criterion of United Nations jurisdiction. Part of the problem may have been the refusal of governments to adopt a view of "recommendation" corresponding to the one that led to its general acceptance at San Francisco as a principal component of the peaceful settlement function. As a part of the continuance of the traditional approach of pressure/counter-pressure, majorities caused the organization to go beyond recommendations in many cases, while target states did not object on this ground but rather attempted to ban all discussion by invoking the rule of non-intervention in domestic affairs. In view of the prominence thus given to this rule, the general attitude may well have developed, among authorities as well as among informed elements of the public, that any proposed pronouncement or measure, if not barred by the non-intervention clause, is legally authorized. As a corollary, similar freedom can be said to be enjoyed as to subjects deemed to be matters of international concern. [24]

It would have been preferable, in view of these developments, if the non-intervention clause had been omitted from the Charter. Such omission would have meant no lessening of the rule of non-intervention had the Charter been properly interpreted. Nor can it be asserted that such omission would have brought about any essential lessening of the misuses of the Charter that have actually occurred. However, it has rendered a disservice in encouraging officials and private individuals to ignore affirmative grants of power in that instrument and the limitations surrounding such grants. The clause was a confusing element that has made efforts at improvement more difficult.

The best solution to this problem is to apply the dispute-handling functions and procedures of the Charter according to proper interpretations such as are here believed to be exemplified in the policy guidelines proposed herein. Such applications would not seek to place artificial and unworkable barriers to the jurisdiction of the organization; they would rather seek, through encouragement of full and free debates, to contribute to the only possible basis for the consistent delimitation of the respective areas of international and domestic competence, namely the development of a degree of world community sentiment that would eliminate intractable disputes and situations.

NOTES

1. Goldberg, "International Law in the United Nations," supra.
2. Id. at 142.
3. Art. 15(8).
4. Ch. VIII, Sec. A, para. 7.
5. Charter of the United Nations: Report to the President, supra, at 44.
6. "Supplement to Report of Rapporteur, Committee I/1 to Commission I," Doc. 1070, I/1/34 (1)(d), 6 U.N.C.I.O. Docs. 486 (1945).
7. See L. Preuss, "Article 2, Paragraph 7 of the Charter of the United Nations and Matters of Domestic Jurisdiction," 74 Académie de Droit International, Recueil des Cours 547, 578 (1949-I), citing L. Oppenheim, International Law: A Treatise (London: Longmans, Green, 1948), vol. 1, at 379, n. 1 (7th ed., H. Lauterpacht).
8. "Supplement to Report of Rapporteur," supra, at 486.
9. "Amendments Proposed by the Governments of the United States, the United Kingdom, the Soviet Union, and China," Doc. 2, G/29, 3 U.N.C.I.O. Docs. 622, 623.
10. "Summary Report of the 16th Meeting of Committee I/1," Doc. 976, I/1/40, 6 id. at 494. For the argument of the Australian delegation, which proposed the amendment, see Doc. 969, I/1/39, id. at 436. The peaceful settlement provision under Ch. VII, with which this "exception" clause is concerned, arises from the authorization to the Council, in Art. 39, to "make recommendations" in regard to situations found to constitute threats to peace, breaches of peace, or acts of aggression.

11. Ch. 5, text at notes 4-6, supra.

12. U.N. SCOR, 1st Year, 46th meeting, at 352 (1946).

13. Id., 1st Ser., Special Supp., Rev. Ed., at 1-2 (1946).

14. J. Howell, "Domestic Questions in International Law," 1954 Proceedings, American Society of International Law 90, 94 (1954).

Discussing early U.N. cases in a legal context, Preuss regretted "the tendency to dismiss constitutional limitations as mere technicalities, to disparage the binding force of international law, and to engage in purely emotional appeals." Preuss, "Article 2, Paragraph 7," supra, at 648. A subsequent legal treatment of the precedents, noting the growth of "international concern" as a supposed legal basis for U.N. competence, expresses alarm concerning the extent to which this approach could be expanded. R. Higgins, The Development of International Law through the Political Organs of the United Nations (London: Oxford University Press, 1963), at 80.

15. W. Hall, A Treatise on International Law (Oxford: The Clarendon Press, 1924), at 346-47 (8th ed., A. Higgins); C. Hyde, International Law Chiefly as Interpreted and Applied by the United States (Boston: Little Brown, 1947), vol. 1, at 253 (2d ed.); Fitzmaurice, "The General Principles of International Law Considered from the Standpoint of the Rule of Law," 92 Académie de Droit International, Recueil des Cours 1, 178-79 (1957-II); Wright, "United States Intervention in the Lebanon," 53 American Journal of International Law 112, 121-23 (1959); E. Lauterpacht, "The Contemporary Practice of the United Kingdom in the Field of International Law—Survey and Comment, V," 7 International and Comparative Law Quarterly 92, 104 (1958).

16. Text at n. 2, supra.

17. Ch. 6, text at n. 28 et seq., supra.

18. E.g., S.C. Resolution 67 (1949) in the Indonesian case, G.A. Resolution 1573 (XV) (1960) in the Algerian case, and G. A. Resolution 1819 (XVII) (1962) in the Angolan case.

19. E.g., G.A. Resolutions 820 (IX) (1954), 917 (X) (1955), 1598 (XV) (1960), 1663 (XVI) (1961), 1761 (XVII) (1962), and 2396 (XXIII) (1968), and S.C. Resolution 181 (1963).

20. The subject of international human rights activity is discussed in Ch. 10, infra. The power of the U.N. to condemn is taken up at the beginning of the same chapter.

21. P. 16 et seq., supra.

22. Fourth paragraph quoted in text at n. 2, supra.

23. Text at notes 5-10, supra.

24. Higgins, The Development of International Law, supra, at 77-81; M. McDougal and W. Reisman, "Rhodesia and the United Nations: The Lawfulness of International Concern," 62 American Journal of International Law 1, 15 et seq. (1968).

8

PURPORTED LEGISLATIVE
AND JUDICIAL POWERS OF
POLITICAL ORGANS

This chapter is concerned with pronouncements by the General Assembly and the Security Council on the merits of disputes, purporting to be binding and made without the consent of some of the parties to particular situations. The actions discussed are essentially assertions of legislative and judicial powers on the part of the organs in question. They are not intermixed with assertions of the "enforcement" power, with applications of force, or with the concept of non-intervention, as were some of the asserted powers discussed in previous chapters. They belong wholly within the peaceful settlement function in the sense that that is the only Charter function authorizing pronouncements on the merits of cases as means of seeking solutions of disputes. However, they are here considered not to be proper exercises of that function.

Pronouncements in this category include:

(1) S.C. Resolution 95 (1951), in which the Council called upon Egypt to desist from barring the Suez Canal to Israeli-connected ships and cargoes. This resolution was taken by some governments to constitute a binding order on Egypt. [1]

(2) Council resolutions in the Katanga and Rhodesia cases holding secessionist movements in those countries to be illegal. [2]

(3) A series of resolutions in which the Assembly and the Council have characterized as illegal certain Israeli actions in Jerusalem. [3]

(4) Resolutions holding discriminatory policies of states or other political entities, directed against ethnic components of their populations, to be illegal. Illustrative is G.A. Resolution 1663 (XVI) (1961), which holds that South Africa's policy of apartheid is contrary to that country's obligations under the Charter.

Resolutions of the last type are somewhat different from the others. They have a bearing on long-continued policies, such as

apartheid and denials of self-determination. The facts of such policies are seldom controverted, and there is wide consensus, outside
the particular states against which the resolutions are directed, as
to the need that the policies in question be changed. Such resolutions
have been defended as contributing to a desirable development of law. [4]
There is obvious warrant for such support insofar as the resolutions
tend to develop a worldwide consensus in favor of equal rights and
self-determination of peoples. They also give a certain appearance
of legitimacy as quasi-legislative or quasi-judicial pronouncements,
in that they appear to bear on generally uncontroverted factual situations and to represent widespread consensus as to rules and principles to be applied. However, it is herein considered undesirable
that they be cast in the form of legally binding decisions. In the first
place, such resolutions can serve as precedents encouraging the use
of such pronouncements in other situations in which consensus as to
facts and applicable principles may be lacking. More generally,
their use in intractable situations tends to engender in various manifestations and degrees, depending on circumstances, the undesirable
consequences outlined in Chapter 1 and discussed in various parts of
this study.

The remainder of this chapter will be mainly concerned with
two cases, that of Namibia and that concerning the liability of member states to pay assessments for the expenses of the peace-keeping
operations in the Suez and in the Congo (Zaire).

NAMIBIA

South Africa obtained control of Namibia (then South West
Africa[5]) following World War I by virtue of a League of Nations
Mandate. Following World War II and the end of the League, it has
been maintained and widely considered that the Mandate continued in
force, with the United Nations entitled to supervise South Africa's
discharge of its responsibilities thereunder. This view was upheld
by an advisory opinion of the World Court in 1950. [6]

A part of South Africa's asserted obligations toward Namibia
was exemplified by the principle, stated in the Mandate, that "the
well-being and development of such peoples form a sacred trust of
civilization."[7] A number of governments, comprising large United
Nations majorities, have claimed that South Africa violated this responsibility by applying to Namibia its policy of apartheid, and in
other ways. Ethiopia and Liberia brought a suit in the World Court
against South Africa with a view to obtaining a legally binding judicial
decision to this effect. The suit was dismissed, however, in 1966,
on the grounds that the two countries did not have a sufficient legal
interest in the matter to entitle them to initiate the action. [8]

The Assembly shortly thereafter declared the Mandate terminated on the grounds that South Africa had failed to fulfill its obligations thereunder and had in fact disavowed the Mandate. [9] Namibia was said henceforth to be directly under the responsibility of the United Nations.

South Africa rejected the resolution, basically on the grounds that the Assembly was without power to decide such an issue. [10]

In 1969 and 1970, several Security Council resolutions affirmed the Assembly's decision and demanded South Africa's withdrawal from Namibia. [11] Among other things, the Council declared that South Africa's continued presence in the territory was not only illegal but an "aggressive encroachment on the authority of the United Nations, a violation of the territorial integrity and a denial of the political sovereignty of the people of Namibia."[12] Other states were called upon to refrain from relations with South Africa inconsistent with these resolutions.

In an advisory opinion of June 21, 1971, requested by the Council, the World Court affirmed the validity of the Assembly's decision terminating the Mandate, and the ensuing Council decisions. [13] It then appeared to go further, passing upon the substance of the major issue in dispute by declaring that the continued presence of South Africa in Namibia was illegal and that other states should refrain from dealings implying recognition of the legality of that presence.

A few months later the Security Council accepted the opinion, at the same time reiterating its own assertion that South Africa's continued administration of Namibia was illegal. [14]

The Assembly's termination of the Mandate can be distinguished from cases in which it or the Council purports to decide with binding effect the merits of disputes. This is because the Mandate was in the nature of an agreement and because the United Nations stood in the role of successor in interest to an original party to the agreement, namely the League of Nations. A party is generally considered entitled to terminate an agreement if it considers that other parties are violating it.

An effort was first made to obtain the decision of the World Court on the question of breach, an effort forestalled by the Court's decision that the complaining states were not competent to bring the suit. [15] The Assembly then proceeded to decide, on behalf of the United Nations, that the conditions had been breached and that, accordingly, the Mandate was terminated. The Court, in its subsequent advisory opinion, upheld this action partly on the grounds that without it there could be no remedy for injustices committed under the Mandate. [16]

This Assembly action here being regarded as justifiable, the present thesis is relevant mainly to the ensuing pronouncements by the Council and the World Court declaring the continued administration of Namibia by South Africa to be illegal and demanding its withdrawal. According to our guidelines, these pronouncements should have been limited to recommendations by the Assembly and the Council.

A dilemma is evident here. The Mandate having been the basis for South Africa's control of Namibia, and having been terminated, why should not the United Nations declare it legally mandatory that South Africa withdraw?

The Security Council, it will be recalled, affirmed the Assembly's decision and demanded the withdrawal of South Africa from Namibia. The advisory opinion upheld these pronouncements as legally valid under Articles 24 and 25 of the Charter, thus raising certain questions somewhat apart from the immediate effect of the pronouncements that South Africa was acting in violation of law.

Taking up, first, this holding, in light of the three criteria herein considered indicative of damaging consequences, the first, straining of relations, undoubtedly occurred. Since South Africa held this territory "merely" as a Mandate, this effect on relations might be thought logically to have been less than it would have been if South Africa could have claimed it outright. Such may indeed have been the case. However, there appears to have been a widespread feeling among the dominant element of the South African population, at the time of the Mandate, that no commitments were undertaken thereby that could lead to definitive findings of breach of the Mandate[17] or, a fortiori, to the actual loss of control of the territory.[18] The United States might have experienced similar surprise and resentment if, during the Panama Canal controversy, the U.N. had made similar findings and demands that it withdraw from the territory.

Confusion generated by this case on the conscious level as to the true nature of relevant U.N. powers might have been limited to the dominant element of the South African population. Most of the rest of the world would have seen the U.N. actions as legal. However, as confusion diminished on this account, illusion correspondingly increased. This must have resulted from the array of institutions—Assembly, Council, and Court—employed to enunciate the supposed rule of law. The case might, for this reason, stand together at the time of writing with that of Rhodesia at the pinnacle of the structure of illusion that has been discussed, forming a focus of attention for people concerned with the search for world peace.

During and after 1975 the effect of these measures became intermixed with the effects of the collapse of the Portuguese colonial

empire in southern Africa. The resulting increased vulnerability of
the South African–Namibian relationship to neighboring states hos-.
tile to that relationship no doubt was the primary reason for a move
toward Namibian independence in that year. Whatever the contribution to this move of the U.N. measures under consideration, they
should be regarded essentially as applications of pressure, representing the traditional approach to the conduct of relations.

The World Court's advisory opinion upholding the legality of
the Security Council pronouncements was based largely on Articles
24 and 25 of the Charter.

Article 24 provides that the Security Council has primary responsibility for the maintenance of peace and security. Paragraph
2 of this article states that the powers available to the Council for
the fulfillment of this responsibility are found in Chapters VI, VII,
VIII, and XII of the Charter. The opinion states that this specifica-
tion of powers does not limit the Council, which has "powers com-
mensurate with its responsibility for the maintenance of peace and
security."[19] The only limitations are said to be the fundamental
principles and purposes found in Chapter I of the Charter. In context, this must be read as saying that when it is fulfilling its responsibility for the maintenance of peace and security, the Council
has decision-making powers with regard to substantive issues within
this very broadly stated limitation.

There is a contradiction here, since Chapter VI of the Charter,
mentioned in Paragraph 2 of Article 24, explicitly limits the peaceful settlement role of the Council to the power of recommendation.
Moreover, this limitation appears to reflect the continuing refusal
of individual member states to be bound, without their consent, by
third-party decisions on substantive issues.[20] This intent of the
Charter, being basic, cannot fail to be incorporated as an essential
component of the principles and purposes set forth in Chapter I of
the Charter, by which, according to the Court's opinion, the Council
is bound. It must, for example, be inherent in the notion of sovereignty contained in Article 2(1) in Chapter I, which provides that
"the Organization is based on the principle of the sovereign equality
of all its Members."

In saying that the Council is not limited to the powers specified
in Article 24(2), and that it is limited only by the principles and purposes set forth in Article 1, the Court was quoting a memorandum
of the Secretary-General of January 10, 1947,[21] in support of the
asserted right of the Security Council to assume, on behalf of the
United Nations, temporary responsibility for the administration of
Trieste pending settlement of a dispute concerning that city between
Italy and Yugoslavia. The assertion of Council power in that case
was quite different from that in the Namibia case, since there had

been no indications, in the preparation of the Charter or elsewhere, that members were inclined to deny to the organization the right temporarily to administer territory. Reasons exist on which I have based an argument that this should be regarded as a category of Charter power that has come into existence by a process of tacit Charter development. At the same time I indicated disagreement with the Secretary-General's memorandum on the grounds that member states had never agreed to the broad and open-ended competence it asserted was the Council's.[22] It is impossible to imagine the United States, for example, deliberately committing itself to a binding third-party decision-making authority of this kind.

The Court also relied in part on Article 25 of the Charter, which provides that:

> The Members of the United Nations agree to accept and carry out the decisions of the Security Council in accordance with the present Charter.

The Court read this provision as referring to the broad power of decision-making it was attributing to the Council under Article 24. It dismissed an argument that Article 25 was intended to apply only to decisions under Chapter VII, claiming that there was nothing in the Charter to sustain this argument.[23] However, the Court's interpretation again runs directly counter to the language of Chapter VI, which, as noted, carried out the generally shared purpose of the members to limit the organization's peaceful settlement function to the power of recommendation. Article 25 could only have been intended to apply to Council pronouncements of a kind generally agreed to be binding.[24]

The Court thus appears to have upheld a broad power of decision on the part of the Council[25] going far beyond any powers explicitly agreed to, and equally far beyond what the generality of states would be willing to accept as applied against themselves. This part of the decision thus seems likely to have created confusion and fostered illusion, as well as to hold the potential for future straining of relations should it be applied against other states.

EXPENSES OF UNEF AND ONUC

Disputes arose in 1961 concerning the question of whether member states were legally bound to pay assessments for their shares of expenses of the United Nations Emergency Force (UNEF) and the U.N. force in Zaire (ONUC).[26] The assessments were made by the General Assembly under the authority of Article 17 of the Charter, which provides in part:

1. The General Assembly shall consider and approve the budget of the Organization.

2. The expenses of the Organization shall be borne by the Members as apportioned by the General Assembly.

The language is that of a treaty obligation on the members to pay their assessments. The obligatory nature of the provision is substantiated by Article 19, which decrees loss of voting rights in the Assembly as a penalty if states fall into arrears, to a defined extent, in their financial contributions.

Several states refused to pay the assessments for UNEF and ONUC on the grounds, generally speaking, that since these were special types of operations dealing with peace and security, their expenses could be assessed only by the Security Council. The Assembly thereupon requested an advisory opinion of the World Court on whether these costs, as assessed by the Assembly, were expenses of the organization within the meaning of Article 17. The Court's affirmative ruling[27]—advisory in character and so not binding—was adopted by the Assembly as the applicable rule.[28]

The appearance thus given of a binding decision by the Assembly was enhanced by the United States and like-minded member states when they sought to apply the penalty decreed by Article 19 by depriving of their vote, in the nineteenth session of the General Assembly in 1964, states that had fallen into arrears by virtue of their refusal to pay assessments for these armed forces.[29] Authorities pressing for the penalty, moreover, argued that it was automatic. The arrears having been found to exist, they said, the Assembly had no alternative but to apply the rule in question.

The totality of these efforts represented a very strong attempt to convey the impression that the recalcitrant states were legally bound to pay the assessments in question and that they were in defiance of such legal obligations. It is submitted that governments forming the majority in these developments made a contribution to the structure of illusion that is a major concern of this discussion and demolition of which is considered essential if international dispute-handling activities are to contribute to permanent world security.

How can this be so when everything that was done was in conformity with explicit Charter provisions? The answer is that the competent authorities, when they framed the Charter, did not anticipate the possibility that budgetary items could give rise to intractable disputes. Had they foreseen this possibility, they would presumably have phrased the relevant Charter provisions more in accordance with those relating to the peaceful settlement function per se. Also unanticipated was the possibility that a budgetary issue could involve a question of Charter interpretation. The Soviet Union here contended that only the Security Council had the right either to take action for the maintenance of peace and security or to assess the costs of such activity; it insisted, moreover, that this was an important question of principle.[30]

The framers of the Charter had taken note of the problem of Charter interpretation per se. A report of the Committee on Legal Problems of the San Francisco Conference, approved by the Conference, recognized that organs of the U.N. were empowered to undertake necessary interpretations of the Charter in the conduct of their business but that:

> It is to be understood, of course, that if an interpretation made by any organ of the Organization or by a committee of jurists is not generally acceptable it will be without binding force. In such circumstances . . . it may be necessary to embody the interpretation in an amendment of the Charter. . . .[31]

The foregoing understanding was a necessary component of the general insistence of states on retaining the right to be their own judges of matters of concern to themselves. This all-embracing rule, part and parcel of the "system" characterized by the occasional emergence of intractable disputes, necessarily and by definition takes precedence over supposed rules of international law whenever the subject-matter of such a rule becomes involved in an intractable dispute.

The case illustrates well two aspects of international law as a component of the structure of illusion. They are interrelated and derive from the appearance that Articles 17 and 19, embodying routinely "necessary" rules to enable the United Nations to finance its activities, and being imbedded in the world's most important treaty, are incontestably rules of law. So, indeed, they may be said to be, pursuant to the usual concept of international law. The illusory nature of the concept appears only from a perspective that takes into account the goal of permanent world security and, in particular, the prerequisite to that goal of an adequate substructure of world community sentiment.

One component of this structure of illusion is exemplified by the probability that the continuing refusal of states at the time of writing, a decade later, to pay the controversial assessment is regarded by many people and governments as constituting a continuing breach of law. Naturally, this is the view of those who favor the payment and oppose the policies of the "delinquent" parties. Under the customary concept of international law, this view is correct. The illusion lies in the tendency to believe that international law shares the essential nature of the predominant concept of law, derived from domestic systems, whereas in fact it lacks the vital attribute of underlying consensus to the extent necessary to ensure general effectiveness.

The second illusory element, well illustrated by this case, is the apparent belief that the application of pressures unacceptable to recipient states can, at the least, do no harm and might prove successful. Immediate damage was caused during the 19th session of the General Assembly as a result of the attempt to enforce Article 19 of the Charter. To prevent a confrontation on this issue, the Assembly attempted to avoid votes on controversial questions and was thus compelled to confine its agenda to matters that could be decided without objection. The session was thus, to a large extent, paralyzed.

The case also produced longer range adverse consequences of the kind discussed in Chapter 1.

The first of these, the straining of relations due to the application of pressures deemed unwarranted, was particularly damaging in this case. There appears, in retrospect, to have been little reason why officials should have anticipated that target governments would be amenable to the type of pressure brought to bear under Article 19. They may have thought that the application of this provision would have held the target states up to world disapprobation for failure to carry out their "legal" obligations and for pursuing policies calculated to damage the United Nations. To what extent such sentiments were engendered throughout the world can only be speculated; however, the target states do not seem to have been perturbed. It seems probable that to most people the dispute was assimilated and absorbed in the major east-west struggle. At the same time, however, the effort of the majority publicly to stigmatize certain other states seems likely to have strained relations; any such effect must have been intensified by the resulting paralysis of the 19th session of the Assembly. The fact that the assessments remain unpaid a decade later is doubtless accounted for in part by the resentments created through the policy followed.

The second disadvantage, the engendering of confusion as to the true powers of the organization, was, as in the case of Namibia, obscure. Peoples and governments supporting the enforcement of Articles 17 and 19 doubtless perceived the case as involving uncomplicated violations of the law. The nature of the confusion may be suggested by asking how the United States would respond if it were in the minority and saw the prospect of United Nations military forces acting in ways that it might deem detrimental to its interests. Would its citizens consider their country to be a law-breaker if it refused to pay for such operations?

Exceptionally damaging must have been the third consequence, the fostering of the illusion that existing dispute-handling institutions represent the best progress that has been possible, given the circumstances, toward world peace and security. The obtaining of the World Court's advisory opinion, the endorsement of that Opinion by the Assembly, and the argument that the application of Article 19 should be automatic must have tended to create the impression that here, if anywhere, true international law exists. Of course it is equally obvious that the supposed law could not be effectively applied, and the case must thus have contributed to the undesirable psychological syndrome of illusion/disillusion characteristic of attitudes toward international dispute-handling. The disillusion in this case has not been sufficient to overcome the illusion if, as is believed to be the case, peoples and governments, apart from those of the countries refusing to pay the assessments in question, generally consider that this failure has been due to wrongdoing and not to any defect in the system itself.

The application of this study's proposed guidelines in this case would have meant that the Assembly would have done no more than recommend that all the member states pay their assessments for the peace-keeping operations. If this course had been followed, damage caused by the dispute would have been greatly lessened.

Does it follow then that the United Nations should never purport to make binding decisions even in routine fiscal and administrative matters? The answer is, in principle, affirmative, for the reason that in the very rare case in which a government would refuse to comply with a demand, the assertion that it was in violation of law would be useless and counter-productive. I refrain from suggesting a guideline of policy to this effect, in the interests of practicality. A step closer to a practical course, but still not in that category, would be a proposal that the word "law" be dispensed with. The general desirability of this course is considered in Chapters 3 and 11.

It would, however, be practical for authorities to maintain a flexible posture so that if a supposedly routine administrative or budgetary issue should unexpectedly escalate into a dispute, they would be in a position to relax pressures and thus facilitate a negotiated settlement and also hold to a minimum the damage that would accrue if the dispute continued unsettled.

NOTES

1. Ch. 4, n. 10, supra.

2. With regard to Katanga see Ch. 6, n. 30 and accompanying text, supra; with regard to Rhodesia see Ch. 3, notes 29 and 30 and accompanying text, supra.

3. S.C. Resolution 252 (1968), S.C. Resolution 267 (1969), S.C. Resolution 298 (1971), and G.A. Resolutions 2253 and 2254 (ES-V) (1967).

4. Higgins, The Development of International Law, supra, at 118-23.

5. On June 12, 1968, the General Assembly resolved that "in accordance with the desires of its people, South West Africa shall henceforth be known as 'Namibia'." G.A. Resolution 2372 (XXII).

6. Advisory Opinion on International Status of South West Africa, [1950] I.C.J. 128.

7. League of Nations Covenant, Art. 22.

8. South West Africa Cases, Second Phase, [1966] I.C.J. 1.

9. G.A. Resolution 2145 (XXI) (1966).

10. See, e.g., Statement of Government of South Africa, U.N. Doc. A/7045/Add. 9, Feb. 19, 1968. Quoted in M. Whiteman, 13 Digest of International Law (Washington, D.C.: Department of State, 1968), at 761-62.

11. S.C. Resolutions 264 (1969), 269 (1969), and 276 (1970).

12. S.C. Resolution 269 (1969).

13. Advisory Opinion on Legal Consequences for States of the Continued Presence of South Africa in Namibia (South West Africa) notwithstanding Security Council Resolution 276 (1970), [1971] I.C.J. 16.

14. S.C. Resolution 301 (1971).

15. N. 8 and accompanying text, supra.

16. Advisory Opinion on Legal Consequences, [1971] I.C.J., supra, at 46-50.

17. Factors entering into this opinion are:
(1) The view of some responsible officials was that Class "C" mandates (which included those pertaining to South West Africa) were not far from annexation. See, e.g., Q. Wright, Mandates under the League of Nations (Chicago: University of Chicago Press, 1930), at 62-63; S. Slonim, South West Africa and the United Nations: An International Mandate in Dispute (Baltimore: Johns Hopkins University Press, 1973), at 36-38. These treatises cite some of the relevant statements made at the time, some of which are also collected in the Preliminary Objections of South Africa in South West Africa Cases . . . Pleadings, vol. 1, at 221-23 (1966). This view seems to be reflected in the statement, in the League of Nations

Covenant (Art. 22), that South West Africa and territories with certain similar characteristics (later to be designated Class "C" Mandates) "can be best administered under the laws of the Mandatory as integral portions of its territory, subject to the safeguards above mentioned in the interests of the indigenous population."

(2) While South Africa agreed, in the Mandate, that any dispute arising between itself and another League member relating to the interpretation and application of the Mandate should, if not otherwise settled, be referred to adjudication by the World Court, judicial history reveals a very close question whether this was meant to apply to any disputes other than those involving specific interests of particular League members. The Court held in its preliminary judgment of 1962 that Ethiopia and Liberia were competent to complain concerning the treatment by South Africa of the indigenous inhabitants of the Mandated territory; this decision was, however, in effect overruled by the definitive decision of 1966. South West Africa Cases, Preliminary Objections [1962] I.C.J. 319; South West Africa Cases, Second Phase [1966] I.C.J. 6. It seems most probable that the generally prevailing opinion on the part of the South African government and people, at the time the Mandate was established, tended to assimilate the commitments of the Mandate with the generality of important international commitments undertaken by states without any binding provisions for determining alleged breaches.

18. See, on this point, the dissenting opinions of Judges Fitzmaurice and Gros in Advisory Opinion on Legal Consequences, [1971] I.C.J., supra, at 264-79 and 334-38, respectively; Acheson and C. Marshall, "Applying Dr. Johnson's Advice," 11 Columbia Journal of Transnational Law 193 (1972).

19. Advisory Opinion on Legal Consequences, [1971] I.C.J., supra, at 52. The passage quoted in the text was taken by the Court from a Secretariat memorandum of Jan. 10, 1947 (U.N. SCOR, 2d Year, 91st meeting, at 44-45), referred to in the text on p. 186.

20. Ch. 1, text following n. 3, supra.

21. Cited in n. 19, supra.

22. Halderman, The United Nations and the Rule of Law, supra, at 27-37.

23. Advisory Opinion on Legal Consequences, [1971] I.C.J., supra, at 52-53. See, in accord, Higgins, "The Advisory Opinion on Namibia: Which U.N. Resolutions Are Binding under Article 25 of the Charter?" 21 International and Comparative Law Quarterly 270 (1972).

24. The legislative history of Art. 25 clearly indicates that, as stated in Charter of the United Nations: Report to the President . . ., supra, at 78-79, the phrase "in accordance with the present Charter" at the end of Art. 25 is intended to mean that "the

precise extent of the obligation of members under Article 25 can be determined only by reference to other provisions of the Charter, particularly Chapters VI, VII, and XII (Article 24, paragraph 2)." See Doc. WD 44, CO/18, 18 U.N.C.I.O. Docs. 47, 62-63; Doc. WD 158, CO/79, 17 id. at 43, 46-47; Doc. 1068, CO/139(2), 15 id. at 69, 71; Doc. WD 422, CO/186, 17 id. at 169, 171-72. See, in general accord, Russell, History of the United Nations Charter, supra, at 665; L. Goodrich, E. Hambro, and A. Simons, Charter of the United Nations; Commentary and Documents (New York: Columbia University Press, 1969), at 208 (3d ed. rev.); D. Bowett, The Law of International Institutions (New York: Praeger, 1963), at 32; "Introduction to the Annual Report of the Secretary General on the Work of the Organization, 16 June 1960-15 June 1961," U.N. GAOR, 16th Sess., Supp. 1A, at 4. Dugard, writing on the advisory opinion in the Namibia case, is in accord in believing that, in the absence of finding of a threat to peace, the Council resolutions are properly recommendatory in character. J. Dugard, "Namibia (South West Africa): The Court's Opinion, South Africa's Response, and Prospects for the Future," 11 Columbia Journal of Transnational Law 14, 29-32 (1972).

25. A more authoritative view is to be found in the separate opinion of Judge Dillard:

> "By invoking Articles 24 and 25 of the Charter . . . [the advisory opinion] does not purport to carry the implication that, in its view, the United Nations is endowed with broad powers of a legislative or quasi-legislative character. The Opinion is addressed to a very specific and unique situation concerning a territory with an international status, the administration of which engaged the supervisory authority of the United Nations," Advisory Opinion on Legal Consequences, [1971] I.C.J., supra, at 150. (Italics in original.)

26. The nature and purposes of these operations are outlined in Ch. 6, supra.

27. Advisory Opinion on Certain Expenses of the United Nations (Article 17, paragraph 2, of the Charter), [1962] I.C.J. 151.

28. G.A. Resolution 1854A (XVII) (1962).

29. For a summary of the dispute see Yearbook of the United Nations 1964, at 3 et seq.

30. U.N. GAOR, 16th Sess., Plenary, at 1155 (1961); id., 19th Sess., Plenary, 1330th meeting, at 25 (1965).

31. "Report of the Rapporteur of Committee IV/2 as Approved by the Committee," Doc. 933, IV/2/42(2), 13 U.N.C.I.O. Docs. 703, 710.

9

LAW AND THE JUDICIARY

The view was indicated in Chapter 4 that in international relations "law" does not exist in the sense ordinarily attached to the word, which derives from domestic law. For this reason it was suggested that the word itself should be de-emphasized in international dispute-handling activities, with the purpose of minimizing the illusions fostered by the pretense that law (in the ordinary meaning of the word) exists as a reality, and as something to be built upon, in international relations. On the other hand, however, law-related concepts such as agreements and customs, and institutions such as courts and tribunals, should be employed as appropriate. The World Court or another third-party tribunal may be the best or only means of solving some disputes.

In regard to such procedures, provided for in the Charter, the following policy guidelines are proposed:

> Judicial organs should be asked to decide disputes only when the parties appear ready to comply with the resulting decisions.
>
> Advisory opinions should not be requested of the World Court when the resulting opinions would give the impression of passing on pending disputes between states or other political entities, unless the parties appear ready to comply with the resulting opinions.

JUDICIAL DECISIONS IN CONTENTIOUS CASES

The first of these guidelines would require that litigation not be instituted in contested cases where there is reason to doubt that the losing party or parties will be willing to carry out the decision. The purpose here is generally the same as that which lies behind

125

the first guideline proposed in Chapter 1, which would limit political organs to the power of recommendation in the exercise of their peaceful settlement function. The guideline proposed in this chapter would have the further effect of limiting all exercises of this function, in intractable cases, to recommendations by political organs. Decisions of the World Court and other tribunals in contentious cases are, under the Charter, legally binding on the parties. Other international tribunals may be similarly empowered. Such decisions in intractable cases can only lead to defiance by the losing parties. The present proposal is to avoid this result by ruling out the reference to adjudication of such cases.

There have been only a few cases, to the time of writing, in which parties have defied decisions of the World Court generally supposed to be legally binding. The paucity of cases is due to the fact that the Court, unlike the Assembly and the Council, does not have jurisdiction in a dispute unless all the parties consent. Some states have modified this general rule by agreeing to accept jurisdiction in advance as automatic in defined categories of disputes. These categories must necessarily be seen, by the governments entering into the commitments, as involving issues as to which their countries and the Court will prove to be in sufficient accord to ensure that resulting decisions can be carried out without undue sacrifice. Governments do not deliberately enter into commitments that might place them in the position of being obligated to carry out decisions involving unacceptable sacrifices. Sometimes, even if rarely, a dispute originally seen as being in the first category proves to be in the second.

The Corfu Channel case illustrates this possibility, as well as the difficulty or impossibility of applying the proposed guidelines in such cases. The case did not appear to be in the intractable category when the Court decided it, since both parties, Albania and Great Britain, had agreed to its jurisdiction. The decision on the merits went against Albania, whereupon that country's representatives proceeded to contest the right of the Court to award damages on the grounds that its acceptance of jurisdiction had not gone this far. Such an award was nevertheless made, and it is this part of the decision that remains unfulfilled. [1]

A second case can be used for illustrative purposes, although the decision in question was a preliminary one and did not prove to be final. This was the South West Africa case brought by Ethiopia and Liberia, seeking a definitive decision that South Africa had violated its agreement under its Mandate of South West Africa. There was reason from the outset to doubt that an adverse Court decision would cause South Africa to change its policy in relevant matters. The principal purpose of the suit seems to have been to

use the judiciary as a means of pressure in a dispute long since
proved to be of the intractable variety.

In a preliminary decision of 1962,[2] the Court found that it had
jurisdiction under a clause in the Mandate itself (dated approximately
forty years earlier) providing that:

> The Mandatory agrees that if any dispute whatever
> should arise between the Mandatory and another Member
> of the League of Nations relating to the interpretation
> or the application of the provisions of the mandate, such
> dispute, if it cannot be settled by negotiation, shall be
> submitted to the Permanent Court of International
> Justice. . . .[3]

The preliminary decision had the effect of confirming the continuing force of the Mandate. Under it, South Africa was bound by
certain obligations. For this discussion's purposes, we may point
to the obligation to make reports, which could be plainly seen by
the world to have been violated by South Africa. The duty to report
to the United Nations, as the successor of the League, had been
confirmed by earlier advisory opinions of the Court. The effect of
the preliminary decision of 1962 was to place South Africa, in the
eyes of world opinion, in the position of violating a decision of the
Court handed down in a contentious case, and thus binding. This
general impression continued in force at least until 1966, when the
Court dismissed the case on the grounds that the complaining states
did not have the requisite legal standing to initiate it.[4]

The disadvantageous consequences that have been mentioned
as resulting from purportedly binding decisions of political organs
also applied here to some extent, although with somewhat different
force and effect.

The straining of relations resulting from this case has been
mentioned in Chapter 8. Particular damage may have resulted from
the judicial decision because of the prestige of law and the judiciary,
carried over from domestic societies, and the resulting embarrass-
ment to the defiant state by appearing to be in violation of law. The
proposed guidelines would seek to reduce or eliminate such damage
by forestalling judicial decisions in intractable disputes.

The second effect, confusion as to the role and powers of the
decision-making organization, could scarcely have existed in overt
form, since there was doubtless widespread agreement that South
Africa was in violation of the law in refusing to report on its administration of Namibia.

The third disadvantageous consequence, the fostering of illusion, here took the form of an illusion/disillusion syndrome in

which people are caused to think that all possible efforts have been made to establish effective law in international relations but that such efforts cannot be successful. This line of thought, in which the illusory aspect must reach a high point when judicial pronouncements are involved, tends to distract efforts from channels that might prove more fruitful.

A case in which the agreements to submit to adjudication and to carry out the decision both proved illusory was the Right of Passage dispute between India and Portugal, decided by the World Court in 1960.[5] The case involved small enclaves of Portuguese territory surrounded by Indian territory. These territories being, in the Indian view, remnants of colonialism rightfully belonging to independent India, their status became controversial. The particular aspect of the dispute of interest here arose when India restricted the use of its territory as a means of communication among the enclaves. Portugal brought the dispute before the World Court as a means of having its right of passage for this purpose confirmed by binding judicial decision. With India contesting its jurisdiction, the Court found that it was competent by virtue of acceptances by the two parties, under the optional procedure provided by the Court's Statute, and proceeded to hand down a decision upholding Portugal's sovereignty over the territories in question.[6] The following year India seized the territories by force, defying the Court's decision.

Some members of the Security Council thought that the Indian action was contrary to the Charter, particularly to Article 2(4), forbidding the use of force as an instrument of policy. A proposed resolution[7] based on this rule, calling for Indian withdrawal, was defeated by a veto,[8] and nothing further was done.

As the denouement proved, the dispute between India and Portugal was at an altogether different level from the case that was brought before the Court. In the real dispute the parties were too far apart to permit peaceful solution by available resources.[9] The decision of the Court was irrelevant to this dispute. It was damaging because it tended to foster the illusion that international law and the World Court provide a fruitful channel in the search for world peace.

The 1980 Case Concerning United States Diplomatic and Consular Staff in Tehran (United States of America v. Iran)[10] was similar to the Judgement of December 15, 1949 in Corfu Channel in that the defendant, after the institution of the proceedings, disavowed an apparent acceptance of the Court's jurisdiction. In the former case, the World Court upheld its jurisdiction in part upon the adherence, by both parties, to the Vienna Conventions on diplomatic and consular relations, and annexed protocols conferring automatic jurisdiction on the Court in the event of disputes.[11]

The cause of the proceeding was the seizure of U.S. diplomatic and consular personnel and property in Iran following that country's revolution of 1979. The U.S. contended, and the Court held, that Iran had violated treaties and general international law in failing to prevent these seizures and their continuance, still in progress, when the case was decided.

Iran did not come into court, but sent letters denying the Court's jurisdiction on grounds that this case was but incidental to a more profound dispute between the two countries.[12] Account would have to be taken of the "deep-rootedness and the essential character of the Islamic Revolution of Iran, a revolution of a whole oppressed nation against its oppressors and their masters." The letters alleged such things as "shameless exploitation of our country, and numerous crimes perpetrated against the Iranian people, contrary to and in conflict with all international and humanitarian norms."

> The problem involved in the conflict between Iran and the United States is thus not one of the interpretation and the application of the treaties upon which the American Application is based, but results from an overall situation containing much more fundamental and more complex elements. Consequently, the Court cannot examine the American Application divorced from its proper context, namely the whole political dossier of the relations between Iran and the United States over the last 25 years. . . .

The letter went on to mention some of the incidents of this history.

The Court proceeded to decide the case, and the judgment was ignored by Iran. It seems to have had little to do with the ultimate release of the hostages eight months later.

The purpose in thus describing the Iranian position is not to suggest that it was either correct or incorrect as an exposition of the Court's proper jurisdiction. It is commonplace in legal order systems for courts to adjudicate portions of disputes. The point to be made is that these systems are essentially different from the situation prevailing in the international realm, which is, in fact, not a system in any comparable sense. The case has a resemblance to Right of Passage, in the existence of an underlying and more basic dispute at a different level from that before the Court. Iran, in effect, took itself out of the limited consensus which had permitted it and other countries to subscribe to rules of diplomatic protection, with automatic third-party adjudication of disputes which might arise.

Informed elements of the world public, being given no alternative, probably accepted the contention of the Court, the United States, and others, that the seizure of the hostages was a violation of valid law. Moreover, it must have become widely understood that the basic rule in issue—the inviolability of embassies—was one of the oldest and best established norms of "international law." The result must be a rather extreme case of the illusion/disillusionment syndrome.

This case, like the others discussed in this section, upholds the first guideline proposed at the outset of this chapter. In particular it reinforces the proposition therein implied that it is undesirable for states to agree in advance to the Court's automatic jurisdiction as to disputes to arise in the future, even when the subject matter seems to be one of total agreement. The important consideration, from the present perspective, is that the parties, at the time of the decision, be willing to carry it out; this can better be estimated at the time the dispute is submitted.

ADVISORY OPINIONS

Our second proposed guideline concerning the judicial mode of peaceful settlement would forbid requests for advisory opinions when the result could reasonably be expected to give the appearance to the world that one or more concerned parties were in defiance of a judicial verdict.

The League of Nations Covenant authorized the Permanent Court of International Justice (P.C.I.J.) to give an advisory opinion on "any dispute or question referred to it by the Council or by the Assembly"[13] and it was recognized from the outset that this jurisdiction could involve issues of pending disputes between states. The Advisory Committee of Jurists of 1920, which prepared the initial draft of the Statute of the Court, proposed that separate treatment should be accorded requests for advisory opinions as between those which did and those which did not involve such issues. The former were to be handled "under the same conditions as if the case had been actually submitted to it for decision."[14] When the proposal came before the Assembly, a suggestion for the deletion of the last-mentioned provision led to the elimination of the whole proposed provision on advisory jurisdiction.[15] The giving of advisory opinions was, of course, authorized by the Covenant of the League of Nations, so that the absence of any provision on the subject in the Statute left the handling of such questions to the discretion of the Court.

As was noted by the Committee of Jurists, when a current subject of dispute is involved in an advisory opinion, certain problems arise.

While such opinions are, by definition, not legally binding, there is reason behind the tendency of people to accept them in some cases as definitive. The point was put as follows by a Judge of the World Court:

> [A]n advisory opinion which is concerned with a dispute between States from a legal point of view amounts to a definitive decision upon the existence or nonexistence of the legal relations, which is the subject of the dispute. . . .[16]

Of similar import was the view expressed by a committee of the Court in 1927 that:

> In reality, where there are in fact contending parties, the difference between contentious cases and advisory cases is only nominal. . . . So the view that advisory opinions are not binding is more theoretical than real.[17]

This problem was not dealt with in either the Statute or the rules of the Court until 1927, when a rule was adopted providing that if an existing dispute between states should become involved in advisory proceedings, a party should be entitled to appoint an ad hoc judge if a judge of its nationality were not already on the Court.[18]

Meanwhile, an aspect of the problem arose in the Eastern Carelia case, in which the Council requested the Court's advisory opinion concerning the interpretation of a treaty between Finland and the U.S.S.R. with respect to the degree of autonomy to be accorded Eastern Carelia by the latter country. The Court declined to entertain jurisdiction of the case, giving as its principal reason that this was an actual dispute between states and that the Soviet Union, one of the parties, had not subscribed to the Covenant of the League and thus had not accepted the jurisdiction of the Court. The Court said the basic principle of the independence of states was involved, as well as the corresponding rule of international law that "no State can, without its consent, be compelled to submit its disputes with other States either to mediation or to arbitration or to any other kind of pacific settlement. . . ."[19] Later in the opinion the Court said:

The Court is aware of the fact that it is not requested to decide a dispute, but to give an advisory
opinion. This circumstance, however, does not essentially modify the above considerations. The
question put to the Court is not one of abstract law,
but concerns directly the main point of the controversy between Finland and Russia. . . . Answering
the question would be substantially equivalent to
deciding the dispute between the parties. The Court,
being a Court of Justice, cannot, even in giving advisory opinions, depart from the essential rules
guiding their activity as a Court.[20]

It thus seems to be implied that if the question posed to the
Court had not involved directly the main point of the controversy,
the advisory aspect would have dominated and the requested opinion
would have been given. The opinion thus seems to leave considerable scope for interpretation as to whether a given question involves
directly the main point of a dispute. As will be indicated below in
regard to the Peace Treaties case, an opinion delivered on this
basis may strain relations and give rise to other consequences
herein deemed disadvantageous to long-term goals of world community, peace, and security.

The United States showed that it perceived the potential contradiction when, in 1926, in connection with a proposal that it
should become a member of the P.C.I.J., the Senate interposed a
reservation that:

[T]he Court shall not . . . , without the consent of the
United States, entertain any request for an advisory
opinion touching any dispute or question in which the
United States has or claims an interest.[21]

The League evidently considered that, as far as disputes to which
the U.S. was a party were concerned, this requirement was satis-
fied by the Court's opinion in Eastern Carelia.[22]

This U.S. reservation no doubt also provided part of the
motivation for a new provision, Article 68, in the Statute of the
Court, which evidently had the purpose of confirming the rule of
Eastern Carelia[23] in a flexible format:

In the exercise of its advisory functions, the
Court shall further be guided by the provisions of the
Statute which apply in contentious cases to the extent
to which it recognizes them to be applicable.

This provision was continued in force as Article 68 of the Statute of the International Court of Justice. This Court further indicated its purpose by the language of the corresponding provision of the Rules of the Court (now Rule 102) that "for this purpose it [i.e., the Court] shall above all consider whether the request for the advisory opinion relates to a legal question actually pending between two or more States."

These and other pronouncements of the time indicate, although the rule was not stated rigidly, that the competent authorities did not intend that the advisory procedure could become an indirect means of obtaining judicial decisions of disputed issues without the consent of the parties. [24]

The policy guideline presently under discussion is close to the rule for which Eastern Carelia seems to have been widely accepted, namely that the sovereignty of states forbids the giving of such opinions on issues of pending disputes without the consent of states concerned. Its motivation is somewhat different, however. The present discussion is interested not in the ill-defined, abstract concept of "national sovereignty" but rather in the impact on world opinion and the consequent effects on prospects for world security that probably result when a state appears to be defying the law. The trend during the period of the United Nations and the I.C.J. has, however, been in the opposite direction.

It should first be observed that the actual powers and procedures for advisory opinions, as agreed to in the basic documents, continue virtually unchanged. The basic power of the Court to hand down such opinions remains discretionary. Article 68 of the Statute, important from the perspective of this discussion, was retained, and, as noted above, the corresponding article of the Rules of the Court (now Rule 102) was amended to emphasize the distinction between questions that did and those that did not involve legal questions actually pending between states.

At a higher constitutional level, however, a change did take place, in that the Statute of the Court was incorporated as an integral part of the Charter and the Court designated as the principal judicial organ of the United Nations.

This development became a factor of importance in the advisory opinions concerning the Peace Treaties in 1950. These involved a dispute concerning compliance by Bulgaria, Hungary, and Romania with human rights clauses of the peace treaties they entered into following World War II, which gave rise to two advisory opinions in 1950. These states were non-members of the United Nations and were thus in the position of the U.S.S.R. at the time of Eastern Carelia. The basic dispute concerned allegations, brought before the General Assembly, that they had violated human rights clauses of the peace treaties. The question asked of the Court, which resulted in the first opinion, concerned alleged obligations of the three countries, under the treaties, to participate in the formation of commissions to determine questions of breach. The opinion[25] found them to be so obligated. They continued, however, their previous refusal to cooperate, thus causing the Assembly to ask the Court for its opinion as to whether certain steps could be taken in order to set up the commissions without the cooperation of the countries concerned. This question gave rise to the second advisory opinion in the case,[26] in which the answer was negative and, in effect, indicated that nothing further could be done to determine the charges of alleged breaches of the treaties.

The first opinion contained the following passage:

> The consent of States, parties to a dispute, is the basis of the Court's jurisdiction in contentious cases. The situation is different in regard to advisory proceedings even where the Request for an Opinion relates to a legal question actually pending between States. The Court's reply is only of an advisory character: as such it has no binding force. It follows that no State, whether a Member of the United Nations or not, can prevent the giving of an Advisory Opinion which the United Nations considers to be desirable in order to obtain enlightenment as to the course of action it should take. The Court's opinion is given not to the States but to the organ which is entitled to request it; the reply of the Court, itself an "organ of the United Nations," represents its participation in the activities of the Organization, and, in principle, should not be refused.[27]

While the main thrust of this opinion was opposite to that of Eastern Carelia, here too the Court proceeded to modify its position so that, in overall effect, the two cases are similar in leaving considerable discretion to the Court in particular cases. Thus, in Peace Treaties:

> There are certain limits, however, to the Court's duty to reply to a Request for an Opinion. It is not merely an "organ of the United Nations," it is essentially the "principal judicial organ" of the Organization. . . . It is on account of this character of the Court that its power to answer the present Request for an Opinion has been challenged.

Article 65 of the Statute is permissive. It gives
the Court the power to examine whether the circumstances of the case are of such a character as should
lead it to decline to answer the Request. In the opinion of the Court, the circumstances of the present
case are profoundly different from those . . . in the
Eastern Carelia case . . . , when that Court declined
to give an Opinion because it found that the question put
to it was directly related to the main point of a dispute
actually pending between two States, so that answering
the question would be substantially equivalent to deciding the dispute between the parties. . . .

[T]he present Request for an Opinion is solely
concerned with the applicability to certain disputes
of the procedure for settlement instituted by the
Peace Treaties, and it is justifiable to conclude that
it in no way touches the merits of those disputes. . . .
It follows that the legal position of the parties to these
disputes cannot be in any way compromised by the
answer that the Court may give to the Questions put
to it. [28]

Some judges dissented from the decision to give the requested
opinion, holding that the principle of state sovereignty forbade judicial pronouncements on issues of pending disputes without the
consent of parties concerned. [29]

Some adverse consequences of the kind previously discussed
herein as likely to arise from binding, or apparently binding,
third-party decisions of intractable disputes, may be assumed to
have arisen in this case.

That relations were strained seems probable. The opinion
was requested as part of a campaign to condemn the three countries
for violation of the pertinent clauses of the peace treaties. This
purpose may, in turn, have been in part perceived as contributing
to pressures and counter-pressures in the intensifying east-west
political struggle. The first advisory opinion was caused to contribute to that end, notwithstanding the Court's view that it concerned a subsidiary and essentially procedural issue. [30] The effect
was accentuated by the implication, evident throughout the second
opinion, that Bulgaria, Hungary, and Romania had violated the
treaties because they had not carried out their legal obligations,
as determined in the first opinion, to appoint their members to the
Treaty Commissions. In its next session the Assembly adopted a
resolution in which it:

2. <u>Condemns</u> the wilful refusal of the Governments of Bulgaria, Hungary and Romania to fulfill their
obligation under . . . the Treaties of Peace . . . which
obligation has been confirmed by the International Court
of Justice;

3. <u>Is of the opinion</u> that the conduct of the Governments of Bulgaria, Hungary and Romania in this matter
is such as to indicate that they are aware of breaches
being committed of those articles of the Treaties of
Peace under which they are obligated to secure the en-
joyment of human rights and fundamental freedoms in
their countries; and that they are callously indifferent
to the sentiments of the world community;

4. <u>Notes</u> with anxiety the continuance of serious
accusations . . . and that the three governments have
made no satisfactory refutation of these accusations.[31]

The second adverse consequence, namely the creation of confusion concerning the powers being exercised, may not have occurred
in this case, at least in the conscious minds of observers. Most
people in the non-communist world may have thought that Bulgaria,
Hungary, and Romania, as defeated states, were rightly subject to
binding treaty commitments on such a universally approved subject
as human rights.

The third consequence, the fostering of illusion, must have
been present and closely combined with disillusionment. There
was here an apparent structure of law and legal institutions of im-
posing dimensions, resting upon a foundation that combined force
with righteousness. Nevertheless, it proved impossible to make
the supposed law effective. Most observers in the non-communist
world were probably not inclined to attribute this failure to any
deficiency in the legal institutions being utilized but rather were
disposed to blame the supposed wrongdoing of the respondent states
and, particularly, of the Soviet Union, which was supporting their
position.

Turning to the question of practicality of applying in such a
case the guidelines herein proposed, it may be observed that had
this been done, the Assembly's initiative would not have gone beyond recommendations that Bulgaria, Hungary, and Romania act in
the manner desired. There would have been no request for an advisory opinion.[32] The practical consequences of this line of conduct, in terms of the goal of improving the observance of the relevant clauses of the treaties, would apparently have been improved.

If the course that was followed had a tendency to strain relations between the parties and to intensify the east-west struggle, these consequences, in their turn, could logically be expected to intensify the repression of human rights in the countries concerned.[33] The course herein recommended would, if followed, have generally reduced these effects of the case.

The dispute that emerged in 1961 concerning the assessment of costs for certain "peace-keeping operations" was considered in its broader context in Chapter 8. The advisory opinion in this case[34] may seem to exemplify the justifiable request for advice needed by a United Nations organ for the conduct of its business. The question was whether the Assembly could make legally binding budgetary assessments against member states for the expenses of operations such as UNEF and ONUC.

There was involved, however, an issue of Charter interpretation that some states considered important to their interests.[35] One delegation, that of the U.S.S.R., indicated that its country would not accept an advisory opinion contrary to those interests.[36] The situation was thus rather clearly one in which the request for the Court's opinion would have been forbidden by the proposed guideline relevant to advisory opinions. As indicated in Chapter 8, the dispute assumed major importance and ranks high among those that have damaged the United Nations and prospects for world security.

The last advisory opinion to be considered in this chapter is the one concerned with the case of Namibia, also discussed, in its broader context, in Chapter 8. Whereas Certain Expenses superficially appeared to involve merely budgetary and fiscal matters, Namibia was patently an important political dispute involving South Africa's control of a large and valuable territory.

The case was first referred to the International Court of Justice in 1950. The reference was in the form of a request for an advisory opinion as to whether the Mandate of South West Africa given to South Africa by the League of Nations continued in force notwithstanding the dissolution of the League. The case differed from Eastern Carelia and Peace Treaties in that South Africa was a United Nations member.

The Court advised that the Mandate continued to force and that the United Nations had succeeded to the supervisory role of the League.[37] While this was legal advice deemed necessary by the political organs to facilitate their further consideration of the case—a fact not contested by South Africa—it must also have been seen by the world as a decision by the highest tribunal as to the rule that properly governed the situation.

Thenceforth, South Africa, in its highly visible refusal to submit reports to the United Nations on its administration of Namibia, conveyed the impression of violating a legal obligation.

The Assembly did not follow the precedent of Peace Treaties in immediately accusing the non-complying state of such a violation. In its Resolution 449(V) of December 13, 1950, it accepted the advisory opinion and urged South Africa to give effect to it.

The pressure was escalated, however, by Assembly Resolution 749A (VIII), of November 28, 1953, in which that organ, inter alia:

> 2. Records with deep regret that the Government of the Union of South Africa continues in its refusal to assist in the implementation of the advisory opinion. . . .

> *   *   *   *   *

> 9. Reaffirms further that the Union of South Africa continues to have the international obligation stated in Article 22 of the Covenant [concerning the Mandate System] . . . the supervisory function to be exercised by the United Nations to which the annual reports and the petitions are to be submitted.

Following the unsuccessful effort by Ethiopia and Liberia to have South Africa declared by the Court to be in violation of the Mandate, the General Assembly decided that such was the case and proceeded to declare the Mandate terminated. Then followed the Council resolutions endorsing the Assembly action and demanding the withdrawal of South Africa from Namibia, and the request for the advisory opinion of the Court on the legal consequences of what was, at the time, the latest of these resolutions.[38] It is the resulting advisory opinion of June 21, 1971,[39] that is of interest in the present chapter. The Court's answers to the question put to it state, in their first paragraph:

> (1) that, the continued presence of South Africa in Namibia being illegal, South Africa is under obligation to withdraw its administration from Namibia immediately and thus put an end to its occupation of the territory. . . .[40]

There follow several other paragraphs setting forth the obligation of other states with respect to recognition of the above ruling and the non-recognition of South Africa's claims.

The opinion thus gives the clear appearance of passing upon the major issues of the dispute. South Africa contended that the request was necessarily for the Court's opinion on these matters and that it should be rejected for this reason, citing Eastern Carelia. The Court rejected this contention on two principal grounds. First, it pointed out that unlike the Soviet Union in Eastern Carelia, South Africa had accepted advisory jurisdiction by subscribing to the U.N. Charter and had, moreover, come into Court and argued its case.[41] Second, it asserted that the Security Council had requested the opinion to obtain judicial advice on the effects of its relevant decisions, and not to obtain assistance in its efforts to settle the case. Therefore, the Court said, the request does not relate to a legal dispute actually pending between South Africa and the United Nations.[42] This latter assertion goes contrary to the plain appearance that the Court was, in fact, passing upon the principal legal issues in the case.[43]

The adverse effects of the impression conveyed by the broader Namibia case, involving the Council and the Assembly as well as the World Court, were considered in Chapter 8.[44] They are believed to have derived largely from an impression that South Africa was in defiance of law. The advisory opinion, the particular subject of this chapter, was perhaps the most important factor in creating this impression.

In conclusion, advisory jurisdiction per se now forms an important component of the illusory structure, composed of supposed organizational structures and legal powers, discussed throughout the present study. As previously stated, the abolition of this structure is essential to progress toward world peace and security by means of the kind discussed herein.

The desired goal would be essentially achieved through a return to the rule of Eastern Carelia, and beyond it to a more basic one, which would forbid requests for opinions that could reasonably be expected to result in the appearance that one or more states (or other entities) were in defiance of law.

The recommended step would also tend to dismantle the structural importance that has been given to the Court as the principal judicial organ of the United Nations. The important relationship of the U.N. to law, at the present time, lies in the potential of the organization for developing law through proper use of its powers in the area of dispute-handling. The advisory procedure is not such a proper procedure when it is used to intervene in the handling of intractable disputes.

NOTES

1. Corfu Channel Case, Judgment of April 9th, 1949, [1949] I.C.J. 4; Corfu Channel Case, Judgment of December 15, 1949, id. at 244. The first of these judgments was on the merits of the dispute; the second awarded damages. Earlier there had been a suggestion of an impasse to come later when Albania disputed the British contention that it had accepted the Court's jurisdiction. The Court held in a preliminary decision that it rightfully had jurisdiction on the basis of an Albanian letter of acceptance. Corfu Channel Case, Judgment on Preliminary Objection, [1948] I.C.J. 15. Had there been no further act of acceptance by Albania, this episode might well, pursuant to our guidelines, have given rise to inquiries as to whether this was, in fact, an intractable dispute. However, Albania and the U.K. proceeded to enter into a special agreement referring certain questions to the decision of the Court. After the Court had proceeded, on this basis, to decide the merits, Albania contested its competence to award damages.

2. South West Africa Cases, Preliminary Objections, [1962] I.C.J. 319.

3. League of Nations, Official Journal, 1921, at 90; reprinted in Wright, Mandates under the League of Nations, supra, at 620; Slonim, South West Africa and the United Nations, supra, at 370.

4. South West Africa, Second Phase, [1966] I.C.J. 6.

5. Right of Passage over Indian Territory (Merits) [1960] I.C.J. 6.

6. Id. at 39.

7. U.N. SCOR, 16th Year, 988th meeting at 21 (1961).

8. Id. at 26-27.

9. Portugal accepted the Court's jurisdiction on Dec. 19, 1955, and three days later instituted the litigation under discussion. A reservation in its declaration of acceptance claimed the right to withdraw it, vis-a-vis any category of disputes, at any time, with immediate effect. I.C.J. Yearbook 1955-1956, at 185-186. India having already filed its acceptance of jurisdiction, the Portuguese acceptance served, as found by the Court, to establish that body's competence to determine the case. In unsuccessfully contesting the jurisdiction, India maintained, among other arguments, that it had been entitled by reciprocity to avail itself of the Portuguese reservation but was prevented from doing so by the shortness of time between the two Portuguese actions that established the jurisdiction of the Court and then instituted the proceeding. Right of Passage over Indian Territory (Preliminary Objections), [1957] I.C.J. 125, 132. The adjudication thus rested on something less than full, free, and mutual submissions to the rule of law. See

Waldock, "Decline of the Optional Clause," 32 British Yearbook of International Law, 1955-6, at 244, 275-77 (1957).

10. 19 Int'l Legal Materials 553 (1980).

11. Vienna Convention on Diplomatic Relations, 1961, 500 U.N. Treaty Series 95; Optional Protocol concerning compulsory jurisdiction of disputes, id. 241; Vienna Convention on Consular Relations, 1963, 596 id. 261; Optional Protocol, id. 487.

12. The Court found it sufficient to analyze the first Iranian letter, dated December 9, 1979, since the second letter, dated March 16, 1980, merely repeated its important points. See the Court's opinion, op. cit., n. 10, paragraphs 34 and 37. The first letter is set forth in Case Concerning United States Diplomatic and Consular Staff in Tehran (United States of America v. Iran): Request for the Indication of Provisional Measures, [1979] I.C.J. 7, 10-11.

13. Art. 14.

14. P.C.I.J. Advisory Committee of Jurists. Proces Verbaux of the Proceedings of the Committee 731-32 (1920).

15. League of Nations. P.C.I.J. Documents Concerning the Action taken by the Council of the League of Nations under Art. 14 of the Covenant and the Adoption by the Assembly of the Statute of the Permanent Court of International Justice. Minutes of the Subcommittee of the Third Committee [of the Assembly, first session] at 113, 156 [1920].

16. Advisory Opinion on Interpretation of Peace Treaties (First Phase), [1950]. I.C.J. 65, 101-102 (Zoričič).

17. "The Rules of Court. Report of the Committee appointed on September 2, 1927, Fourth Annual Report of the Permanent Court of International Justice," [1928] P.C.I.J., Ser. E. No. 4, at 75, 76.

18. Originally in Art. 71, which later became Art. 83 of the rules of both the P.C.I.J. and the I.C.J.; presently Art. 102 of the rules of the latter court.

19. Advisory Opinion on Eastern Carelia [1923] P.C.I.J. Ser. B., No. 5, at 27.

20. Id. at 28-29.

21. U.S. Sen. Doc. No. 45, 69th Cong., 1st Sess. The initiative, by the President, was never carried into effect because of the lack of the two-thirds majority required for Senate approval.

22. Minutes of the Conference of the States Signatories of the Protocol of Signature of the Statute of the Permanent Court of International Justice (L. of N. Doc. V. Legal. 1926.V.26) at 75, 79; Annex 4 to Committee of Jurists on the Statute of the Permanent Court of International Justice: Minutes of the Session Held at Geneva, Mar. 11 to 19, 1929 (L. of N. Doc. C.166.M.66.1929.V), at 99, 100.

23. S. Rosenne, The Law and Practice of the International Court (Leyden: Sijthoff, 1965), vol. 2, at 652.

24. Anand cites several authorities to this effect, including A. Hammarskjold, "The Permanent Court of International Justice and Its Place in International Relations," 9 Journal of the Royal Institute of International Affairs 467 (1930); R. Anand, Compulsory Jurisdiction of the International Court of Justice (New York: Asia Publishing House, 1961) at 264-72. Rosenne, op. cit., although placing more stress on the discretion accorded the Court, appears to be of the same opinion as to the intent of Art. 68.

25. Advisory Opinion on Interpretation of Peace Treaties with Bulgaria, Hungary, and Romania (First Phase), [1950] I.C.J. 65.

26. Advisory Opinion on Interpretation of Peace Treaties with Bulgaria, Hungary, and Romania (Second Phase), id. at 221.

27. Advisory Opinion (First Phase), [1950] I.C.J., supra, at 71.

28. Id. at 71-72.

29. Id. at 79 (Azevado); 89 (Winiarski); 98 (Zoričič); 105 (Krylov).

30. Lauterpacht questioned the Court's view that it was concerned only with a procedural issue not touching the merits of the case. This, in his view, could scarcely be said of a finding of breach of treaty such as this one. H. Lauterpacht, The Development of International Law by the International Court (London: Stevens, 1958) at 353-54.

31. G.A. Resolution 385 (V) (1950).

32. In accord is Anand's conclusion that "it would have been better if the Court had given no opinion in the Interpretation of Peace Treaties case." Anand, Compulsory Jurisdiction, supra, at 280. He elaborates arguments pro and con at 273-280.

33. They probably contributed to such repression not only in communist countries but in the U.S., where the phenomenon known as McCarthyism was then current.

34. Advisory Opinion on Certain Expenses of the United Nations (Article 17, paragraph 2, of the Charter), [1962] I.C.J. 151.

35. Ch. 8, n. 30, and accompanying text, supra.

36. U.N. GAOR, 16th Sess., 5th Comm., at 289 (1961).

37. Advisory Opinion on International Status of South West Africa, [1950] I.C.J. 128, 143.

38. Ch. 8, notes 9-12 and accompanying text, supra.

39. Advisory Opinion on Legal Consequences for States of the Continued Presence of South Africa in Namibia (South West Africa) notwithstanding Security Council Resolution 276 (1970), [1971] I.C.J. 16.

40. Id. at 58.

41. Id. at 23-24.

42. Id. at 24.

43. In the subsequent advisory opinion on the Western Sahara, Spain contended that the Court should refuse the request, on the grounds that it had refused a Moroccan proposal to adjudicate the territorial dispute concerning which the Assembly was now requesting an advisory opinion. The Court rejected this contention, distinguishing Eastern Carelia on the grounds, inter alia, that all the parties in the instant case were members of the U.N. and had accepted advisory jurisdiction and had also, unlike the situation in Eastern Carelia, supplied all information necessary to an opinion. The Court also pointed out that in Western Sahara the opinion was not requested on a current dispute between states but rather was one that had arisen during the Assembly's consideration of the dispute, and concerned an earlier legal situation of the territory in question. Western Sahara [1975] I.C.J. 12, 28-29.

44. Namibia, Ch. 8, supra.

10

SOME RECENT DEVELOPMENTS

Consideration of some recent trends may help to fill in the outline of the thesis being presented. These trends are, first, politicization of the United Nations and, second, increased attention to the problem of human rights.

POLITICIZATION OF THE U.N.

First we may take up the problem posed by proposals which led to the adoption of G.A. Resolution 3151 G (XXVIII), condemning "the unholy alliance between Portuguese colonialism, South African racism, zionism and Israeli imperialism," and G.A. Resolution 3379 (XXX), "determining" that "zionism is a form of racism and racial discrimination." This last resolution has evoked a strong emotional protest. It was characterized as "evil"[1] and opposed on the grounds that it attacked a democratic state, namely Israel.[2] Ideological and political conflict was thus exacerbated.

A proper grounds for opposing these resolutions, but one not employed, was that no power of condemnation of its members had been conferred on the U.N. In particular, states formulating the Charter and joining the organization had obviously never intended to subject their ideologies and policies to such actions. Early condemnations of Nazism and Fascism[3] are not cases in point, since states espousing these doctrines were not accepted as members of the U.N. These condemnations may, however, have facilitated the later views of majorities that the organization is free to take such actions against fellow members or other states or political entities.

The several condemnations of <u>apartheid</u> by the organization are, rightly in my view, considered morally justified by the vast majority of the world's peoples and governments. They serve, however, as precedents for other condemnations, such as those of

Zionism, which to many members of the anti-_apartheid_ majority seem unjustifiable.

The United Nations can best serve its long-range goals by adhering to the powers agreed to by the members as generally acceptable. Recommendations that _apartheid_ be abandoned would appear appropriate; a recommendation that Zionism abolish itself would be so absurd that the proposal would probably not be made and, if made, would invite quick defeat. The same would be true generally of ideologies of, or pertaining to, member states.

As far as the human rights issues exemplified by _apartheid_ are concerned, adherence to agreed-to powers from the beginning would have brought about a changed world environment more conducive to observance of such rights than the one that has actually prevailed and could, conceivably, have advanced such observance beyond what has been seen in fact, up to the time of writing.[4] (Very little progress would have been required to exceed the actual performance.)

The General Assembly, beginning in 1970 and through 1973, rejected the credentials of the South African delegation[5] without, however, barring it from participation in the proceedings. This action was described by Assembly presidents as strong condemnation of the policy of _apartheid_.[6] In 1974, in its 29th session, the Assembly continued this practice vis-a-vis South Africa and, in addition, barred that country from participation in its proceedings.[7] This course of action has been continued up to the time of writing.[8] The Secretariat pointed out that the Charter did not authorize suspension of a member from its rights and privileges by the Assembly acting alone.[9] Various members, basing their objections on this lack of power under the Charter, went on to argue that the barring of a member from participation deprived it of basic rights of membership, as well as obstructing the desirable goal of U.N. universality. The case thus combines two wrongful acts of politicization: the condemnation of a member for its policies and the breach of some of its rights of membership, as an expression of this condemnation.

In 1975 the United States prevented consideration by the General Assembly of the question of Puerto Rican independence. By its own account, it did this by informing the appropriate governments that it would regard the inscription of the item on the agenda as an unfriendly act, thus intimidating them.[10]

Since the status of Puerto Rico as part of the United States was established in full conformity with the Charter principle of self-determination, U.N. consideration of the question might properly have been objected to as wrongful intervention in the domestic affairs of a state. Given the political climate existing at the time, as well as the trend of past practice, it can only be assumed that the objection would have been overruled;[11] moreover, it may be assumed that had the substantive issue been taken up by the United Nations, a resolution adverse to the United States' position might well have resulted. In the event of such an outcome, the United States should have explained the organization's limitation to the power of recommendation in such matters and should then have asserted and exercised its right to reject the recommendation.[12]

Such a course of action would have been beneficial, in the first place, on the grounds that it would have been contributing to the development of a system. As was suggested in Chapter 1, a rudimentary system, capable of growth, could be brought into being to the extent that issues are debated in the U.N. and resulting pronouncements limited to recommendations. It would be desirable, of course, if cases could be eliminated that have propaganda as their main purpose, or are otherwise improper. Frequently, however, there is no way consistent with the Charter of doing this. An ultimately effective system is better promoted by considering such cases than by excluding them by means not provided for in the Charter. As debates become more full and free, the tendency would be for the incidence of improper cases to diminish.

The recognition by the General Assembly, in 1975, of the right of the Palestine Liberation Organization to participate in proceedings pertaining to the Palestinian dispute was protested by Israel and tended to exacerbate the dispute. Both Jewish and Arab non-governmental groups did participate in some of the early discussions in this case,[13] pursuant to what appears to have been recognition of the desirability of hearing all sides of the dispute. The politicization of this move in 1974-75, and the resulting exacerbation of the conflict, is indicative of how the international environment has deteriorated in the intervening years. The sharp edge of such an issue would be blunted to the extent that full and free debates on the relevant issues became possible. Such debates are a major intermediate goal of our proposed guidelines; however, their realization would represent a more advanced stage of development than that in which these guidelines would initially be applied.

As trends crystallize and worsen by reason of the increasing politicization of United Nations dispute-handling resources, it might seem that prospects for the proper and effective use of these functions and procedures would diminish. On the other hand, however, these trends create conditions in which the impact of such proposals as might be made would be increased. Within the world public, as distinguished from governments, where the ground for change must be prepared, the more proposals seem to controvert unfavorable trends, the greater may be the attention they will command. There might therefore be a potential audience ready to listen attentively to arguments and proposals holding out the hope that the United Nations might still bring about, or at least contribute significantly to, its major goal of world peace and security.

HUMAN RIGHTS

Since the United States government headed by President Carter embarked in 1977 on a program designed to improve human rights practices throughout the world, this subject has naturally assumed enhanced importance. While it has made some use of the United Nations and promised to make more use of international organizations,[14] the campaign has been, up to the time of writing, mainly bilateral between the United States and other particular countries.

Human rights practices look as if they would be relatively amenable to efforts for their improvement. It appears that governments have it within their power to bring about such changes simply by amending relevant laws or interpretations. The human rights problem is nevertheless herein regarded as so closely related to the central problem of international relations as to be merely a facet of it. The aspect of principal concern to this study is the fragmentation of humanity into separate communities. Efforts to solve either of these problems would, if successful, solve the other. There are, obviously, severe difficulties attendant upon such efforts directed to any portion of the central problem. The most severe problem in the human rights context is the attachment of states to their traditional sovereign rights, particularly the sentiment that their human rights practices are matters of domestic jurisdiction.

The powers specifically conferred on the United Nations for the promotion of human rights seem to have been intended, generally, to fall in the cooperative and non-controversial area of activity devoted to improving conditions of life, and not in the controversial political arena, largely devoted to the handling of disputes. In the former area, the U.N.'s powers under the Charter include the making of recommendations, the initiation of reports and studies, the drafting of conventions, and the calling of international conferences.[15] Concerning the power to make recommendations,[16] it appears to be reasonably in keeping with general attitudes prevailing at the time to assume that this was not intended to be directed to particular states but rather to the generality of states. It will be recalled that the non-intervention clause of the Charter was modified and its location changed, as compared to the earlier corresponding clauses of the League Covenant and the Dumbarton Oaks Proposals, to ensure that the Charter provisions on economic, social, human rights, and related matters would not lead to intervention in the domestic affairs of states.[17]

Even "mere" recommendations directed to individual states could lead to disputes, and the exact intent of the framers as to the right of the U.N. to entertain disputes on human rights is not clear from the record. Certain points are clear, however. First, the feeling has been strong and widespread on the part of governments and dominant elements of national populations that the human rights practices of their own states are matters of exclusively domestic jurisdiction. Second, any power given to the United Nations to deal with disputes and situations concerning the practices of particular states are limited to discussion and recommendation. Third, majorities have caused the organization to appear to be exceeding these limits in numerous cases involving human rights.

On the last point, whereas the sensitivity of human rights issues might logically have caused majorities to exercise caution regarding the exercise of pressures, in practice this factor, by reason of its emotional and political effects, may actually have had the opposite effect of causing U.N. human rights resolutions and measures to exceed, more than in the generality of cases, the relevant limitations of the Charter.

Two cases that have already been mentioned are those of Spain[18] and Rhodesia,[19] in which the U.N. initiated measures appearing to seek the overthrow of the respective regimes of those countries as means of improving human rights practices. In some other cases the General Assembly sought to initiate tangible pressures for the same purpose, and called upon the Council to impose formal sanctions.[20]

On the level of moral and verbal pressure, there have been numerous condemnations of state practices and other pronouncements purporting to decide such issues. The limitation to recommendations imposed by the Charter's provisions relating to human rights and by those relating to peaceful settlement in general have been notable more for being broken than for being observed.

As to the results of these activities, the case of Spain may be particularly revealing. The international measures initiated in 1946 against the Franco regime failed and were withdrawn after a few years,[21] and the oppressive regime continued for a generation. Following Franco's death, a new regime, much more inclined to observe human rights, came into power. Rather obviously, the outside pressure failed, whereas the change, when it eventuated, came from within.

As to the result of international efforts on the world scale, the following assessment was made in 1977 by the Commission to Study the Organization of Peace in its 25th report, entitled "New Aspects of the International Protection of Human Rights":

> Framers of the United Nations Charter gave
> human rights a new international status and all signa-
> tories pledged themselves to promote universal re-
> spect for, and observance of, human rights. However,
> the record of these last thirty-two years gives cause
> for grave concern. A rapidly changing international
> community continues to witness atrocities and mass
> murders, as well as the denigration of the dignity and
> worth of individuals and groups. . . . The practice
> of torture is widespread, the incidence of terror has
> never been greater. . . . Gross violations of human
> rights around the world virtually rival the totalitarian
> excesses of the interwar years and patently demon-
> strate that the peoples of the United Nations have not
> yet made good on their promise to promote basic
> human rights. [22]

Also in 1977, the Nobel Prize Committee, in awarding the peace
prize to Amnesty International, said that since the adoption by the
U.N. of the Universal Declaration of Human Rights in 1948, the
world had "witnessed an increasing brutalization, an internationali-
zation of violence, terrorism and torture. . . ."[23]
This record seems to cast at least some doubt on the effectiveness of international pressures as a means of advancing human
rights. More than this: there is the doubt, explicit in the present
study in its entirety, whether the application of unacceptable pressures in human rights cases will not have the same or greater effects than the application of such pressures in other cases in contributing to the downward spiral of security that seems characteristic of our times during periods between major wars. It seems very
likely that this downward trend of general world security brings with
it deterioration in the observance of human rights.
On the other hand, adherence to Charter limitations in the
handling of disputes could be expected to promote world community
sentiment and to do so by democratic means—explicitly, through improved effectiveness of the debating process. One facet of such a
strengthening of world community sentiment would be the improvement of world security; another, the improvement of human rights
observances as understood by democratic societies.

NOTES

1. G.A. Plenary, U.N. Doc. A/PV.2400, at 152, Nov. 10,
1975.

2. Interview with Ambassador Daniel P. Moynihan, U.S. Representative to the U.N., CBS News, "Face the Nation," Oct. 26, 1975.

3. An implied condemnation of "Hitlerism" is found in "The Declaration by United Nations," signed Jan. 1, 1942. Yearbook of the United Nations, 1946–47, at 1. See to similar effect G.A. Resolution 39(I) (1946).

4. See text at notes 22 and 23, infra.

5. The first decision is recorded in GAOR, 25th Sess., Plenary, 1905th meeting 11 (1970).

6. The first such statement is recorded in id., 1901st meeting at 25.

7. G.A. Plenary, 29th Sess., U.N. Doc. A/PV. 2281, at 76, 86 (Nov. 12, 1974). For discussion in plenary session see id. 72-101. (A/PV refers to provisional records of General Assembly meetings.) Describing the Statute of the International Court of Justice, the U.N. Charter (Art. 92) states that the Court "shall function in accordance with the annexed Statute, which . . . forms an integral part of the present Charter." This Court's predecessor, the Permanent Court of International Justice, established pursuant to the League of Nations Covenant, was based in part on a similar Statute which was not, however, declared to be an integral part of the Covenant. Both Courts are usually referred to herein as the World Court.

8. For the summary of a debate at the 35th session, in 1981, leading to a decision to continue the practices in question, see 18 U.N. Monthly Chron. 5-8 (April 1981).

9. U.N. GAOR, 25th Sess., Annexes, Agenda Item 3, at 3, U.N. Doc. A/8160 (1970).

10. Interview with Ambassador Moynihan, supra.

11. This trend is discussed in Ch. 7.

12. Without prejudice to the desirability of uniformly referring all unsettled disputes to the United Nations, it may be observed that the U.S., because of its compliance with the self-determination principle, happened to be in a strong position to debate the Puerto Rican case on its merits. It could, moreover, have pointed out that this principle was not always observed by the "anti-colonialist"-minded countries, which generally formed the opposition to the U.S. on this matter. See, e.g., Ch. 3, n. 9 and accompanying text, supra, concerning the opposition of many of these countries to recognizing the principle in the case of West Irian. Although not on the agenda, the Puerto Rican case did come up in the General Assembly debates in 1975, and the U.S. delegation took the occasion briefly to explain its compliance with the self-determination principle and previous U.N. recognition of the fact. G.A. Plenary, 30th Sess.,

U.N. Doc. A/PV.2380, at 116 (Oct. 8, 1975). The principal U.S. Representative to the U.N. strongly supported this course on the part of his delegation, as well as the earlier efforts to keep the matter off the agenda. Interview with Ambassador Daniel P. Moynihan, U.S. Representative to the United Nations, ABC News, "Issues and Answers," Dec. 7, 1975. These two courses of action are, however, at opposite poles as far as correct use of the U.N., as herein perceived, is concerned.

13. See, e.g., Yearbook of the United Nations, 1946-47, at 281-86.

14. Address by President Carter to the United Nations, Mar. 17, 1977, 76 Department of State Bulletin 329, 332-33 (1977).

15. Art. 62. See Ch. 11, n. 19 and accompanying text, infra.

16. A separate power of recommendation on human rights matters is conferred by Art. 62(2), in addition to a more general power of recommendation in Art. 61(1).

17. Ch. 7, text at n. 3 et seq., supra.

18. See Ch. 1, n. 10 and accompanying text, supra.

19. Ch. 3, text at n. 27 et seq., supra; Ch. 4, text at n. 26 et seq., supra.

20. See Ch. 5, text at notes 20 and 21 et seq., supra.

21. G.A. Resolution 386(V) (1950).

22. New Aspects of the International Protection of Human Rights: Twenty-fifth Report of the Commission to Study the Organization of Peace at 9 (The Stanley Foundation, 1977).

23. Matchbox [publication of Amnesty International USA], Fall 1977, at 1.

11

INSTITUTIONS FOR
HANDLING DISPUTES

The idea of handling disputes by means of institutions is a commonplace derived from domestic societies. It is easy to overlook the fact that two components are involved: first, the consensus of the people concerned, or a dominant element of them, and second, the institutional structure built upon that consensus.

In some limited international areas it has proved possible to create organizations infused with a sufficient degree of underlying consensus to enable them to solve disputes and situations among their members to the extent of preventing disorder and violence. On the world scale, this degree of consensus has never existed. Consideration of how to build an effective world dispute-handling structure must involve separate consideration of the two factors, consensus and structure.[1]

To this end, and for present analytical purposes, international dispute-handling activity may be divided into two categories: efforts to solve particular disputes and efforts directed to the building of structures.

The preceding chapters have been largely concerned with activities in the first category.

The subject matter of the present chapter, activity directed primarily to institution-building, consists largely of statements attempting to promote or strengthen particular institutions, functions, or procedures and unrelated to efforts to resolve particular disputes.

This study, having as its overall concern the potential of the United Nations for fulfilling its major purpose, is necessarily based on an institutional premise. Its more particular concern with means of building such consistency of world thought patterns as to bring all disputes within manageable proportions also appears to necessitate an institution fulfilling some of the functions of the United Nations. Efforts to formulate policy guidelines to this end seem to be almost hopeless as long as governments are the sole actors and there is no international forum capable of applying some significant pressure in the direction of mediation and accommodation.

Institutions capable of maintaining order are normally produced by requisite degrees of community sentiment on the part of concerned populations. These elements of systems of order, consensus and institutions, may usefully be envisioned as components of equations. In the international realm, leaders constructed institutions before a requisite degree of consensus existed on the other side of the equation to ensure world order. However, the institutional side was essentially limited to discussion and recommendation, and this limitation balanced the existing degree of consensus on the other side. A central question is whether the use of the institutions within their limitations can contribute to the further growth of consensus to the degree required to become the basis of an effective system of order. The notion of the equation may be useful to emphasize the probable necessity to this end that the two sides be kept in balance.

There is, therefore, a difference between recognizing the importance—indeed, the essentiality—of the United Nations and placing emphasis on it as an institution, per se. The difference may be perceived by contrasting the commonplace tendency to regard the world organization as having failed in its purpose of maintaining peace and security with what is herein perceived as its proper purpose, namely that of steadily contributing to conditions in which world peace can be preserved.

Conceding, then, the general institutional framework of the study, it is proposed as a guideline of policy:

> Emphasis should not be placed on dispute-handling institutions as a means of seeking world peace and security.

An American newspaper said, in regard to the Sino-Japanese conflict over Manchuria in 1933:

> There is . . . in this country . . . a belief that the affair is that of the League to which the United States does not belong. [2]

It might be thought that if this statement were valid at the time, the attitude thus reflected has long since changed. The United States dropped its isolationist attitude after Pearl Harbor, it accepted international responsibilities involving heavy sacrifices, and it became a leading supporter of the United Nations. The quoted statement nevertheless contains an element that remains valid today, namely, the wish of people to transfer to others the responsibility for peace and security. This attitude might involve conscious or subconscious admissions that the people concerned do not know how to go about achieving this goal. The feeling might be that since the League of Nations, and later the United Nations, was created for the purpose, it should know; and that therefore the responsibility can rightfully be placed on it. To the extent that there is any validity in this conclusion, the attitude in question would probably entail a disinclination to think seriously about possible lines of action that are unfamiliar. The League and the United Nations perhaps filled a psychological need. The League was, of course, new after World War I. However, many considered that it was tangible and comprehensible and could serve a purpose as the repository of responsibility for peace and security. When that organization failed, its successor was designed to play a stronger role, being supposedly endowed with the power to enforce peace. Efforts to use these dispute-handling mechanisms strongly, and to strengthen them further, were inherent in the attitude governing their use in the ensuing period.

It seems to have been widely and routinely accepted from the outset that the machinery of dispute-handling is in itself of critical importance as a means of settling disputes, and thus of seeking peace and security. Statements incorporating this assumption in regard, for example, to the League, the United Nations, and the supposed institution of international law, have in fact been counterproductive in that they have directed public attention in wrong directions. The basic fallacy is in the assumption that it is possible to create institutions that will be able to deal with any disputes that might arise, and that the primary channel for seeking peace and security lies in their creation. Instead, it is submitted, the primary goal must be to create a world climate in which intractable disputes will not arise. If this is not done, and if the traditional climate continues to prevail, some disputes will already have passed beyond any possibility of peaceful solution by the time they become visible. It is merely a truism that institutions cannot resolve intractable disputes. Moreover, even if we take into account the great majority of disputes and situations that are successfully solved, the institutions that are employed to handle some of them are, at their most useful, of secondary importance when considered in light of the overall problem here under discussion. The peaceful settlement function of the United Nations, as defined in the Charter, can be called an institution of primary importance, but for a different purpose, namely that of contributing to the change of world climate referred to.

Dispute-handling mechanisms of the United Nations have been the subject of considerable efforts to strengthen them. Such efforts have been consistent with the view prevailing at the outset that these institutions should be strong.

To indicate the nature of the basic assumption concerning the importance of these institutions, reference may be made to the following statement concluding an article written at the time the Covenant of the League of Nations was being formulated:

> Any international organization that is set up will
> necessarily be imperfect, and will fail, to some
> extent, in putting an end to the reign of violence.
> It can hardly be more imperfect, however, than
> were the beginnings of national organization from
> which have developed the civilized state. It has been
> a characteristic of all vigorous races in their early
> days, and in modern times especially of the English-
> speaking peoples, to go ahead with ill-constructed
> political machinery, without taking much heed of its
> defects, and improve it piecemeal as they went
> along. In this course they have been surprisingly
> successful. Will they be the leaders now in a world-
> wide experiment?[3]

This paragraph seems to indicate the view that the machinery of international organization was the crucial factor in establishing law and order. Whatever may have been the author's actual intent, other parts of the article seem to raise a question as to whether such is in fact the case. Thus, it says:

> [A] glance at the history of legal institutions is in-
> structive. Most of us live in surroundings so far
> removed from the primitive that it is hard for us to
> realize that courts of law flourished, and dealt with
> a multitude of cases in a manner satisfactory to the
> people, when their power of compelling obedience was
> so imperfect as sometimes to touch the vanishing
> point. [4]

At another point the author considered, as a factor in the effective-ness of international tribunals, the "scarcity" of substantive prin-ciples available to such tribunals, and went on to say:

> The history of both early courts of law and of
> modern international arbitrations shows that the

> legal rules to be applied, as well as the means of en-
> forcing judgments, may be left somewhat indefinite
> without preventing the judicial machinery from work-
> ing effectively. In international arbitrations, when
> once a question has been submitted, a conclusion has
> always been reached, and that conclusion, though fre-
> quently unsatisfactory to one side, and sometimes
> rendered by a divided court, has almost always been
> accepted.[5]

This statement, like the previously quoted passage, can be interpreted as downgrading the importance of the tribunals as compared
with the degree of agreement existing between the parties.

The fact that two states agree to submit a dispute to the binding decision of a third-party tribunal means, in effect, that the
dispute is in the manageable rather than in the intractable category.
However meager may appear to be the principles on which the
tribunal can base its decision, the parties must necessarily be
sufficiently in agreement, and sufficiently sure of the limitations
within which the tribunal will decide, to be willing to accept an adverse decision rather than have the dispute continue unresolved.
The tribunal in such cases plays an indispensable role, but it is
not the essential factor in reaching the agreement. Before 1919,
when the above article was published, all international tribunals
were set up ad hoc by concerned parties for the decision of particular disputes. The number of successful arbitrations in the latter
nineteenth and early twentieth centuries is an indication that when
states are sufficiently agreed to proceed by this method, the setting
up of tribunals is not a serious problem.

Therefore the article under discussion suggests in some of
its parts a conclusion somewhat different from that stated in its
final paragraph to the effect that people have had surprising success
in causing imperfect institutions to contribute to law and order.
The alternative and perhaps preferable conclusions might be that
the success of a "system" depends on the degree of community
existing among its members and that, if a requisite degree exists,
imperfect machinery may well prove to be workable.

An example of the kind of pronouncement herein considered
undesirable was the statement, in a British memorandum presented
to the Dumbarton Oaks Conversations in 1944, that one of the purposes of the future United Nations organization should be "to
guard and enlarge the freedom of man by institutions for the removal of social wrongs."[6] The intent may have been to suggest
that the organization should assist and facilitate the growth of
understanding and consensus as to what are social wrongs; however,

the statement must have had a tendency to convey the impression that the institution is the essential factor in the prevention of such wrongs.

Secretary-General Hammarskjold was a strong contributor to the "institutional" approach to peace and security. In a statement of 1956, for example, concerning former U.S. President Wilson, he said:

> As he so clearly understood, the international interest had to be institutionalized if it were to have a reasonable hope of prevailing in the course of time. No matter how solemn the engagement to common purposes and universal aims, whether expressed in a Covenant for a League of Nations or in a Charter for the United Nations, institutions functioning continuously in the service of these purposes would be needed to give them effect. [7]

Hammarskjold stressed his own view of the institutional approach in his important University of Chicago speech of May 1, 1960, saying, inter alia:

> However primitive a basic institutional pattern may be, it carries within it seeds for the growth of higher social organisms, covering wider areas and groups of peoples. . . . [S]uch an institutional system for co-existence, stage by stage, may be developed and enriched until, on single points or on a broad front, it passes over into a constitutional system of cooperation. [8]

It is submitted that a distinction must be made in this respect between an "institutional pattern" and a functioning system capable of maintaining peace and security. The latter concept no doubt exerts a force on behalf of its own acceptance. [9] In such a system, the institutional pattern is based on a requisite degree of community sentiment; a reciprocal interchange ("input" and "feedback") of ideas and sentiments is then established so that it can be said that each element exerts a force on the other that, if the system is successful, strengthens it by enabling it to adapt to changing conditions. In the international realm, however, no basic consensus has ever been established, and in such a situation, an institutional pattern is unable to contribute to the growth of an effective system. Hammarskjold recognized, in his Chicago speech, that the institutional approach being advocated was experimental. He said that the experiment should be pushed by all means.[10] By 1980 it seems possible to suggest that this approach is not fruitful and is, more-over, counter-productive, since it tends to distract attention from other approaches that might be more conducive to success.[11]

An effective statement of the prevailing view on the role of institutions in the search for peace and security is contained in the concluding sentence of an article by Professors McDougal and Reisman, approving of United Nations actions in the Rhodesian case:

> [W]ith respect to international governmental organiza-
> tions . . . one of the conditions of progress toward
> major objectives may be that authoritative reach
> must sometimes exceed effective grasp.[12]

We may consider this statement in relation to Secretary-General Hammarskjold's belief that certain parallels between the United Nations Charter and the United States Constitution were a cause of optimism for the former:

> When the United Nations was created, the
> founders had the experience . . . of such a highly
> evolved constitutional pattern as that established
> on the American continent. A strong influence
> from [this experience] can be seen in the Charter
> of the United Nations.[13]

He went on immediately to point out the rudimentary legislative, executive, and judicial functions of the United Nations. The United States government, in fact, possesses dispute-handling machinery with far greater "effective grasp" than anything in prospect for the international realm. It was also possessed of such apparently strong institutions in the years just prior to 1860; however, these institutions proved wholly incapable of solving the dispute that erupted into civil war in that year. Legislative efforts to do so included the Missouri Compromise[14] and the Kansas-Nebraska Act,[15] while an outstanding judicial effort resulted in the Dred Scott decision of the Supreme Court.[16] It appears not to have been the weakness of these institutions, in any objective sense, that caused the failure; it was rather the fact that the parties were too far apart in their concepts of justice in the premises to permit peaceful solution.

This episode of civil war thus seems to support the thesis of this discussion that efforts to strengthen dispute-handling institu-tions, per se, are essentially irrelevant. It may be objected, on the other hand, that the example is insufficient to prove the point.

With respect to much weaker international institutions for handling disputes, it might be suggested that there is room for efforts directed toward strengthening them.

It might also be suggested that the American Civil War, as just one breakdown in the life of a state with very strong institutions, proves little. However, most of United States history has been a demonstration that neither are dispute-handling institutions per se the solution to its racial issues or to the more general problem of maintaining law and order. During the first part of this history, up to the Civil War, the slave population was suppressed by force, governmental and non-governmental. While dispute-handling institutions thus produced a semblance of law and order, they did not produce "peace and security," as was proved by the outbreak of the Civil War itself.

United States history since the Civil War is even more revealing as regards the thesis under consideration. Shortly after that war the Fourteenth Amendment, providing that all citizens are equal before the law, was incorporated into the written Constitution. The constitutional law thus enacted was itself an institution for dispute-handling, as were, of course, the older institutions of the legislative, judicial, executive, and administrative components of the government. While competent authorities of these institutions naturally contended that their actions conformed to law, dispassionate observers would scarcely agree that equality under the law was, in fact, provided for the black and certain other ethnic minority components of the population. The reason for this apparent failure was that the consensus of the dominant element of the population went in a different direction from that of the equality requirement of the Constitution as it would be interpreted by later generations. Another illustration of divergence between institutions and actions occurred in 1941-42, following the the Japanese attack on Pearl Harbor, when the United States government placed many citizens of Japanese descent under physical restraints as a measure of wartime security. The United States became engaged in war with Germany and Italy at the same time; however, citizens of German and Italian descent were not so restrained.

There may be interpolated here, somewhat out of context, the observation that the present phase of the discussion pursues problems of law at a level on which domestic and international law must merge if either is to be fully effective. By contrast, in their treatment of more immediate applications of the notion of law, other parts of the discussion are largely devoted to demonstrating that "international law" is in essence quite different from domestic law. In this view, of course, the world does not possess effective international law. Neither, however, does it possess wholly effective domestic law; nor can it as long as domestic affairs can be impinged on by international crises. The legal justification of the United States government for restraining its citizens of Japanese descent was that they were seen to present a threat to security.[17] It might be generally agreed that measures deemed necessary would be taken against any group in the country perceived as presenting such a threat. Consequently, the citizens of Japanese descent can be said to have been treated on the basis of equality. The only means of permanently eliminating the kind of external threat that precipitated this legal dilemma would be to establish the requisite degree of world community sentiment to ensure against intractable international disputes. This case demonstrates that in the pursuit of order, an indissoluble link exists between domestic and international realms.

A change in the attitude of the United States government toward the country's black population was heralded by the decision of the Supreme Court in 1954 that banned as unconstitutional the deliberate racial segregation of schools.[18] Further judicial decisions upholding equality of rights followed, as did some important legislative enactments. Stemming from the fact that the United States has an effective, if yet imperfect, system, such governmental acts have basically different force and effect from efforts to build and use international institutions to handle disputes in present world conditions. Even in the case of the United States, as was shown by the slow implementation of the original court decision on school desegregation, law per se cannot bring about change contrary to prevailing community sentiment. However, given some significant degree of community support, laws can be enacted and enforced that directly change the conditions of life. In the international realm, on the other hand, policy pronouncements on such subjects are relatively divorced from the changes they seek.[19] Most such pronouncements can become effective only with the consent of the states concerned. Individual cases sometimes become the subject of dispute-handling activity involving pronouncements by the Security Council or the General Assembly, and sometimes of more tangible measures, with the uncertain results characteristic of this area of international activity.

It may be concluded that attempts to strengthen international dispute-handling processes by strengthening dispute-handling institutions—including efforts to impress the world public as to their importance—are counter-productive and undesirable because they tend to draw attention away from more fruitful channels of endeavor, including the area of activity concerned with conditions of life.

The concept of international law forms the framework for certain kinds of efforts toward institutionalization herein deemed undesirable. Some background considerations consistent with the present approach have been set forth in Chapter 4.

Efforts to advance international law as an institution fall into two principal categories. The first has to do with the prevailing notion of law as a body of rules and the second with institutional means of applying these rules effectively.

Both aspects have undergone change since World War II as the result of the emergenceof newly independent countries. These countries have tended to aloofness toward the pre-existing body of rules and toward the World Court, which had been regarded as the centrally important institution for the application of the rules. This attitude derived from the view that both the rules and the Court were the creations and instruments of the former colonial powers.

Effective efforts to institutionalize both the notion of law per se as a body of rules and that of the World Court as the primary institution for applying the rules, reached their peak in the Covenant of the League of Nations, the Charter of the United Nations, and the Statutes of the two versions of the World Court: the Permanent Court of International Justice and its successor, the International Court of Justice.

A crucial step in the institutionalization of law was taken when some world leaders conceived the idea that the substantial number of successful arbitrations in the nineteenth and early twentieth centuries represented effective applications of international law and that such applications might be made more effective if a permanent world court could be established, of as high caliber and as completely impartial as possible, and strictly limited to deciding in accordance with law. These officials were, perhaps, impressed with the customary expressions by governments of their devotion to law. It was anticipated that if the political aspects of ad hoc arbitrations could be eliminated and such third-party proceedings placed on a more purely legal basis, governments would be willing to submit more of their disputes—and more important disputes— to the judicial process.[20]

INTERNATIONAL LAW AS A BODY OF RULES

An essential fallacy of this approach lay in the assumption that a body of rules of law already existed, which it would be the duty of the Court to identify and apply in particular cases. Leaders thus placed before the world's people the hope that by pursuing the notion of law they could achieve effective law in a sense comparable to that of law in their domestic societies, that is to say, of rules of law and the means of applying them with the effect of maintaining law and order.

However, the rules and dispute-handling institutions of domestic societies are effective because they rest upon a base of community sentiments. People perceive the enactment, modification, interpretation, and application of the rules as being the essence of law and order, but in fact they are the visible manifestations of a deeper and more crucial process that must, to be successful, maintain viable constitutional patterns of public opinion.[21] International peace and security have the same basic requirement.[22] It is erroneous to think that they can be achieved through concentration on the legal forms of rules and the more tangible instruments of dispute-handling. The reverse is the case.[23] World leaders of the earlier twentieth century made an understandable but deleterious mistake when they thought that it was the arbitral tribunals that produced successful solutions of such disputes as the Alabama Claims and North Atlantic Coast Fisheries cases. The crucial contributing factors were the pre-existing agreements between the parties, which permitted solutions of particular disputes. When attention was focused on how to strengthen institutions, instead of on the question of how to broaden the area of agreement among nations, the world tended to be diverted into a wrong channel in the search for world peace.[24]

Important tangible results were the establishment of the World Court, with its mission of deciding disputes in accordance with the rules of law, and corresponding provisions of the League of Nations Covenant and the Charter of the United Nations that explicitly postulated the existence of a body of rules of law. The sources of the rules to be applied by the Court were stated in Article 38 of the statutes of both Courts to be custom, treaties, the general principles of law recognized by civilized nations, judicial decisions, and the writings of qualified jurists.

A statement in the preamble of the Charter that stresses the need to create suitable conditions for maintaining respect for the obligations of treaties and other sources of international law is relatively desirable insofar as it stresses the need for creating the conditions in which law may be effective, but relatively undesirable in its affirmation of the prevalent conception of international law as an existing institution and the desirability of maintaining it as a condition for peace. The latter idea is further affirmed in Article 1 of the Charter, where it is said to be the duty of the United Nations to bring about solutions of disputes "which might lead to a breach of the peace" in accordance with the principles of justice and international law, and in Article 13, where the Assembly is directed to take steps to encourage the development of international law and its codification.

This concept of law as an institution received further confirmation in the Declaration on Rights and Duties of States, adopted by the United Nations General Assembly on December 6, 1949,[25] which declares at its outset that "the States of the world form a community governed by international law" and that "the progressive development of international law requires effective organization of the community of States," and concludes by saying:

> Every State has the duty to conduct its relations
> with other States in accordance with international law
> and with the principle that the sovereignty of each
> State is subject to the supremacy of international law.

With the ensuing emergence of newly independent states in Asia and Africa, such efforts directed at the institutionalization of international law and emphasizing a supposed pre-existing body of rules tended to be superseded by declarations and treaties that emphasize principles in which the new states were interested, particularly the end of colonialism and of racial discrimination.

Such pronouncements are undesirable only when they promote the notion of law per se. This occurred in a number of instances. One such statement adopted by the Assembly during its 25th anniversary observance is entitled "Declaration on Principles of International Law Concerning Friendly Relations and Cooperation among States in Accordance with the Charter of the United Nations."[26] After affirming some of the principles of the Charter— the prohibition of the use of force and of wrongful intervention, the duty to settle disputes peacefully, etc.—it concludes by stating the "principle" that "States shall fulfill in good faith the obligations assumed by them in accordance with the Charter" and goes on to place stress on the obligations of states under general international law, treaties, and the Charter.[27]

A second method by which authorities seek to enhance the stature of international law as a body of rules is maintaining that all amicable relations of states are regulated by law and that all settlements of disputes and all agreements concluded are to be regarded as accretions to law.

An apparent use of this approach in the hope of building law as an institution, and thus in turn of strengthening world peace and security, was made by the United Nations Secretary-General in an address of 1968 entitled "International Law and the United Nations," in which he said, <u>inter alia</u>:

> [W]hat role does law play in keeping the peace today?
> At best it can be said that it can be likened to the
> candles which light the darkness. The Rann of Kutch
> dispute . . . has recently been settled by arbitration.
> A territorial dispute between Argentina and Chile has
> likewise been settled by the same means. The dis-
> pute between the Republic of Indonesia and the Kingdom
> of the Netherlands regarding West Irian, which had
> already broken out into armed clashes, was solved by
> an agreement negotiated by the parties in 1962. The
> more these examples are followed, the sooner the
> darkness will be dispelled. [28]

The reasons for disagreeing with the statement that these
settlements represented advances for law is indicated, in part, in
the above-quoted passage where the Secretary-General noted that
solution of the West Irian case had been preceded by armed clashes.
The general incompatibility of the handling of this case with the
growth of an effective rule of law has been indicated in Chapter 3. [29]
As there stated, it is impossible to conceive of a viable legal system capable of maintaining peace and security in which a state can
gain its ends by the threat or use of force, or in which two states
can settle a dispute in a manner impinging on the interests of a
third party without consulting the wishes of the latter. The rule of
law has requirements altogether different from a mere aggregation
of rules. The handling of the West Irian case demonstrates that the
mode of reaching a rule that can be agreed on may be detrimental
to progress toward an effective rule of law.
    The aspect of the problem here under discussion, however,
is the undesirability of statements that, like that of the Secretary-
General quoted above, seek to build up the notion that the reaching
of agreed-on solutions is, per se, an advance for law and consequently represents progress toward world security.
    The Secretary-General's address of 1968 proceeds to illus-
trate, separately, the treaty institution as a supposed means of
advancing international law and as an institution in its own right.
    The first aspect was illustrated by the following passage of
the address:

> With the conclusion of the Antarctic Treaty in Wash-
> ington, on 1 December 1959, this potential source of
> strife and conflict was converted into an area of peace
> and co-operation. . . . [T]he Treaty on Principles

> Governing the Activities of States in the Exploration and
> Use of Outer Space . . . was concluded in 1966. . . .
> The process of law has neutralized this possible source
> of conflict, and has converted it into an area of peace
> and cooperation.[30]

If, however, treaties were to have this effect, there would have to
be general and comprehensive provisions for determining disputes
of interpretation. Efforts to achieve such general competence for
the World Court have not succeeded;[31] neither do important treaties
generally contain provisions for their own interpretation by third
parties. Disputed situations do not often become static simply
because a settlement is reached, by treaty or otherwise. If any
change in the situation governed by a treaty takes place, disputes
of interpretation are likely to arise. If such disputes cannot be
settled, the treaty might become inoperative; the relationship
would then be likely to rest on force.[32] Such a situation may exist
even though the treaty appears to continue in force, since the
stronger party may desire to have the treaty continue, and act
accordingly, while the weaker might wish to alter or terminate it
but lack the power to do so. The general refusal of states to agree
to automatic dispute-settling procedures with respect to their
treaties can be said to reflect a preference for relying on force,
rather than on law, if disputes arise as to the interpretation or
application of particular treaties. It also reflects the absence in
international relations of law in its predominant meaning in domestic usage, i.e., that of effective law.

One aspect of the United Nations program for the promotion
of human rights had as its result an attempt to build up the treaty
institution as a form of law and as superior, in principle, to
recommendations. This was the policy that envisioned the Universal Declaration of Human Rights as a first step to be followed by
a treaty that would incorporate those rights as binding law and contain provisions for determining breaches. The matter is mentioned here because of the general agreement that the treaty would
result in binding legal status for the rights specified therein and
that this status would represent a clear step of progress over the
Universal Declaration, a "mere" statement of aspiration.[33] Concerned people were probably not so unanimous as to exactly how
this result was to be achieved.[34] There was probably no general
anticipation that states, on subscribing to the treaty, would immediately be unanimous as to the interpretation of particular provisions, or in complying therewith; it was anticipated, however, that
the existence of the legal obligation would be a persuasive factor in
hastening general world compliance.[35] The point of concern to this

discussion is the clarity of the general view that the second, or treaty, stage would be a step of progress from the recommendatory stage represented by the Universal Declaration.

Such statements are here considered undesirable as a general rule because they represent the erroneous tendency to institutionalize law and treaties as means of advancing international law.

As to the value of the particular treaties under reference, they came into force too recently,[36] at the time of writing, to warrant any conclusions as to their effects on human rights practices. However, if it is true, as was suggested in Chapter 10, that such practices are part of the core problem of international relations, the further conclusion suggests itself that human rights do not constitute the kind of problem that can be solved by treaties. Such apparently comprehensive treaties as these might, therefore, create illusions that they represent substantial progress toward solution of the world's human rights problems; indeed, it seems likely that arguments for the Covenant and the Charter advanced by competent authorities have had this effect. The treaties can, accordingly, be expected to divert attention and effort from lines of endeavor that might have proved more fruitful.[37]

They might have the further disadvantage of straining relations, since disputes may have this effect to a greater extent if they involve allegations of treaty violation. States may also remain sensitive about their human rights practices even though, by entering into treaties on the subject, they might seem to have foregone the argument based on domestic jurisdiction.[38]

Turning to a second aspect of the institutionalization of treaties, it may be observed that, in the address mentioned earlier in this chapter, the Secretary-General expressed the hope that the successful conclusion of some important international treaties—on Antarctica, on the exploration and use of outer space, and on the non-proliferation of nuclear weapons—would provide incentive for the conclusion of further treaties for regulation of the use of the seabed and for the control of arms.[39] It seems rather certain, however, that governments, in deciding on treaty commitments, are guided almost exclusively by considerations of self-interest. This fact would not necessarily prevent certain treaties from motivating others. For example, a treaty might be seen as embodying a new and useful concept; a similar factor might be involved here, as when governments are motivated to adhere to multilateral treaties of quasi-legislative effect. It is difficult to anticipate, however, that the conclusion of a treaty on one subject, such as space exploration, could stimulate the conclusion of treaties on quite different subjects, such as the exploration and use of the seabed.[40] In fact the latter has proved, to the time of writing, a more difficult subject for agreement than the former.

The foregoing are, however, but subsidiary aspects of a major fallacy, namely the view that international peace and law are advanced by building the treaty institution per se. It is, of course, essential to build law, and international agreements would no doubt have an important place as an aspect of effective law. However, the building of either world security or world law—different aspects of a single hoped-for eventuality—would require changes in the format of international relations in regard to which the institutionalization of either law or treaties is irrelevant. Efforts toward such institutionalization are, moreover, harmful in that they create confusion and foster illusions.

One such illusion might well be the notion, based on the proposition that law is a stabilizing factor, that treaties, since they embody law in the form of obligations deliberately undertaken and precisely stated, are to be sought as a means of securing world stability. While it is here believed that if the world were to make significant progress toward peace and security the number of international agreements could be expected to increase, expectations concerning their durability might be decreased in such circumstances. Disputes over interpretation might be resolved with increasing frequency through amicable negotiations, arbitration, or the conclusion of new agreements. Agreements, per se, would gradually lose the formidable character hitherto attributed to them as the intended means of establishing fixed and stable relationships and assume an appropriate role as an integral aspect of a system capable of maintaining order in a changing world. The growth of community sentiment might logically be expected to have as a consequence the replacement, to some degree, of written agreements by generally accepted, and generally unwritten, norms of conduct; the relationship between law and treaty would tend to resemble that existing between the laws and constitutions of states on one hand and private contracts on the other.

The present thesis, accordingly, as an aspect of its search for means of causing both law and treaties to play their effective roles in the building and maintenance of a secure world, opposes placing emphasis on the institutionalization of treaties, as it does placing it on that of international law.

INSTITUTIONAL MEANS OF APPLYING LAW

The second principal category of efforts to institutionalize the concept of law consists of the search for organizations and procedures capable of applying in practice the supposed body of rules that forms the first category. The growth of the second category was inevitable if the first was not to be merely an abstraction. It may also have received enhanced attention from a desire of people to externalize their responsibilities and to seek, as the repository of particular responsibilities, institutions as tangible and concrete as possible.

The present phase of the discussion follows logically what was said earlier in this chapter about evolutionary thinking concerning arbitration, which led to the founding of the World Court.

Advocates of that institution were disappointed in that it proved impossible to confer on it general automatic jurisdiction comparable to that enjoyed by judicial systems of states. The grant of such competence would have meant that participating states committed themselves to binding judicial decisions of certain disputes to arise in the future, with no further consent to particular adjudications required. Agreement on such a grant of power was prevented by some of the major powers—primarily the Soviet Union, in the case of the new embodiment of the Court, the International Court of Justice, set up after World War II—whereas the majority appeared to favor the proposal. [41] The latter position is believed to have been based on an unwarranted expectation that after World War II the world would prove capable of being governed by law. [42]

When it proved impossible to endow the World Court with general automatic jurisdiction, efforts tended to focus on obtaining agreement to such jurisdiction by states on an individual basis pursuant to an optional procedure provided by the Statutes of the two Courts.

A gradual narrowing of focus may be observed. The proclaimed desire has been to develop an effective regime of international law. However, as if unwilling to concentrate attention on this subject in its obvious vastness and complexity, people have turned their attention first to the creation of a World Court and then to the task of obtaining the acceptance by states of the automatic jurisdiction of the Court. Of course, all the complexities of the original aspiration are packed into the latter issue; however, the tendency has been to present it as a rather simple question.

Illustrative of the innumerable statements favorable to the acceptance of such jurisdiction is the following by Secretary-General Hammarskjold in his important University of Chicago speech of 1960:

> [T]he International Court of Justice . . . would have possibilities to develop into a more important element in the settlement of international conflicts than it now is, were the unfortunate and self-defeating reservations against its jurisdiction made by some Member countries to be withdrawn. [43]

This jurisdictional issue has gradually diminished since it became evident that most peoples and governments newly independent after World War II were unwilling to accept the Court's jurisdiction, and since the United States was forced by elements of its own public to abandon its role of leadership.[44] As indicated by a statement of the U.S. Secretary of State in 1970, that country has redirected attention to the Court per se (as distinguished from "compulsory jurisdiction") as a focus of efforts to advance international law. The Secretary advocated efforts to bring more cases before the Court as a means of promoting the rule of law and thus providing the basis for world community. He said that the basic cause of the relative non-use of the Court was the reluctance of states to refer disputes to it for adjudication. Governments, he said, have been unwilling to adopt the practice of adjudication, with its accompanying expectation of winning some cases and losing some. Thus, there has been a failure to grasp the long-term advantage of establishing a system for settling disputes in accordance with law.[45]

The impression was thus given by the Secretary of State, as earlier by the Secretary-General in his University of Chicago address, that the decision to submit regularly and routinely to adjudication of legal disputes is one within the free discretion of governments. This approach ignores the real source of difficulty, which consists of the occasional emergence of disputes in which the parties are too far apart to permit prompt and effective solutions. A government party to such a dispute, considering that an adverse judicial decision would entail unacceptable sacrifice or the risk of such sacrifice, will refuse in most cases to submit to that procedure. Therefore, instead of having a solution to the problem of law—and a consequent major step in the direction of world security—within easy reach of governments in the form of discretion to accept jurisdiction in proper legal disputes, the world has not even looked in the direction in which the search for such a solution must begin.

The World Court presents a particular problem in relation to the thesis under discussion, since, representing as it does the crystallization of a dream never realized, it is indissolubly linked with the notion of law. It is limited by the Charter and its Statute to deciding in accordance with law except in regard to those cases as to which the parties might agree that it should decide ex aequo et bono. Such language tends to promote the illusion that an established law, capable of being distinguished from equity, exists in the international realm.

NOTES

1. A proposal for the development of international institutions in the security field, based on consideration of both components (and, incidentally, drawing significantly on the NATO precedent), is put forth in L. Beaton, The Reform of Power: A Proposal for an International Security System (1972). Well considered though this proposal is, it appears to call for changes in world thought patterns too great to be practical in the prevailing conditions.

2. Bangor Daily Commercial, Feb. 25, 1933; cited in D. Fleming, The United States and World Organization: 1920-1933 (New York: Columbia University Press, 1938), at 458.

3. R. Gray, "International Tribunals in the Light of the History of Law," 32 Harvard Law Review 825, 834 (1919).

4. Id. at 826.

5. Id. at 831-32.

6. Foreign Relations of the U.S. 1944, vol. 1, at 670, 671.

7. "Woodrow Wilson and the United Nations," address by Dag Hammarskjold, May 20, 1956, W. Foote, ed., Servant of Peace: A Selection of the Speeches and Statements of Dag Hammarskjold, Secretary-General of the United Nations 1953-1961 (New York: Harper & Row, 1962) at 108, 109.

8. "The Development of a Constitutional Framework for International Cooperation," address by Dag Hammarskjold, id. at 251, 252.

9. R. Hutchins, The Constitutional Foundation for World Order (Denver: Social Science Foundation, University of Denver, 1947), at 13-14.

10. Hammarskjold, "The Development of a Constitutional Framework," supra, at 255.

11. The continued importance accorded institution building is indicated by G.A. Resolution 2734 (1975) and the annexed Declaration on the Strengthening of International Security, adopted as part of the observance of the 25th anniversary of the Organization, and by the statement of the Secretary-General in 1976 that:

>   The Charter concept of world order is based on respect for the decisions of the principal organs of the United Nations and for international law, principles, and procedures. . . . We have had many recent experiences of the wide discrepancy between the unanimity, or near unanimity, of decisions of the Security Council or the General Assembly and the practical effect which such decisions have on the issues to which they are addressed. This is a development which, if

allowed to continue, will . . . once again put in jeopardy
the security of the world community. It is therefore in
the interests of all Governments, even at the cost of some
short-term disadvantages, to support and respect the
authority of the Security Council and to contribute to its
central role in developing a system of world order. . . .
["Introduction to the Report of the Secretary-General on
the Work of the Organization," August 1976, U.N. GAOR,
31st Sess., Supp. 1A (A/31/1/Add. 1), at 4.]

12. M. McDougal and W. Reisman, "Rhodesia and the United
Nations: The Lawfulness of International Concern," 62 American
Journal of Int'l Law 1, 19 (1968).

13. Hammarskjold, "The Development of a Constitutional
Framework," supra, at 255.

14. 3 U.S. Statutes at Large 545 (1820).

15. 10 id. at 277 (1854).

16. 60 U.S. (19 How.) 393 (1856).

17. Korematsu v. United States, 323 U.S. 214 (1944).

18. Brown v. Board of Education of Topeka, 349 U.S. 294
(1954).

19. U.N. activities in this area are outlined in Chapters IX
and X of the Charter, entitled respectively "International Economic
and Social Cooperation" and "The Economic and Social Council."
As observed in Ch. 10, text at n. 15, supra, this area was intended
to be generally non-controversial and is thus to be distinguished
from the other major area of U.N. activity, the handling of disputes.

20. Instructions to the American Delegates to the Hague Conference, 1907, Foreign Relations of the U.S., 1907, Pt. II, at 1128,
1135; P. Jessup, Elihu Root, vol. 2, at 75-76 (1938).

21. E. Carr, The Twenty Years' Crisis 1919-1939 (London:
Macmillan, 1946), at 177-180 (2d ed.). Edmund Wilson, speaking
of the early phase of communism in Russia, said:

[E]ven where a group of socialists come to the helm,
they are powerless by themselves either to instill their
ideals or to establish their proposed institutions. Only
the organic processes of society can make it possible
to arrive at either. [E. Wilson, To the Finland Station:
A Study in the Writing and Acting of History (New York:
Harcourt, Brace, 1940), at 323.]

22. Carr, The Twenty Years' Crisis, at 177-80. See also
Ch. 10, text at n. 21, supra, in regard to the development of human
rights in Spain.

If there is any great lesson we Americans need to learn with regard to the methodology of foreign policy, it is that we must be gardeners and not mechanics in our approach to world affairs. We must come to think of the development of international life as an organic and not a mechanical process. [G. Kennan, Realities of American Foreign Policy (Princeton: Princeton University Press, 1954), at 93.]

Reference might also be made here to the well-known passage in Luke 17:20-21, beginning: "The kingdom of God cometh not with observation; Neither shall they say, Lo here! or lo there. . . ." If we interpret the "kingdom of God" as meaning international peace, some of the observable things that will not bring it about are not only bullets and bombs but also rules and tribunals, taken by themselves, "for, behold, the kingdom of God is within you." (The possibility that the gospel message was, in fact, concerned in part with international relations [specifically the Israelite's Roman problem] is discussed in V. Simkhovich, Toward the Understanding of Jesus (New York: Macmillan, 1925).

23.   The statement by a prominent statesman ("The Rule of Law and the Settlement of International Disputes," address by William Rogers, U.S. Secretary of State, 1970 Proceedings, American Society of International Law 285), to the effect that world community should be based on international law, reverses the real relationship of these elements of systems of order. The context of the statement indicated that the speaker was viewing international law in its traditional sense of a body of rules.

24.   [T]he fundamental point for us to notice in connection with this systematization of the law is that our reasonings upon it in large masses cannot extend farther than the facts of our observation: we cannot make any progress toward building the law up out of reasonings of that kind any more, for instance, than the student of the evolution of animal life could build up the succession of forms except by studying the facts of the pathway that life has followed. Within their great systems of facts both biologist and student of law can bridge gaps, supply missing links, and work over the material to a very limited extent. But the student of law like the others must stop there, even in his study; much less has he the right to attribute to the system as such any self-realizing capacity. [A. Bentley, The Process of Government, supra, at 286-87.]

25. G.A. Resolution 375 (IV) (1949).

26. G.A. Resolution 2625 (XXV) (1970).

27. The fact that officials of the newer "anti-colonialist" countries were largely responsible for such efforts does not contradict the statement ventured at the beginning of this section that they tended to be aloof from the pre-existing body of rules and the World Court. They have, at the same time, apparently shared the general view of the nature of law held by officials of the older countries and have endeavored to give it a new orientation more favorable to their perceptions of their countries' interests.

28. U.N. Monthly Chronicle, vol. 5, Aug.-Sept. 1968, at 114, 117.

29. Ch. 3, text at n. 4 et seq., supra.

30. U.N. Monthly Chronicle, vol. 5, supra, at 117.

31. Ch. 3, text at notes 18 and 19, supra.

32. A. David, The Strategy of Treaty Termination: Lawful Breaches and Retaliations (New Haven: Yale University Press, 1975), at 173-74.

33. The Secretary-General said in 1968 that by virtue of the treaty (which had become two "covenants" adopted and opened for ratification by the General Assembly in G.A. Resolution 2200 A (XXI), in 1966) "the principles proclaimed in the Universal Declaration and the right of self-determination of all peoples were placed in an incontestable legal context." "Address by Secretary-General in Commemoration of Twentieth Anniversary of Adoption of Declaration of Human Rights," U.N. Monthly Chronicle, vol. 5, May 1968, at 65, 67.

The two treaties are: The International Covenant on Economic, Social and Cultural Rights and The International Covenant on Civil and Political Rights. For texts see annexes to G.A. Resolution 2200A (XXI) (1966).

34. In keeping with the original intent of the proposal that led to the Covenants, a draft of the Covenant on Civil and Political Rights prepared by the Human Rights Commission in 1954 would have conferred jurisdiction on the International Court of Justice to make binding decisions on questions of alleged breach. U.N. Economic and Social Council, Official Records, 18th Sess., Supp. 7, at 71 (Art. 46) (1954). It also provided that, at an earlier stage, the Human Rights Committee (provided for in the presently adopted text) should, if a settlement could not be reached in a particular case, be empowered to give its opinion as to whether there had been a breach (id., Art. 43, at 70-71). These provisions are omitted in the final adopted text, although it does contain some milder provisions of implementation.

35. G.A. Resolution 2788 (XXVI) (1971). R. Gardner, In Pursuit of World Order: U.S. Foreign Policy and International Organizations, at 149-54 (1964); press conference of Marc Schreiber, retiring Director of the U.N. Division of Human Rights, Apr. 7, 1977, U.N. Monthly Chronicle, vol. 14, May 1977, at 39, 40.

36. The International Covenant on Economic, Social and Cultural Rights came into force Jan. 3, 1976. The International Covenant on Civil and Political Rights came into force Mar. 23, 1976, as did the Optional Protocol concerning an aspect of implementation of that treaty. For texts see annexes to G.A. Resolution 2200A (XXI) (1966).

37. Professor Corbett has said, with regard to the Covenants, that "the danger is that the paper semblance of accomplishment will stand in the way of progress towards effective international promotion of human rights." P. Corbett, The Individual and World Society, at 51 (1953). He also doubted the utility of the Universal Declaration. Id. at 52-53.

38. The U.S. apparently strained relations with the U.S.S.R. by alleging that the latter had violated human rights clauses of another instrument, the Final Act of the Conference on Security and Cooperation in Europe. This debate took place at the 1977 Belgrade meeting of Representatives of participating states. N.Y. Times, Mar. 10, 1978. Whether these provisions of the Final Act were, in fact, binding treaty obligations is itself debatable, and there is no agreed forum with competence to decide such disputes about this instrument. Relations were strained because the Soviet Union knew that it was seen by much of the world as having been accused, with accompanying proofs, of violating treaty obligations to observe the human rights in question.

39. U.N. Monthly Chronicle, vol. 5, supra, at 118-19.

40. An argument has, however, been made that goes beyond the Secretary-General's position to maintain that the U.S., by adhering to the law of the sea treaty being negotiated in 1977, might be virtually forced into further and undesirable international commitments. R. Darman, "The Law of the Sea: Rethinking U.S. Interests," 56 Foreign Affairs 373, 386-88 (1977). This argument is countered in J. Charney, "United States Interests in a Convention on the Law of the Sea: The Case for Continued Efforts," 11 Vanderbilt Journal of Transnational Law 39, 42 (1978).

41. Ch. 3, text at n. 18, et seq., supra.

42. See, e.g., Ch. 3, text at n. 18, supra.

43. Hammarskjold, "The Development of a Constitutional Framework," supra, at 256.

44. Ch. 3, text at n. 21, et seq., supra. However, in a memorandum of 1976, presented to the U.S. Congress, the U.S. Department of State reiterated its advocacy of effective compulsory jurisdiction, and suggested certain amendments to the Charter and the Statute calculated to strengthen the role of the Court. "Widening Access to the International Court of Justice," 16 International Legal Materials 187, 203 (1977).

45. Rogers, "The Rule of Law and the Settlement of International Disputes," supra, at 286.

12

DISPUTE-HANDLING
INSTITUTIONS IN COMPETITION
WITH THE UNITED NATIONS

We turn in this chapter to consider non-United Nations dispute-handling resources and some uses of these that tend to build them up as institutions competitive with that world organization. One linked cause and effect of such practices has been the attempted use of the former as means of keeping disputes out of the latter.

Some preconceptions from the drafting stage of the Charter continue to contribute to this practice. A pervasive supposition was that the United Nations would be able to use force if necessary to maintain peace and that, consequently, it could ensure the satisfactory solution of all disputes. There having been no question on this point, attention could be turned to the choice of methods for the settlement of particular disputes. This line of thought has no place for the distinction between disputes that are and that are not capable of prompt and effective settlement. Of these categories it is, of course, the second that is of particular concern to this study.

PROPER ROLE OF THE UNITED NATIONS

To deal with this problem, as posed by the question whether given disputes should be referred to the United Nations or to another organization, the following guideline is proposed:

All significant international disputes not promptly and effectively settled by other means should be referred to the United Nations without prejudice to the right of the parties to resume negotiations or to refer particular disputes to other means of settlement.

All intractable disputes should be referred to the United Nations, not because the world organization is necessarily best equipped for their solution, but rather because its dispute-handling resources are better qualified than any others to handle such disputes in ways conducive to the long-range goal of permanent world security. This view has in mind, of course, proper uses of United Nations dispute-handling resources as outlined earlier in this study. In fact, these procedures are here believed to represent, as a rule, the best that can be done in difficult cases not only in the interests of long-range goals but also in the practical interests of achieving agreed-on solutions.

The above-proposed guideline involves but a small modification of Article 37(1) of the Charter, which provides:

> Should the parties to a dispute of the nature referred to in Article 33 fail to settle it by the means indicated in that Article, they shall refer it to the Security Council.

Article 33, referred to in the foregoing paragraph, provides:

> 1. The parties to any dispute, the continuance of which is likely to endanger the maintenance of international peace and security, shall, first of all, seek a solution by negotiation, enquiry, mediation, conciliation, arbitration, judicial settlement, resort to regional agencies or arrangements, or other peaceful means of their own choice.
>
> 2. The Security Council shall, when it deems necessary, call upon the parties to settle their disputes by such means.

In the perspective of the present discussion, Article 37(1) is the Charter provision to be given emphasis. Article 33 is to be de-emphasized. In its simplest interpretation its first paragraph can be said to do no more than express, first, the basic truth that solutions of disputes require agreement between the parties and, second, the basic Charter concept that parties to disputes should, first of all, seek solutions among themselves. In this sense, the provision is harmless. The enumeration of modes of settlement, however, is undesirable in that it tends to enhance their importance—to "institutionalize" them. There is a similar tendency in the phrase "first of all," which can be read as emphasizing the need for resorting to one or the other of the listed procedures. Paragraph 2 completes a provision that gives states an apparent basis for claiming that particular cases should be submitted to one of the enumerated procedures instead of to the United Nations and that the Security Council may properly order parties to do so.

Another provision to be de-emphasized is Article 36, authorizing the Council to recommend that the parties refer their disputes to "appropriate procedures or methods of adjustment." This authorization is reiterated in Article 37(2). Article 37(1), which was quoted above and is here considered the relevant provision to be emphasized, is thus followed by one that tends to mitigate it and give it a circular effect. That is to say, pursuant to these provisions, a dispute that proves incapable of solution by other means should be referred to the Security Council, which may then immediately recommend that it be referred to some other procedure it deems appropriate.

The Charter provisions presently under discussion, Articles 33, 36, and 37, are in Chapter VI, which defines the peaceful settlement function and particularly that of the Security Council. Another group of relevant provisions that falls under Chapter VIII, concerning regional arrangements, will be discussed shortly.

From the perspective of this discussion, an inappropriate use was made of Article 33 by the Soviet Union, in 1945, in an effort to keep its dispute with Iran out of the United Nations and have it handled by negotiations between the parties. The case involved the allegedly wrongful presence of Soviet troops in northern Iran, demands by the former country that the troops remain there, support for an alleged local autonomy movement, demands for Soviet oil concessions, and related matters.[1] When Iran brought the dispute to the Council, the U.S.S.R. asserted that the matter was being handled by negotiations between the parties, that efforts of this kind were required by Article 33 of the Charter, and that there was accordingly no foundation for placing the dispute on the Council's agenda.[2] The Council acquiesced to some extent, leaving the case within the bilateral negotiating framework. However, it placed the item on its agenda, kept it there despite Soviet objections, and called for progress reports.[3]

The Soviet position seems rather patently to have been designed to keep the organization from handling the case and to allow the dispute to be settled through bilateral "negotiations" between a great power and a weak state, the former already having troops stationed on the territory of the latter.

That the case was ultimately resolved in a manner satisfactory to Iran[4] is by no means due exclusively to the negotiations that were ostensibly the basic mode of settlement. An essential contribution appears to have been made by the United Nations in focusing world attention on the case with the effect of contributing to the ultimate decision of the U.S.S.R. to yield.[5]

The case is cited here not to suggest that the United Nations erred in its handling of the case but rather to illustrate how a state can use Article 33 as an argument for keeping a dispute out of the United Nations. Though the outcome was successful from the point of view of the organization, the case may have contributed in some degree to building "negotiation" as an institution, and thus to increasing the ability of parties, in some situations, to insist on its use even when other parties object.

Perhaps encouraged by the Soviet position in the Iranian case, as well as by some Charter provisions, a statement by the Indian delegation in the West Irian case may, in its turn, have tended to encourage subsequent efforts by states to keep intractable disputes out of the United Nations:

> When two Member States are deadlocked in a long-
> standing dispute of this character, there is no sub-
> stitute for negotiations. Any dictation by the United
> Nations would be pointless, unwise and contrary to
> the spirit of the Charter. Indeed, there is no instance,
> as far as I know, in which the United Nations has
> sought to settle a dispute between two Member States
> over the head of one of them. . . . [6]

The Netherlands, in this case, had indicated its readiness to relinquish its control of West Irian and turned the debate in the General Assembly to consideration of the proposal that any solution should recognize the right of self-determination of the West Irian people. [7]

It is true that in the vote that followed soon after the above statement was made the Netherlands proposal was rejected, the member states of "anti-colonial" persuasion supporting the position of Indonesia that, since it claimed to be sovereign of the territory, the right of self-determination did not apply. There was, accordingly, no Assembly majority on which to base a suggestion that, in this particular case, the Assembly should have continued to exercise surveillance.

Neither is it desirable, however, to deny that it has this power as an attribute of its basic peaceful settlement function. The effort of the Indian delegation to pose policy alternatives, in terms of either Assembly "dictation" or total relinquishment in favor of negitiations between the parties, is unwarranted. The last sentence of the above-quoted statement is contradicted by United Nations insistence, year after year, on the right of self-determination of peoples in such political entities as Algeria, Morocco, Rhodesia, South Africa, and Portuguese overseas territories.

The guideline proposed in this chapter is formulated so as to recognize the right of the United Nations to remain cognizant of disputes even when they are proclaimed to have been settled by the parties, or by states claiming to be the sole parties. This right should be exercised when requisite majorities perceive "settlements" as disposing of the rights of third parties who have not been properly consulted, or as being in any significant manner contrary to the long-range goals that it is the purpose of the United Nations to secure.

REGIONAL SECURITY ORGANIZATIONS

Regional security organizations comprise an important dispute-handling institution which may be given roles in competition with the world rule of the United Nations for the maintenance of peace and security.

While they are juridically separate from the United Nations, such institutions are the subject of Chapter VIII of the latter organization's Charter, a fact that, apart from the detailed contents of that chapter, must tend to enhance the general importance of such organizations. This chapter of the Charter is largely devoted to defining the relationship between the United Nations and regional organizations with respect to dispute-handling activities.

These relationships, as thus defined, reflect the relative importance customarily attached to collective measures, or "enforcement" activity, as compared with peaceful settlement. Regional exercise of the latter function was considered potentially useful, and it was not feared that it would be disruptive of the role of the world organization. Article 52, the first Article of Chapter VIII, encourages the use of such procedures.

Regional "enforcement" activity was also considered potentially useful but at the same time potentially dangerous to the role of the United Nations; it was accordingly provided in Article 53 that it should be employed only with the authorization of that organization. A provision containing this limitation had been included in the Dumbarton Oaks Proposals.[8] Another section provided that the future U.N. Charter should not preclude "action taken or authorized in relation to enemy states as a result of the present war by the Governments having responsibility for such action."[9] At the San Francisco Conference the U.S.S.R. and France, as states immediately concerned with this authorization, insisted that it be written into Article 53 as an exception to the "authorization clause" of that provision. The exception, in fact, refers explicitly to possible action by regional organizations. At the same time, the American states, other than the United States, mounted strong pressure for an exception authorizing independent enforcement action by the inter-American system.[10] This demand, especially when juxtaposed to the Soviet-French demand, created a dilemma for the United States delegation.[11] As one delegate said:

> [T]he Security Council would be a very weak body if it was deprived of jurisdiction over events in this hemisphere. On the other hand, it was difficult to see how this hemisphere could be left under the Security Council and Europe outside.[12]

On the broader Conference scene, fears were expressed that the whole concept of a world security system would be undermined if regional organizations were allowed to take independent "enforcement action."[13]

The debate, one of the most intense and comprehensive of the Conference, led to a compromise[14] of which one component was the inclusion of the "authorization clause," limited by recognition of the right of European states to take regional security measures vis-a-vis former enemy states; another was a new provision, Article 51, which recognizes the right of individual and collective self-defense in the event of armed attack.[15] While this provision avoided direct mention of regional organizations, its principal purpose was to enable such organizations to act in emergencies without waiting for United Nations authorization.

Regional Peaceful Settlement Function

The solution embodied in the Charter also includes the following paragraphs of Article 52, which encourage resort to the peaceful settlement functions of regional organizations:

> 2. The Members of the United Nations entering into such [regional] arrangements or constituting such agencies shall make every effort to achieve pacific settlement of local disputes through such regional agencies before referring them to the Security Council.

> 3. The Security Council shall encourage the development of pacific settlement of local disputes through such regional arrangements or by such regional agencies either on the initiative of the states concerned or by reference from the Security Council.

These carefully formulated provisions were a manifestation of the tendency, also exemplified by Article 33, of the framers to draw up categories of processes by which disputes should be settled in accordance with their circumstances, while overlooking the categorization here considered of overriding importance, namely the distinction between disputes that can be promptly and effectively settled and those that cannot.

Efforts between 1954 and 1968 to have a series of American cases referred to the Organization of American States (OAS) were successful to an extent that doubtless convinced many people that, in regard to regional matters, regional organizations rightfully enjoy priority over the United Nations.

In 1954 Guatemala complained to the Security Council that it was the victim of military aggression from neighboring countries.[16] Some members of the Council invoked the above-quoted paragraphs of Article 52 and cited Article 33 as grounds for the contention that the dispute should first be considered by the OAS. A draft resolution with this intended effect was vetoed by the Soviet delegation,[17] but opponents of Council consideration of the dispute were able to confine the debate to this issue until the dispute was terminated by the collapse of the Guatemalan regime.[18] The states responsible for preventing a substantive debate in the Council were led by the United States, which opposed the Guatemalan regime on the grounds that it embodied the threat of communist infiltration into the western hemisphere.[19] Supporters of the Guatemalan regime in a Council debate might have influenced world opinion by arguing that the attack on that country represented violations of the Charter with respect to the use of force and aggression, and that it was a wrongful intervention in a matter of domestic concern. In such a case opponents of the Guatemalan regime could have seen the Security Council as a hostile forum, and thus have desired to confine the dispute to the more sympathetic environment of the OAS. In this aspect, a resemblance can be seen between this case and the Soviet-Iranian dispute of a decade earlier, in which the Soviet Union attempted to restrict the discussion to bilateral negotiations, excluding the United Nations.[20]

The Guatemalan case was no doubt damaging to the United Nations in that world opinion must have seen it as a defeat for the organization's major purpose of applying collective measures to deal with violence and threatened violence. Secretary-General Hammarskjold objected to the proposition that a regional organization could supersede the Security Council in its major responsibility for the maintenance of peace and security.[21]

From the perspective of this discussion, a damaging aspect was the intermixing and confusion of the collective measures and peaceful settlement functions of the organization. Such intermixtures more customarily take place by the unwarranted interjection of some elements of "enforcement" into situations that should be handled by the peaceful settlement function, properly limited to powers of discussion and recommendation. In this case it took place in the opposite direction, by attempts to force a justified appeal to the collective measures function into the category of peaceful settlement.

Cuban complaints against the United States, beginning in 1960, gave rise to debates as to whether the United Nations or the OAS was the proper forum for their consideration. Cuba alleged that the United States was giving aid to Cuban counter-revolutionary elements and had committed violations of Cuban air space and that it was responsible for economic aggression, diplomatic pressures, [22] and, later, preparations for aggression [23] and actual aggression. [24] Eventually embracing the Bay of Pigs episode, the dispute was of the intractable variety and should have been referred to the United Nations as soon as this fact became evident. The United States and like-minded representatives in the Security Council succeeded for a time in preventing substantive debates on the complaint in the United Nations by claiming that the case should first be considered by the OAS. Substantive debates in the United Nations ultimately took place, but the argument concerning the proper forum was resumed intermittently, with the effect of contributing to the prestige and standing of the OAS and probably strengthening the impression, on the part of some, that it was the proper organ to consider the case, notwithstanding Cuba's refusal to resort to it. A Security Council resolution of July 19, 1960, [25] provided, inter alia:

The Security Council

*   *   *   *   *

Noting that this situation is under consideration by the Organization of American States,

1. Decides to adjourn the consideration of this question pending the receipt of a report from the Organization of American States;

2. Invites the members of the Organization of American States to lend their assistance toward the achievement of a peaceful settlement of the present situation in accordance with the purposes and principles of the Charter of the United Nations. . . .

This resolution was referred to in Assembly Resolution 1616 (XV), in April 1961, following the Bay of Pigs episode. Paragraphs referring more directly to the desirability of using the OAS forum were passed by Committee 1[26] and deleted only by reason of failure to meet the two-thirds voting requirements in the plenary session.[27]

The OAS itself, at the Seventh Meeting of Consultation of Foreign Ministers, adopted the "Declaration of San Jose, Costa Rica," proclaiming that "all member states of the regional organization are under obligation to submit to the discipline of the inter-American system" and declaring that "all controversies between member states should be resolved by the measures for peaceful solution that are contemplated in the inter-American system."[28] Also, in Resolution II of that meeting, an inter-American Good Offices Committee was established, to which the United States made several subsequent efforts to have the case referred.[29]

A prominent argument in favor of referring the case to the OAS was that, as stated by the United States Representative in the Security Council:

> [I]t is not a question of which is greater or which is
> less—the Organization of American States or the
> United Nations. The point is that it makes sense—
> and the Charter so indicates—to go to the regional or-
> ganization first and to the United Nations as a place of
> last resort. . . .[30]

The French Representative said that under Article 33 of the Charter it was mandatory that the case be taken first to the OAS.[31] The Italian Representative said that "if the regional organization were bypassed, a situation could be implicitly brought about in which the responsibility and functions of the Organization of American States might be disregarded and their effectiveness and prestige impaired."[32]

The statements of the actors in these situations seem to be predicated—as is the Charter itself—on the proposition that all disputes are soluble, and that they are merely engaged in selecting the proper forum for the settlement of particular situations. At the same time, it is plain to informed observers that some of these situations are beyond available means of settlement, and that officials are endeavoring to push given situations into one forum or the other in the hope of gaining political advantage. The situation is favorable to the growth of the illusion/disillusion syndrome.

Confusion and the straining of relations also seem to be likely consequences when states wishing to bring disputes into the United Nations for handling pursuant to the peaceful settlement function encounter efforts to force them into other forums where they do not wish to go. Their claims of right to access to the United Nations appear to be at least as valid as the claim of other parties to have recourse to other forums. Article 103 of the Charter[33] is here believed to be indicative of a broader general intention on the part of the framers to give to the United Nations at least the position of primus inter pares in such issues. To these considerations may be added the poor prospects for settling disputes by forcing them into procedures unacceptable to some of the parties.

Tangible Pressures by Regional Agencies

Whereas the Charter encourages resort to regional procedures for peaceful settlement, regional "enforcement action" is forbidden by Article 53 except with United Nations authorization.[34]

The guideline proposed in this chapter is in accord with the latter provision. A dispute in which the application of tangible pressures is contemplated has not been effectively settled. It is, therefore, one that should be referred to the United Nations. Article 53 was intended to recognize the United Nations as the competent organ to decide whether measures of tangible pressure should be applied.

The debate at San Francisco that led to the broad compromise solution under discussion involved several misconceptions that became imbedded in the Charter.

One was the stating of the rule just referred to in terms of "enforcement action." This phrase, as well as the preferable "collective measures," lends itself to efforts to categorize particular measures on the basis of political expedience, in such a way as to authorize actions deemed by majorities to be desirable and exclude those deemed undesirable. The real intent of advocates of the rule was to prevent independent regional measures that could tend to subvert the world role of the United Nations. This purpose is not served if such pressures can be applied on the pretext that they do not conform to particular definitions of "enforcement action." The rule should, accordingly, have been stated as requiring authorization for all regional applications of tangible pressures.

A second misconception was a general failure to recognize that some disputes being handled pursuant to peaceful settlement functions of competent organizations may prove intractable and that persistence in attempting to apply this regional function in such cases can be just as damaging to the world role of the United Nations as can regional "enforcement action." This misconception accounts for the fact that at San Francisco the relevant debate took place in connection with the regional collective measures function.

The following provision for the Charter was proposed by the French delegation but was not adopted:

> Should the Council not succeed in reaching a de-
> cision, the members of the Organization reserve to
> themselves the right to act as they may consider
> necessary in the interest of peace, right and justice.[35]

A resemblance is to be observed between this paragraph and Article
15(7) of the Covenant of the League of Nations:

> If the Council fails to reach a report which is
> unanimously agreed to by the members thereof,
> other than the Representatives of one or more of
> the parties to the dispute, the Members of the League
> reserve to themselves the right to take such action as
> they shall consider necessary for the maintenance of
> right and justice.

The French proposal was considered in the context of possible exceptions to the "authorization clause" of Article 53. Other suggested exceptions included various combinations of provisions that
would recognize the general right of self-defense, the right of regional self-defense, and the latter right as applicable in particular
to the inter-American system. The United States was active in the
discussion in part because of the interest of other American states.
Some members of the United States delegation expressed apprehension that such a "wide open" exception as that embodied in the French
proposal could wreck the United Nations.[36]
    The British delegation indicated strong apprehension toward
independent measures by regional organizations:

> [E]mbodying in the Charter a draft of the character
> brought forward by the United States[37] could only
> have the effect of encouraging groups of states
> everywhere to enter into regional arrangements and
> organizations. The whole concept of world organi-
> zation would be thus undermined. . . .
>
> He had thought that the French formula would meet
> the situation satisfactorily. He was intensely afraid
> of any formula which draws attention to regional or-
> ganizations. Regionalism is the thing which fright-
> ened him.[38]

    The compromise adopted, forbidding regional collective mea-
sures independent of the United Nations except for measures necessary in self-defense, is here considered correct in principle. The
exception will be considered shortly.

The cases that best illustrate the reason for the rule are those of Hungary in 1956, the Dominican Republic in 1965, and Czechoslovakia in 1968. The first and third were military takeovers of the countries by the Soviet Union in order to halt what the latter country feared as anti-communist trends of government. In the latter case, to a much greater extent than in the former, the Soviet Union sought to legitimize its action and share its responsibility by invoking the "socialist community" as the responsible actor.[39] In turn this response merged into the "Brezhnev Doctrine," which holds that socialism is the common cause of all socialist countries and that all should come to the defense of the regime in any socialist country in which it is threatened.[40] In neither case was Security Council authorization sought or given.

It seems possible that the Soviet Union was encouraged in this course by a series of western hemisphere cases in which the OAS applied measures without United Nations authorization. The case of the Dominican Republic may have been particularly relevant, since in it the United States originally applied force in a civil conflict for the stated purpose of preventing the establishment of a communist regime in the Dominican Republic.[41] Soon thereafter, on United States initiative, the OAS established a military force that replaced the American force and continued to function in the Dominican Republic until elections could be held and a new regime installed.

Following are the preamble paragraphs that seek to explain the purpose of the OAS resolution establishing the force:

> The formation of an inter-American force will signify ipso facto the transformation of the forces presently in Dominican territory into another force that will not be that of one state or of a group of states but that of the Organization of American States, which Organization is charged with the responsibility of interpreting the democratic will of its members;

> The American states being under the obligation to provide reciprocal assistance to each other, the Organization is under greater obligation to safeguard the principles of the Charter [i.e., the charter of the OAS] and to do everything possible so that in situations such as that prevailing in the Dominican Republic appropriate measures may be taken leading to the re-establishment of peace and normal democratic conditions;

> The Organization of American States being competent to assist the member states in the

preservation of peace and the re-establishment of
normal democratic conditions, it is also competent
to provide the means that reality and circumstances
require and that prudence counsels as adequate for
the accomplishment of such purposes. . . .[42]

The emphasis on "peace" in this statement was perhaps intended to indicate that the measure in question was not in the "enforcement" category and therefore did not require Security Council
authorization. To similar effect was the statement of the Malaysian
delegation in the Security Council that "an operation undertaken for
the pacific settlement of a dispute may conceivably involve a minimum amount of the use of force."[43] Authorities have also maintained that this operation fell outside the "enforcement" category on
the basis of the World Court's limitation on the scope of that function in Certain Expenses and its consequent holding that ONUC was
not in that category.[44]

The operation in the Dominican Republic nevertheless had the
clear appearance of an intervention, a subject concerning which
Latin American countries have been traditionally sensitive. Strong
opposition within those countries to the OAS action concentrated on
this principle. Some governments that upheld it did so with the purpose of ending what they considered wrongful intervention by the
United States.[45] The OAS could not justify its action more precisely on an alleged right to ensure democracy within the hemisphere,
because such a role had been considered for it by its members and
rejected as incompatible with the principle of non-intervention.[46]

It seems possible, in view of the foregoing considerations,
that the Soviet Union invoked the "socialist community" in the case
of Czechoslovakia with considerable assurance that it would not be
challenged on grounds of non-compliance with the "authorization
clause" of Article 53 of the Charter.[47]

This situation may, in turn, have contributed to the markedly
lesser protest in the United Nations in regard to the action in
Czechoslovakia as compared to that which resulted from the take-
over of Hungary in 1956. Not only was the immediate protest
greater in the earlier case, but it continued for several years, a
phenomenon that did not occur in the case of Czechoslovakia.

It is not suggested that the lesser protest in the later case was
directly due to the inability of opponents of the action to claim violation of the "authorization clause" of Article 53. It may have been
due in part to this circumstance; it was also brought about by the
simple fact that the United Nations had been displaced in the Dominican case and other American cases and its role allowed to be superseded by a regional organization. The grounds of protest were thus

lessened for those who objected to a regional action in the Czechoslovak case.

This last consideration should eliminate any tendency to think
that because other grounds, based on the Charter, were brought
forward in opposition to the Soviet action—particularly with respect
to wrongful intervention and wrongful use of force—the non-avail-
ability of the grounds here under discussion was a matter of relatively minor importance. The requirement of United Nations authorization for regional enforcement is a rule of unique importance intended to ensure that the world role of the United Nations could not
be subordinated to regional activities. It thus, in a sense, encapsu-
lates the need for a world security organization as perceived by the
framers of the Charter. It also provides a means by which, in appropriate circumstances, this need can be laid before the world's
people.

Another part of the compromise solution of which the "authorization clause" formed a part was Article 51 of the Charter, providing as follows:

> Nothing in the present Charter shall impair the
> inherent right of individual or collective self-defense
> if an armed attack occurs against a Member of the
> United Nations, until the Security Council has taken
> measures necessary to maintain international peace
> and security. Measures taken by Members in the ex-
> ercise of this right of self-defense shall be immediate-
> ly reported to the Security Council and shall not in any
> way affect the authority and responsibility of the Secur-
> ity Council under the present Charter to take at any
> time such action as it deems necessary in order to
> maintain or restore international peace and security.

The "quarantine" applied by the OAS in the Cuban missile
crisis of 1962 is illustrative of the kind of case in which the exception could be useful, though it was not invoked in that case. This
was a crisis precipitated by the shipment to Cuba, and the planned
installation there, of nuclear missiles that could threaten most of
the western hemisphere. The United States government, on becoming aware of the threat, informed the OAS, which authorized its
members "individually or collectively" to take measures, including
the use of force, to prevent the continued receipt by Cuba of the
military equipment in question, and to prevent missiles already in
Cuba from becoming an active threat.[48] Under this authority, the
"quarantine"—involving the visit and search at sea of ships approach-
ing Cuba, with the intent of stopping any found to be carrying missiles—was carried out, largely by United States military forces.

It is believed that the "quarantine" should have been regarded as an exercise of regional collective self-defense, notwithstanding the facts that Article 51 of the Charter, which recognizes this concept, limits it to cases of armed attack and that the situation being dealt with did not consist of such an attack. This view results from an attempt to answer the question of which course of action will be most conducive, or least damaging, to the goal of an adequate degree of community sentiment to ensure world peace and security.

Invocation of collective self-defense as justification for this action was rejected because no imminent attack seemed to be threatened by the missiles and, therefore, resort to this theory would represent too broad a construction of "armed attack" and would establish a bad precedent. [49]

The present discussion holds that this apprehension departed from the reality of international relations. A greater danger lay in the course followed, which allowed the U.N. to be superseded by a regional organization in a matter involving international peace and security, and thus damaged it in its ability to perform its basic role.

The clause of Article 51 that limits collective self-defense to cases of armed attack is a manifestation of the misconception, reflected in various parts of the Charter, that the organization would prove capable of dealing effectively with all significant disputes. The need for individual or collective action in self-defense was seen as arising only in emergency situations involving armed attack; in all other cases requiring force it was evidently thought that the United Nations would be able to preserve peace in accordance with Charter principles. Had this in fact proved to be the case, and were states interested in employing the right of self-defense only in cases of bona fide need, the rule of Article 51 would have been adequate, and states would have acquiesced in it. However, the underlying reality applicable to the whole concept of self-defense is that states will take such action as they deem necessary for their security. [50] Since the United Nations has not, to the time of writing, eliminated the need states feel to rely on themselves for their security, its members must have tacitly retained their traditionally claimed right of self-defense.

Consequently, had the "quarantine" been officially recognized as an exercise by the OAS of the right of self-defense notwithstanding the absence of an armed attack, the effect would have been merely to interpret Article 51 in accordance with the underlying reality and would have been generally so recognized.

The question whether it is preferable to resort to regional organizations for collective self-defense or for concerned states to act on their own responsibilities outside of international organizations, is hypothetical rather than practical. The impracticality of

a guideline seeking to carry out the latter policy is indicated by the
various defensive alliance systems that have been constructed during the period of the United Nations. Such a system forms an integral part of the Organization of American States, and regional
solidarity in the western hemisphere has been, at least at times, a
policy with strong emotional overtones. It would not be practical to
suggest regional collective defense apart from this organization,
nor European defense outside of the North Atlantic Treaty Organization.

The framers of the Charter, recognizing the overriding problem of safeguarding the world role of the United Nations, saw no
recourse in this dilemma but to recognize a right of self-defense as
an exception to the general prohibition against independent enforcement measures by regional organizations. As far as our proposed
guidelines are concerned, an equivalent proposal is made at the end
of the present chapter.

What, then, was the legal nature of the quarantine measure?
Several officials of the U.S. Department of State, writing on the
subject shortly after the crisis, concentrated their arguments on the
non-applicability of the "authorization clause," thus in effect indicating that this was a regional "enforcement action" taken independently of the United Nations.

The reasons generally advanced for the alleged non-applicability of the "authorization clause" were, first, that the "quarantine"
did not fall within a proper definition of "enforcement action" as employed in Article 53 and, second, that the clause had become outmoded, or in any event should not be applied, at least in cases of
western hemisphere concern.

The first line of argument derogates from the scope of the
authorization requirement but does not controvert the principle it is
based on. Several arguments of this kind had been advanced in earlier cases involving the Dominican Republic and Cuba, which will be
considered below, and were referred to where appropriate in the
statements concerning the missile crisis. The principal one in the
latter context was that the OAS action initiating the blockade was
recommendatory and thus could not be "enforcement action."[51]

The second line of argument seeks, in effect, to erase the
"authorization clause" from the Charter; it is more damaging,
since it has the effect of proclaiming that a regional organization
may rightfully and constitutionally act independently in regional
matters, thus displacing the United Nations.

The principal argument along this line advanced at the time
was set forth in an article by the Legal Adviser of the U.S. Department of State.[52] It invoked the theory of the Uniting for Peace
resolution, which holds that the responsibility of the Security Council

for the maintenance of peace and security is "primary," and not exclusive. It also took note of the fact that the Assembly has been
held to have a residual power to act when the Council is prevented
by its unanimity rule (i.e., the veto) from fulfilling its primary responsibility in particular cases. This view is here considered
sound, and applicable as well to the granting of authorization, pursuant to Article 53, for regional measures. However, the argument under discussion goes on to hold that, in addition to the Assembly, regional organizations, pursuant to the provisions of Chapter
VIII of the Charter, may be employed to fill the gap created by the
inability of the Council to act. Since Article 53 explicitly forbids
"enforcement action" by the regional organizations that are the subject of Chapter VIII, this argument apparently seeks to sell the pass
that that provision was specifically designed to defend.

That the hinterland thus left undefended, namely the world
security role of the United Nations, is here regarded as important
to the achievement of permanent world security need not be reiterated. It is equally clear that this view differs from that of the government responsible for the arguments presently under consideration. In its view, given the paralysis of the Security Council,
"other organizational peacekeeping efforts" could be resorted to.[53]
However, insofar as these efforts result in giving priority to other
organizations, they are here considered undesirable as subversive
of the role of the U.N., which is irreplaceable. The fact that, as
was pointed out in the statements under consideration, the U.N. remains the paramount organization and could call the OAS to account
for wrongful acts, does not remedy the situation. The harm was
done in this case by indicating to interested observers that in an important dispute or situation the U.N. could properly be, as it was in
fact, superseded by a regional organization.

These arguments concerning the "quarantine" tended to "legitimize" the subsequent OAS decision to deploy troops in the Dominican
Republic without seeking United Nations authorization. This OAS
force replaced the U.S. troops and served, in its turn, to "legitimize" the original United States intervention in that crisis, widely
regarded as wrongful. Both of these cases would seem inevitably to
have contributed to the Brezhnev Doctrine, which was precipitated
by the Czechoslovak case in 1968.

The two American cases mentioned were part of a series of
cases between 1960 and 1967 in which the OAS applied tangible pressures without United Nations authorization. They also, therefore,
advanced the same theme of supersession of the United Nations by
the regional organization though for the most part less vividly.

In considering these cases, an additional policy course to
those just suggested may be assessed for its possible applicability

and desirability. It will, incidentally, enable this chapter to be concluded on a more positive note than would otherwise be possible. The policy in question is the application, in appropriate cases, of the principle underlying the Uniting for Peace resolution. According to that resolution, when the Council is prevented by the unanimity rule from fulfilling its primary responsibility in a situation deemed by the Assembly to require the application of measures, the latter body may exercise a residual responsibility by proceeding to initiate the action deemed necessary. The same theory could apparently with perfect logic be applied to the "authorization clause" of Article 53, with the effect that if the Council is prevented from exercising its primary role in the granting of authorization as stipulated in that Article, the Assembly possesses a residual authority to do so.[54] The potential of this possible course of action may be suggested by some of the cases now to be considered. Other possible courses of action to be kept in mind, depending upon the case, are regional collective self-defense and independent state action.

In 1960 the Trujillo regime of the Dominican Republic was found by the OAS to be guilty of wrongful acts against Venezuela amounting to intervention and aggression; in consequence, regional diplomatic and limited economic measures were applied against the Dominican Republic.[55] In the United Nations Security Council, the Soviet Union, without objecting to the measures, proposed that they called for that body's authorization under Article 53 of the Charter. The American states denied that this was necessary, apparently foreseeing possible future cases in which the Soviet Union might wish to use the "authorization" requirement as a means of obstructing necessary regional measures. The latter group of states, along with other like-minded states in the Council, were successful in defeating the Soviet proposal and obtaining passage of a resolution in which that organ merely took note of the OAS measures.[56]

Members of this Council majority brought forward both of the lines of argument advanced in connection with the "quarantine" measure, namely that the action did not fit the definition of "enforcement action" under Article 53 of the Charter and that the "authorization clause" of that provision should be regarded, in effect, as nonexistent.

Details of the first line of argument are, again, not strongly relevant to our discussion. However, one contention may be mentioned as showing that the approach being followed was based on expediency rather than on any consistent theory. This was the argument that the phrase "enforcement" refers only to measures of force[57] and that, since force was not involved in the measures against the Dominican Republic in 1960, United Nations authorization would not be required. According to the same rule, authorization would have been required for the "quarantine" measure in 1962 and the OAS force deployed in the Dominican Republic in 1965, since both involved the use of force. Authorization was not, however, sought in either case, and the claim that it was required in the Dominican case was strongly resisted.

More important to the present thesis is the second line of argument, which apparently sought to eliminate the "authorization clause" as an effective Charter provision. The United States delegation, in this connection, said that:

> It is noteworthy that Article 54 clearly envisages the possibility of activities by regional agencies for the maintenance of international peace and security, in regard to which the responsibility of the regional organization to the Security Council is purely that of keeping it informed. [58]

Article 54, in fact, requires that the Council be kept informed of regional actions undertaken for the maintenance of peace and security; it in no way derogates from the requirement of the preceding article that "enforcement actions" of regional organizations have United Nations approval.

The Argentine Representative said that the Council's taking note of the OAS action would amount to a "complete demonstration of the coordination which should exist between the regional agency and the international Organization," and went on to say that "however Article 53 . . . may be interpreted in the future, legally organized regional groups . . . must have sufficient authority to solve problems confined within the limits of the region involved."[59]

The Ecuadoran Representative said that:

> Article 53 . . . cannot and should not be used to make a regional agency's action rigidly dependent upon authorization by the Security Council. On the contrary, the relations between the Council and the regional agencies should be so flexible as to permit these agencies to take effective action for the maintenance of international peace and security in the light of regional conditions and without necessarily bringing regional problems before a world forum. [60]

Such downgrading of the "authorization clause," and thus of the entire role of the United Nations, should have been avoided if possible. It could have been avoided without sacrifice in this case, viewed on its own facts, since there was no opposition to the measures. It was the precedent that the majority in this case sought to avoid.

As to the situation that would have existed if the Soviet Union had intended to veto the planned regional action, this case has some instructive aspects and could illuminate some of the potentialities and problems of invoking the possible courses of action presently under discussion. Since, however, essentially the same factual situation, with some additional aspects of interest, was presented as real issues in the ensuing cases involving Cuba, we may pass to these.

In the first such case, an arms embargo was applied by the OAS against Cuba at the Eighth Meeting of Consultation of Foreign Ministers of that organization, held at Punta del Esta, Uruguay, early in 1962.[61] The U.S. delegation, which outlined the complaint against Cuba, mentioned aggression but did not allege Cuban intervention in specific countries. The major charge seems to have been that Cuba, by its adherence to the Marxist-Leninist bloc, had endangered the security of the hemisphere.[62] The most important action taken at the meeting, in regard to this issue, appears to have been the exclusion of Cuba from participation in the OAS.

Cuba and the Soviet Union argued in the Security Council that the arms embargo was an "enforcement action" that required United Nations authorization under Article 53. Opponents of this position, who were successful in preventing application of the clause, argued along the lines earlier employed in the Dominican Republic-Venezuelan case, sketched above.[63] Cuba proposed that the question of applicability be referred to the World Court,[64] but this suggestion was brushed aside. The United States delegation argued on this point that the question submitted by Cuba posed no substantial issue, that it was already decided by the Security Council, and that it was motivated by political rather than legal considerations.[65]

In 1964 an investigating committee of the OAS reported that Cuba was guilty of "terrorism, sabotage, assault, and guerrilla warfare" against Venezuela with the purpose of subverting Venezuelan institutions and of overthrowing that country's government.[66] On the basis of this report, the Ninth Meeting of Consultation of Ministers of Foreign Affairs decided that Cuba was guilty of aggression and intervention, and initiated OAS diplomatic and economic pressures against that country.[67] In 1967, again on the basis of an investigation, the OAS found that Cuban subversive actions had continued and that, in addition, wrongful interventions by that country against Bolivia and other American states had occurred. In consequence, the previous measures against Cuba were strengthened, and non-member states were asked to collaborate in making them more effective.[68]

Neither in the 1964 nor in the 1967 episode did the OAS seek authorization for its measures from the Security Council. More remarkable is the fact that neither did Cuba or the Soviet Union. The issue went through by default. This may appear to have been a victory for the American policy pursued in the cases of 1960 between the Dominican Republic and Venezuela and of 1962 involving Cuba, in which erasure of the "authorization clause" of Article 53 from the Charter was apparently sought. On the other hand, a factor in the situation may have been that in the later case against Cuba, American states were in possession of hard evidence of flagrant acts of terrorism and related activities by Cuban agents, and dissemination of information concerning those acts would have been damaging to that country in the eyes of world opinion. Consequently, Cuba and the Soviet Union may have considered it to their advantage that the issue be debated in the restricted forum of the OAS rather than in the world forum of the United Nations. This view tends to vindicate the guideline proposed above in this chapter, which relies for its "practicality" on the proposition that at least one party in an intractable dispute is likely to be opposed to its reference to a regional organization. In this view, even though the American states did not move to take the case to the world organization, it would have been in their interest to do so.

The OAS itself appears to have adopted this view to some degree in its Resolution IV of the Twelfth Meeting of Consultation of Foreign Ministers, in 1967, recommending that allegations of wrongful intervention by Cuba be referred to the United Nations.[69] The immediate motivation appears to have been the consideration that Cuba, having been denied participation in the OAS, was not under the jurisdiction of that organization, whereas it was within the jurisdiction of the United Nations. Since OAS measures of tangible pressure were in force against Cuba, it seems that, in adopting the resolution under discussion, that organization was seeking moral sanctions against Cuba on the part of the world organization. Indeed, this motivation was made explicit by the Colombian delegation, one of the resolution's sponsors and the first to speak in support of it in the Meeting of Consultation.[70] He said that even if Latin America should be defeated in United Nations votes, the discussion of the moral issue in the world forum could only have beneficial effects on public opinion.

Whatever the mixture of motives, the mere expression of the desirability of referring disputes to the United Nations seems to mark an important change in the previous policy of endeavoring to maintain a monopoly of jurisdiction for the OAS in regional matters. As one authority has said:

> In recommending that acts of Cuban intervention be
> taken to the United Nations, . . . the governments
> for the first time recognized U.N. activity in such
> cases to be appropriate. At the very least, this
> created an important precedent. If followed con-
> sistently, it could bring about a very significant
> abdication of regional action in the security field. [71]

It seems of some significance that at the same time as the OAS
was engaged in applying tangible pressures against Cuba, its members should have been seeking a means of applying moral pressures
against that country in the world forum of the United Nations. Resolution IV of the Twelfth Meeting can be said to have represented a
modification of a previous decision in favor of the former of these
courses. It can, by the same token, be regarded as a step in the
direction of recognizing the applicability of the "authorization
clause" of Article 53 and the possibility of applying to it the principle of the Uniting for Peace resolution.

Acts of Cuban agents of the kind under discussion seem to have
diminished after the Twelfth Meeting of Consultation in 1967. Was
there a connection, and if so, can the diminution be attributed to a
greater extent to the "enforcement" measures or to the threat that
if continued, the Cuban actions would be discussed in the United Nations? The possibility that the latter was the stronger influence is
at least suggested by two considerations. First was the fact that
these actions did not end as a result of the measures applied in 1964;
as a result of their continuance it was found necessary to strengthen
and extend those measures in 1967. Second was the indication by
Cuba and like-minded states of their preference for avoiding debate
in the United Nations by refraining from invoking the "authorization
clause" in regard to these OAS measures. [72]

Resolution IV of the Twelfth Meeting of Consultation therefore
appears to have been a step that was practical in terms of immediate
policy goals and had constructive potential for longer range goals.
It has this latter potential in that it represents a move to keep disputes within the United Nations and to prevent the displacement and
superseding of that organization by regional organizations. It might
therefore constitute virtually the only step of progress, from the
perspective of this discussion, among the various dispute-handling
activities that have been discussed in this study.

The tendency of states, prior to this resolution, to turn away
from the United Nations may have reflected a view that the world organization had proved incapable of fulfilling its world role. The turn
toward the American regional organization may similarly have reflected the view that it was, relatively speaking, the more useful

organization for dealing with the issues of the real world. However, the fact that governments turned away from the world organization did not mean that the problems that had led to its establishment had been solved. They remained just as urgent as before, and indeed, if the nuclear arms race is a criterion, they have progressively worsened to the time of writing.

There may be no way of solving these problems without confrontation on moral issues, both within the minds of concerned individuals and in the form of public debates. The American cases under discussion provided opportunities for confrontations of this kind in varying degrees and forms; however, these were avoided by a turning away from the role and responsibilities of the United Nations in favor of resort to regional groupings that could be more readily employed in pursuit of traditional approaches. It is of interest to note that the Colombian delegation, in introducing Resolution IV in the Twelfth Meeting of Consultation, said that it was important to present a moral issue to the international community.

The following addition to the policy guideline proposed earlier in this chapter seeks to strengthen the requirement for United Nations authorization for tangible pressures initiated by regional organizations and also recognizes that in situations in which the United Nations would neither act nor authorize action by others, some states might nevertheless insist on the application of tangible pressures:[73]

> If the United Nations refrains from applying or authorizing measures of tangible pressure deemed by some governments to be essential for the maintenance of peace and security, and if those governments feel impelled to act, they should not invoke other international organizations for this purpose except in situations clearly justifying action in self-defense.

NOTES

1. See documents submitted to the Security Council at its third meeting, 28 Jan. 1946, by the Delegate from Iran (Doc. S/3), U.N. SCOR, 1st Year, 1st Ser., Annex 2B, at 25; Letter from . . . Representative of Iran, to . . . Secretary-General (Doc. S/25), Report of the Security Council to General Assembly covering the period from 17 January to 15 July 1946, U.N. GAOR, 1st Year, 2d Part, Supp. 1, Annex 2, at 102. The document last cited summarizes the history of the case for the indicated period.

2. U.N. SCOR, 1st Year, 1st Ser., 3d meeting, at 42 (1946).

3. S.C. Resolutions 2, 3, and 5 (1946).

4. The conclusion of the case is outlined in R. Van Wagenen, The Iranian Case 1946 (New York: Carnegie Endowment for International Peace, 1952), at 81-88; B. R. Kuniholm, The Origins of the Cold War in the Middle East: Great Power Conflict and Diplomacy in Iran, Turkey, and Greece (Princeton: Princeton University Press, 1980).

5. Van Wagenen, The Iranian Case, supra, at 89-102; Kuniholm, The Origins of the Cold War, supra, at 380.

6. U.N. GAOR, 16th Sess., Plenary, at 845 (1961).

7. The case is summarized in Ch. 3, text at notes 4-13 et seq., supra.

8. Ch. VIII, Sec. C, para. 2.

9. Ch. XII, para. 2.

10. See, e.g., Doc. 2, G/28, 3 U.N.C.I.O. Docs. 620; The Private Papers of Senator Vandenberg, Arthur H. Vandenberg, Jr. ed. (Boston: Houghton Mifflin, 1952), at 186-93.

11. Minutes of the 31st, 32d, and 38th meetings of the U.S. Delegation, San Francisco, May 7 and 14, 1945, Foreign Relations of the U.S., 1945, vol. 1, at 617-24, 631-40, 707-10.

12. Foreign Relations of the U.S., 1945, vol. 1, at 618.

13. E.g., statement of British Foreign Minister, text at n. 38, infra.

14. L. Claude, "The OAS, the UN, and the United States," International Conciliation, No. 547, 3-15 (Carnegie Endowment for International Peace, Mar. 1964); Russell, supra, at 688-712; T. Franck, "Who Killed Article 2(4)? Or: Changing Norms Governing the Use of Force by States," 64 American Journal of International Law 809, 822-35 (1970).

15. See Minutes of Third Five-Power Informal Consultative Meeting on Proposed Amendments, San Francisco, May 12, 1945, Foreign Relations of the U.S., 1945, vol. 1, at 691-707.

16. U.N. SCOR, 9th Year, Supp. Apr.-June 1954, at 11 (U.N. Doc. S/3232).

17. Id., 675th meeting, at 15, 37.

18. For the debate see id., 675th and 676th meetings. The collapse of the Guatemalan regime was brought to the attention of the U.N. in a communication from the Chairman of the Inter-American Peace Committee, July 5, 1954. (U.N. Doc. S/3262).

19. Attitudes of actors in the case are described, somewhat differently, in D. Eisenhower, The White House Years: Mandate for Change 1953-1956 (Garden City: Doubleday, 1963), at 421-27; and in Urquhart, Hammarskjold, supra, at 88-94 (1972).

20. Text at n. 1 et seq., supra.

21. See references to an unpublished memorandum in Urquhart, Hammarskjold, supra, at 92-93.

22. U.N. SCOR, 15th Year, Supp. July-Sept. 1960, at 9 (U.N. Doc. S/4378).

23. Id. , Supp. Oct.-Dec. 1960, at 107 (U.N. Doc. S/4605).

24. U.N. GAOR, 15th Sess., 1st Comm., 1150th meeting, at 57 (1961).

25. S.C. Resolution 144 (1960).

26. U.N. GAOR, 15th Sess., Annexes, Agenda Item 90, at 10 (1961).

27. Id. , Plenary, 995th meeting, at 497 (1961).

28. 43 U.S. Department of State Bulletin 407, 408 (1960).

29. E.g., id at 747.

30. U.N. SCOR, 15th Year, 874th meeting, at 28 (1960).

31. Id, 875th meeting, at 4-5.

32. Id. at 2.

33. Art. 103 provides:

In the event of a conflict between the obligations of Members of the United Nations under the present Charter and their obligations under any other international agreement, their obligations under the present Charter shall prevail.

34. Text at notes 8-15, supra.

35. Doc. 2, G/7 (o), 3 U.N.C.I.O. Docs. 376, 385.

36. Annex 1 to Minutes of the Third Five-Power Informal Consultative Meeting, supra, at 702.

37. One of the proposals that led to the inclusion of Art. 51. Minutes of the Third Five-Power Informal Consultative Meeting, supra, at 691. Unlike Art. 51, it would have specifically referred to the right of self-defense of regional groups, naming, in this connection, the inter-American system. See also text at n. 15, supra.

38. Minutes of the Third Five-Power Informal Consultative Meeting, supra, at 696.

39. The Soviet position in the Czechoslovak case was stated in U.N. SCOR, 23d Year, 1441st meeting, at 7 et seq. (1968). In the earlier case of Hungary, the U.S.S.R. invoked the Warsaw Pact, but mainly to explain the presence of its troops in Hungary and not as a source of shared responsibility for the Soviet action of 1956. See U.N. GAOR, 2d Emergency Special Sess., at 10 (1956).

40. Pravda, Sept. 26, 1968; English translation (by the Soviet Press Agency) in N.Y. Times, Sept. 27, 1968, p. 3, col. 1.

41. Another and a quite different motivation was indicated by the U.S. in addition to the one mentioned in the text, namely that of safeguarding American lives. This danger soon ended, but military force continued to be applied, first by the U.S. and then by the OAS (see text immediately below). Both U.S. motivations were advanced

by President Johnson (52 <u>Department of State Bulletin</u> 744-48 [1965]) and by Ambassador Stevenson (U.N. SCOR, 20th Year, 1196th meeting, at 13-17 [1965]).

42. 52 <u>Department of State Bulletin</u> 862-63 (1965). The reader may note how easily the Soviet Union could have adapted this argument to suit its purposes in the Czechoslovak case.

43. U.N. SCOR, 20th Year, 1222d meeting, at 25 (1965).

44. A. J. Thomas and Ann Van Wynen Thomas, Working Paper in <u>The Dominican Republic Crisis 1965: Background Paper and Proceedings of the Ninth Hammarskjold Forum</u>, at 58-59 (1967). On this aspect of <u>Certain Expenses</u> see Ch. 6, text at n. 35, <u>supra</u>.

45. M. Ball, <u>The OAS in Transition</u>, at 474-75, 480 (1969).

46. <u>Id.</u> at 485-95; A. Thomas and A. J. Thomas, Jr., <u>The Organization of American States</u>, at 214-22 (1963).

47. The clause was, in fact, alluded to in this connection in a statement of Sept. 12, 1968, by the U.S. Representative in the U.N. Special Committee on the Principles of International Law concerning Friendly Relations and Co-operation among States, equating it with another supposed rule authorizing regional agencies to use armed force "within the rules laid down in Chapter VIII of the Charter." The statement denied both that the action in Czechoslovakia was in accord with the Charter and that the Warsaw Pact had or claimed status as a regional organization. 59 <u>Department of State Bulletin</u> 394, 399-400 (1968). The criteria properly justifying the categorization of groups of states as "regional arrangements or agencies" pursuant to Ch. VII are discussed in Franck, "Who Killed Article 2(4)?", <u>supra</u>, at 827-35.

48. Resolution of October 23, 1962, 47 <u>Department of State Bulletin</u> 722-23 (1962).

49. A. Chayes, <u>The Cuban Missile Crisis: International Crises and the Role of Law</u> (New York: Oxford University Press, 1974), at 62-66. Mr. Chayes was Legal Advisor of the U.S. Department of State at the time of the crisis.

50. The resulting view coincides with that of an important school of thought holding that the right of self-defense should not be considered to be limited by the U.N. Charter to cases of armed attack. D. Bowett, <u>Self-Defence in International Law</u> (Manchester: Manchester University Press, 1958), at 187 <u>et seq.</u>; J. Stone, <u>Aggression and World Order: A Critique of United Nations Theories of Aggression</u> (Berkeley: University of California Press, 1958), at 43-44; M. McDougal and F. Feliciano, <u>Law and Minimum World Public Order: The Legal Regulation of International Coercion</u> (New Haven: Yale University Press, 1961), at 232-38. Two authorities who consider that the "quarantine" measure should, or at least could, have been designated collective self-defense are W. Mallison,

"Limited Naval Blockade or Quarantine-Interdiction: National and Collective Defense Claims Valid under International Law," 31 George Washington Law Review 335 (1962) and D. Partan, "The Cuban Quarantine: Some Implications for Self-Defense," 1963 Duke Law Journal 696.

51. L. Meeker, "Defensive Quarantine and the Law," 57 American Journal of International Law 515 (1963). See also Ch. 6, at n. 62, supra.

52. A. Chayes, "Law and the Quarantine of Cuba," 41 Foreign Affairs 550 (1963). See also the earlier address by Mr. Chayes, "The Legal Case for U.S. Action on Cuba," 47 Department of State Bulletin 763 (1962).

53. Chayes, The Cuban Missile Crisis, supra, at 58.

54. Partan, "The Cuban Quarantine," supra, at 718.

55. 43 Department of State Bulletin 358 (1960).

56. S.C. Resolution 156 (1960). For the debate see U.N. SCOR, 15th Year, 893d to 895th meetings (1960).

57. Id., 893d meeting, at 15-16.

58. Id. at 9.

59. Id. at 6, 7.

60. Id. at 12.

61. English texts of resolutions of this meeting may be found in 46 Department of State Bulletin 278-82 (1962).

62. Statement by U.S. Secretary of State Rusk, Jan. 25, 1962, id. at 270, 273-77.

63. For the Council debate see U.N. SCOR, 17th Year, 992d to 998th meetings (1962).

64. Letter dated 8 March 1962 from the representative of Cuba to the President of the Security Council, U.N. SCOR, 17th Year, Supp. Jan.-Mar. 1962, at 88, 89 (U.N. Doc. S5086).

65. Id., 993d meeting at 24.

66. Quoted in Final Act of Ninth Meeting of Consultation of Ministers of Foreign Affairs. English text in 51 Department of State Bulletin 179, 181 (1964).

67. Id. at 181-82.

68. Final Act, and particularly Resolution III, of the Twelfth Meeting of Consultation of Ministers of Foreign Affairs. English text in 57 id. at 493, 496-97 (1967).

69. Id. at 497.

70. Duodécima Reunión de Consulta de Ministros de Relaciones Exteriores, Actas y Documentos, at 504, 505-509 (1968).

71. Ball, The OAS in Transition, supra, at 482.

72. The causal relationship here suggested is speculative, and some may say it is negated by Cuba's willingness to embark on its African adventures in 1976. However, the intervening period

saw little in the way of positive follow-up to the tendency of Resolution IV of the Twelfth Meeting of Consultation to strengthen the United Nations. More recent developments have instead tended in the opposite direction, as was discussed in Politicization of the U.N., Ch. 10.

73. See text at n. 35 et seq. , supra.

13

PROPOSED GUIDELINES
AND SOME QUESTIONS OF
PRACTICALITY

The major thesis of this study, set forth in Chapter 1, embraces the following chain of thought:

A downward spiral of world insecurity led to both world wars and has been again in progress since World War II, as exemplified by the continuing nuclear arms race.

This trend will probably lead to World War III if allowed to continue.

It can be changed only by building a requisite degree of community sentiment among the peoples of the world.

A conceivable means of doing this is improving the atmosphere and quality of international debates on international disputes and situations.

It is difficult to envision such a development without an international agency capable of mediating direct state-to-state conflicts.

The United Nations may have the potential to carry out this role; however, it has never been tested.

To test it, it is necessary to apply the U.N.'s dispute-handling powers and procedures in ways generally acceptable to all concerned.

To this end it is necessary to endeavor to apply Charter interpretations that are, or will become, through debate, generally acceptable to all concerned. The following proposed policy guidelines indicate such interpretations, as here perceived, of relevant Charter provisions:

In proposing solutions or methods of solution of substantive issues of international disputes, non-judicial organs of the United Nations (usually the Security Council or the General Assembly) should neither exceed nor give the appearance of exceeding the powers of discussion and recommendation.[1]

Judicial organs should be asked to decide disputes only when the parties appear ready to comply with the resulting decisions. Advisory opinions should not be requested of the World Court when the resulting opinions would give the impression of passing on pending disputes between states or other political entities, unless the parties appear ready to comply with the resulting opinions. [2]

When tangible pressures are applied by the United Nations in the handling of international disputes and situations, such measures should be visibly directed to the purposes laid down in the Charter for such measures (i.e., to deal with aggressions, other breaches of peace, or threats to peace). Such measures should not be given the appearance of being designed to enforce substantive decisions on the merits of disputes; all efforts should be made, when necessary, to avoid such an appearance. [3] Although it is not always necessary to state the legal category of such measures, tangible pressures initiated by the United Nations in the handling of disputes and situations should never be placed in any legal category other than that of collective measures. [4]

In seeking the participation of member states in the application of collective measures, the Security Council should limit itself to recommendations. The Council should likewise limit itself to recommendations in the exercise of the provisional measures function. [5]

Emphasis should not be placed on dispute-handling institutions as a means of seeking world peace and security. [6]

As a means of preventing the erosion of the world security role of the United Nations by undue emphasis on dispute-handling functions of other organizations, all significant international disputes not promptly and effectively settled by other means should be referred to the United Nations without prejudice to the right of the parties to resume negotiations or to refer particular disputes to other means of settlement.

If the United Nations refrains from applying or authorizing measures of tangible pressure deemed by some
governments to be essential for the maintenance of
peace and security, and if those governments feel im-
pelled to act, they should not invoke other international organizations for this purpose except in situations clearly justifying action in self-defense. [7]

Implementation of these guidelines would also have the more
general but basic consequence of establishing a new format of international relations in which goals of actors would be pursued in accordance with agreed-on procedures embodying uniform restraints.
The proposal is therefore for a course of action calculated to bring
about, in the course of time, a transformation of the format of international relations from one of anarchy to one embodying basic—
and, it is here believed, indispensable—elements of a system of
order or a rule of law. [8]

The final paragraphs will be concerned with some questions of
practicality.

Our discussion of the problem of implementing the thesis, toward the end of Chapter 1, stressed the role of debate in overcom-
ing the resistance of parties to abiding by Charter procedures and
the limitations on them. Substantive arguments appropriate to such
debates, depending on the given case, might often be that peaceful
and rational solutions are more likely when the negotiations are
within limits acceptable to all concerned than when they exceed those
limits. Such a prospect could be expected to appeal to at least some
of the parties in most disputes, especially when contrasted with the
failure that has attended most efforts to apply stronger measures.

An important aspect of this problem relates particularly to
defendant states. It is, of course, a major component of our thesis
that states in this position should accept the right of the Council or
the Assembly to debate the issues and make recommendations. Essential to this acceptability is the proposition, fully understood when
the Charter was adopted, that the recommendations would not be
binding. In practice, states initiating disputes, and commanding
majorities, have not consistently restricted the competent bodies to
discussion and recommendation. Partly in consequence, no doubt,
defendant states have frequently sought means of avoiding United
Nations proceedings on situations they do not want changed. It seems
likely that this attitude accounts for many claims that consideration
by the U.N. would constitute wrongful intervention in domestic affairs. [9] In a few cases Security Council resolutions have been defeated by vetoes by permanent members, even though such action
has appeared to violate the rule of Article 27(3) of the Charter,

according to which, "in decisions under Chapter VI [i.e., pursuant to the peaceful settlement function] . . . a party to a dispute shall abstain from voting."[10] Reference was made in Chapter 10 to a warning that the United States would consider the bringing of the case of Puerto Rican independence before the U.N. to be an unfriendly act.[11]

The primary responsibility for solving this kind of confrontation seems to rest with the willingness of majorities to limit their pronouncements on the merits of disputes to recommendation. Arguments in favor of a solution should, however, emphasize the potential benefits of a system in which both sides would participate fully and freely in debates.

The most important problem in this area may be simply the strangeness with which officials may view a proposal that they accept uniform and agreed-on restraints in their conduct of disputes and situations. One aspect is the history and reality of a competitive world. This competitive approach, in functioning societies, is shaped and channeled by community norms into non-violent patterns; in the international realm, where such patterns are lacking on the world scale, the same competitive approach sometimes leads to intractable disputes and wars. While some restraints have been formulated and agreed to, notably those of the U.N. Charter, which forms the basis of the present discussion, we have no history of efforts by leaders to ensure that the benefit of these restraints is given to their opponents in given cases. Perhaps the best hope for the practicality of the present approach is that it is far more rational than the one that has prevailed in the past. Considering that the consequences of our irrational practices, even in this century, run into the scores of millions of lost lives, to say nothing of other losses and dislocations, the basis exists for rational argument and the hope that it will prevail if pursued with dedication and persistence.

A world possessed of such a degree of community as to ensure the peaceful solution of all disputes would obviously be quite a different place from what it has been in the past, and it is undoubtedly too much to hope that such a transition could be made without practical problems arising along the way. Most might prove unforeseeable. Some risks and sacrifice might be entailed, although such dangers would be minimized by the procedures herein advocated, since these are based on agreements entered into deliberately by states with the understanding that they would be applicable in future disputes and situations. A particular problem of practicality in this range of considerations is that however fair the rules may be in general, some governments will argue that they should be suspended out of considerations of justice applicable in particular situations. Such arguments would have to be resisted, even in the face of strong emotions and apparent justifications, on the grounds that if exceptions were made in one case there would be no way of resisting demands for exceptions in others.

Another question of practicality, at a different level, is whether the proposed program would result in a decrease, or possibly an increase, in the average of successfully settled disputes. Since we are only proposing to change practices that exceed mutually agreed-to powers of the organization, the question is really whether the abandonment of such practices would result in a decline in the percentage of successfully resolved disputes and situations. A number of cases involving such practices have been described in preceding chapters of this study, and it is my view that they have not been very successful. Their effects can be assessed correctly only by going to a deeper level of practicality in which it is recognized that these methods are merely variants of the traditional approach, in which states apply such pressures as they have available and deem appropriate in particular cases. Naturally, in some cases the pressures are successful; however, the system itself produces some intractable disputes in which, by definition, it cannot succeed. While it is not the purpose of the present proposals to bring about an immediate improvement in the batting average for successful settlements, it would be logical to expect some improvement on the grounds that states are generally more amenable to pressures resulting from the application of powers that have been agreed on than to those viewed as exceeding those powers. There would be no "leap into darkness" concerning what many doubtless regard as the most reliable bases of security, namely arms and alliances, since the present proposals are not concerned with these matters. Faith in these bases is, of course, here believed to be misplaced, and it is the purpose of the present proposals to render them unnecessary.

Another question of practicality might be whether on the basis of the United Nations record there is any reason to think that its dispute-handling resources could be used with rationality and restraint. The only possible answer at present is that we do not know what the effect might be of consistent leadership and argumentation in favor of applying uniform restraints and consistent practices in the interests of long-range goals. We have no history of efforts in this direction. Past state practices have been self-centered and have exalted expediency in the interests of immediate policy goals. The results would surely be different if strong leadership were provided in support of bringing all significant disputes before the U.N. and there handling them in accordance with provisions agreed on as acceptable to all concerned. The results would further be improved to the extent that these proceedings could rationally be linked in relevant discussions with the longer range goals of full and free debates, the development of world community, and the establishment of permanent world security.

Finally, and at a higher level, ultimate goals being sought might involve questions of practicality. Although the proposed course of action would entail only minor procedural changes in the handling of individual cases, the longer range effect of such changes would ultimately tend to engage basic ideologies. Indeed, achievement of the goal of significantly increased world community would necessitate modifications of at least some ideologies.[12] One reason for seeking such changes is that it is desirable to remove such conflicts from physical battlefields to a free market place of ideas. The possibility that such a process might precipitate major upheavals has to be considered. However, the adoption of a plan such as is here advanced, involving only procedures agreed to by all concerned, seems likely to bring about change by gradual and imperceptible steps and to involve only minimal risks compared to those evidently entailed in continuing on our traditional course.

NOTES

1. Ch. 1, supra.
2. Ch. 9, supra.
3. Ch. 1, supra.
4. Ch. 2, supra.
5. Ch. 2, supra.
6. Ch. 11, supra.
7. Ch. 12, supra.
8. Ch. 1, supra.
9. Ch. 7, supra.
10. This rule, which was strongly supported by the United States (see Foreign Relations of the U.S., 1944, vol. 1, at 748; id., 1945, The Conferences at Malta and Yalta, at 68), clearly presupposed that Security Council pronouncements on the merits would be recommendatory only.

The proviso of Art. 27(3) was nevertheless apparently violated by the general acceptance as a veto of a U.S. vote in 1973 against a proposed Council resolution asserting that Panama was sovereign of the Panama Canal Zone and urging the parties to the dispute to reach a settlement. U.N. SCOR, 28th year, 169th meeting 13; id., 1704th meeting 7 (1973). Since the draft contained no elements of U.N. dispute-handling functions other than that of peaceful settlement and clearly fell within that category as an effort to promote the solution on the merits of a dispute, the U.S. was apparently obliged under

Art. 27(3) to abstain in the vote. Its proper course, and possibly a turning point in international relations, would have been to do so and then, if it found the resulting resolution unacceptable, to exercise its right to reject it.

A precedent for the above case, at least to some degree, was the general acceptance as a veto of a Soviet vote in the Council against a proposed resolution having the support of a numerical majority, dealing with the invasion of Czechoslovakia by the U.S.S.R. and associated states in 1968. U.N. SCOR, 23d Year, 1443d meeting, at 29 (1968). Since the resolution would have "called for" the withdrawal of the troops in question, it could be interpreted as a proposal for provisional measures, a category to which the veto applies. However, this call for withdrawal would have been part of a broader resolution, affirming the sovereignty and independence of Czechoslovakia, which could have been interpreted as having the overall effect of an exercise of the peaceful settlement function recommending a change of policy—from one of intervention to one of non-intervention—that would bring about a solution of the situation. Id., 1442d meeting, at 3. The case constitutes an undesirable precedent in that the Soviet vote was accepted as a veto without question or discussion.

See also Ch. 3, text at n. 32.

11. Ch. 10, text at n. 10 et seq., supra.

12. The possibility that some "ideological erosion" may be a condition of peace is suggested in S. Hoffmann, Primacy or World Order: American Foreign Policy since the Cold War (New York: McGraw-Hill, 1978), at 343.

INDEX

arbitration, 155-56, 161, 162, 168 (see also judiciary, tribunals)

armaments, 4

Austin, Warren: U.S. Senator, 44

Australia, 105-07

"balance of power," 13

Brezhnev Doctrine, 187, 192

Brown v. Board of Education, 160

Bulgaria (see peace treaties with Bulgaria, Hungary, and Romania)

Certain Expenses of the United Nations: advisory opinion of World Court, 77-78, 81-82, 83-84, 90, 118, 121, 137, 188

charter, United Nations (see United Nations Charter)

China, Peoples Republic of (see Korea, Sino-Japanese conflict, 1930)

cognizance of disputes and situations, retention of, by United Nations, 179-80

collective measures: regional organizations (see regional enforcement measures)

collective measures function: United Nations, 5-8, 10, 18-23, 33-36, 42-44, 45, 52-53, 57-59, 60, 62, 67-68,

73, 76, 78-80, 81-83, 85, 86-92; breaches of peace, 52: General Assembly, 19-20, 57-59, 63-64, 67-68, 76-77, 91-92; participation by member states, 20-23, 36; recommendation as mode of initiating, 20-23, 57-59, 60-61, 63-64, 67-68; threats to peace, 44, 52, 65-66 (see also tangible pressures by member states; Uniting for Peace resolution)

collective security (see collective measures, United Nations; peaceful settlement function, United Nations; peaceful settlement of disputes)

Colombia, 196-99, 198

community sentiments as basis for world order, 1-4, 7-8, 28, 35, 110, 147, 152, 167, 209; Scandinavia and Finland as model, 4

condemnation: by United Nations, 144-45, 148

Congo (see peace-keeping operations)

"Connally amendment," 31

consensus (see community)

constitutional systems: democratic, 1, 2, 4, 11, 18; debates, role of, 11-12; international, potential, 1-5, 7-8, 10-12; U.S., as precedent, 158-59, 160

ABOUT THE AUTHOR

JOHN W. HALDERMAN, as a member of the U.S. Department of State, participated in the early planning for and formation of the United Nations. He subsequently worked on various aspects of this and other international organizations, particularly in the fields of legal and human rights and peaceful settlement of disputes.

After retiring from the U.S. Foreign Service, he pursued peace studies as a research associate of Duke University. He is the author of The United Nations and the Rule of Law (Dobbs Ferry: Oceana, 1966) and of several articles and is editor of The Middle East Crisis (Dobbs Ferry: Oceana, 1969).

He is a graduate of the University of Oregon and its school of law, and of the National War College.